Getting Started With Team-Based Learning

Getting Started With Team-Based Learning

Jim Sibley and Peter Ostafichuk
With Bill Roberson, Billie Franchini, and Karla A. Kubitz

Foreword by
Larry K. Michaelsen

STERLING, VIRGINIA

COPYRIGHT © 2014 BY
STYLUS PUBLISHING, LLC

Published by Stylus Publishing, LLC
22883 Quicksilver Drive
Sterling, Virginia 20166-2102

The Immediate Feedback Assessment Technique (IF-AT) is a registered trademark of Epstein Educational Enterprises. The sample IF-AT forms included in first-printing copies of this volume are generously provided courtesy of Epstein Educational Enterprises.

For more information about the IF-AT or to order forms for your own classes, visit www.epsteineducation.com.

Library of Congress Cataloging-in-Publication Data
Sibley, Jim.
Getting started with team-based learning / Jim Sibley and Pete Ostafichuk With Bill Roberson, Billie Franchini, and Karla Kubitz ;
foreword by Larry Michaelsen. -- First edition.
    pages cm
Includes bibliographical references and index.
ISBN 978-1-62036-195-5 (cloth : alk. paper)
ISBN 978-1-62036-196-2 (pbk. : alk. paper)
ISBN 978-1-62036-198-6 (consumer e-edition)
ISBN 978-1-62036-197-9 (library networkable e-edition)
1. Group work in education. 2. Team learning approach in education. I. Title.
LB1032.S485 2014
371.3'6--dc23
                                                                2014007480

13-digit ISBN: 978-1-62036-195-5 (cloth)
13-digit ISBN: 978-1-62036-196-2 (paperback)
13-digit ISBN: 978-1-62036-197-9 (library networkable e-edition)
13-digit ISBN: 978-1-62036-198-6 (consumer e-edition)

Printed in the United States of America

All first editions printed on acid-free paper
that meets the American National Standards Institute
Z39-48 Standard.

Bulk Purchases

Quantity discounts are available for use in workshops
and for staff development.
Call 1-800-232-0223

First Edition, 2014

10   9   8   7   6   5   4   3   2   1

To Amanda—she believes in me and that makes me happy.
—Jim Sibley

To my parents, I owe everything to you.
—Pete Ostafichuk

Contents

Foreword

Nearly 35 years ago, when I started using Team-Based Learning (TBL) for the very first time, I was surprised and excited about the level of student engagement in my classes. Something almost magical was happening. My students were taking responsibility both for their own learning and for each other as both learners and fellow human beings. Today, I'm still excited about what is happening in my classes, but I'm even more excited about what has happened as the joy of TBL has spread to other faculty all over the world.

The very most exciting aspect of TBL, however, is the development of a true community of TBL users. Day after day, as I watch the interaction on the TBL LISTSERV, I am amazed and gratified by the sincere and impassioned posts that are aimed at effectively helping improve others' understanding of and our ability to implement TBL.

In many ways, this book is an extension of that TBL user community. Jim and Pete's hope in putting it together was to capture and share the combined TBL community wisdom. Without question, they have achieved that objective. The starting point was Jim conducting hour-long interviews with 46 TBL veterans all over the world to gather information on the barriers and breakthroughs they had experienced implementing TBL in their classes. Instead of a case of "the devil is in the details," this book is a case of "the *delight* is in the details." The book does a terrific job of covering all the basics, but it also does much more. In almost every page, it sprinkles in amazingly helpful tidbits. The icing on the cake is the quotes and vignettes that make the ideas come to life. In every chapter, I found a number of ideas that I will be using to improve my own teaching—and so will you.

—Larry K. Michaelsen
David Ross Boyd Professor Emeritus, University of Oklahoma
Professor of Management, University of Central Missouri

Preface

The idea for this book grew out of an experience I had during a workshop at a local college. The participants were excited by what they had seen in the morning's Team-Based Learning (TBL) workshop and were asking the next logical question: How do we get started? We spent a wonderful afternoon writing activities and questions and trying the activities out on each other, but at the end of the day, I thanked them for their energy and engagement—and left. This is a common story. When we encounter an intriguing idea, we are often left to find our own way of taking it to our classroom. However you discover TBL, whether through a book or through the website (www.teambasedlearning.org) or a workshop, you might not know how to get started. I hope the answer is this book. I hope this book helps fill the gap between that initial exciting contact with the ideas in TBL and successfully taking TBL to your own classroom.

Discovering TBL was a life-changing event for me. I kept looking up from my first reading of the original *Team-Based Learning* (Michaelsen, Knight, & Fink, 2004) and wondering why no one had told me about TBL sooner.

Some aspects of TBL will instantly resonate with your values and beliefs as a teacher, and other aspects may contradict your intuition. I invite you to consider TBL with as open a mind as possible. I was amazed by what I found when I discovered TBL and when I saw how well it worked in the classroom.

Writing a book like this is a collaborative endeavor. Five TBL teachers came together to write about what they have learned along the way. Another 46 TBL teachers contributed their wisdom through interviews. Quotes are peppered throughout the book to tie our advice to stories of real classroom practice. I hope what you hold in your hand is an accurate representation of the current "state of the art" about TBL and how you can be successful at it.

I have had the good fortune of sharing TBL with groups all over the world. What is clear to me is how versatile, adaptable, and fun TBL can be. Please let me know how your journey goes.

—Jim Sibley
August 2013
Vancouver, Canada

When Jim asked me if I'd be interested in coauthoring this book with him, I immediately said "yes." This is largely because I have a deep respect for Jim and relish the opportunity to work with him, but it is also because I truly believe in TBL. As I reflected on my decision, it occurred to me the same thing happened about 10 years earlier as I was assigned to codevelop and coteach my first course as a new faculty member. Jim had discovered TBL, and he suggested to my colleague and me that we should consider building our new course in the TBL format.

Thinking back to my initial experiences, I realize the thing that sold me on TBL most and compelled me to give such a quick "yes" to adopting it was that TBL just made sense. Even as a new faculty member, I recognized there had to be a better way to teach than by passive lectures. As a student, I remember sitting in class thinking "this makes sense" as the teacher lectured away, only to pull my hair out at home as I tried to apply some of the concepts on my own. Flipping this so the students cover the basic stuff on their own before class and then they have the support of a team—as well as the insight and guidance of the subject "expert"—as they actually *apply* the course material to challenging problems seems so obvious and natural that I wondered why I hadn't been exposed to this approach before.

Overall, my journey through TBL has been an immensely positive one. It was a step into the unknown at first, and it was hard work. Yet, year after year, my students continue to report they overwhelmingly prefer the TBL approach. In a typical course survey, about 80% of my students favor TBL, 10% are neutral, and 10% favor conventional lectures. There are a couple of important messages in these numbers: First, no matter what you do, you cannot expect to please everyone, and second, you can expect some resistance. At first, I questioned, "Why don't 100% of my students love TBL? What am I doing wrong?" Now I understand I didn't have realistic expectations to start with, and I also didn't do a good job of preparing and supporting my students for the role change they would be going through to become active learners. What I really needed was a book built from the wisdom of those who had already traveled the TBL path.

I hope this book can be such a source of insight, inspiration, and reassurance for you. You can take comfort that if you say "yes" to adopting TBL, you have in this book the knowledge and experience of many TBL teachers from many disciplines and contexts to help you on your journey.

—Pete Ostafichuk
August 2013
Vancouver, Canada

Acknowledgments

If it takes a village to raise a child, then it must take a community to build a good book. We would like to thank everyone who contributed to this book.

CONTRIBUTING AUTHORS

Bill Roberson, Billie Franchini, Karla A. Kubitz, Larry K. Michaelsen

INTERVIEWEES

Gail Feigenbaum, Allyson Brown, Marie Thomas, Cynthia Evetts, Larry Michaelsen, Mary Gourley, Ruth Levine, Frank Gersich, Janet Stamatel, Liz Winter, Trudi Jacobson, David Raeker-Jordan, Judy Kissack, Meghan Gillette, Lindsay Davidson, Peter Balan, Ron Carson, Chris Burns, Simon Tweddell, Michael Nelson, Karla A. Kubitz, Brent MacLaine, Jenny Morris, Mary Gilmartin, Holly Bender, Mary Hadley, Sandy Cook, Bill Brescia, Tim Dwyer, Lynne Esson, Dean Parmelee, Brenda Collings, Mark Freeman, Joel Dubois, Melanie Carlson, Mark Stevens, Peter Smith, Esam Agamy, N. Kevin Krane, Brian Dzwonek, Shawn Bushway, Sarah Mahler, Judy Currey, Rick Goedde, Paul Koles, Mary Gourley, William Ofstad, Pete Ostafichuk, Laura Madson, Bill Roberson, Cenk Aral, Melissa Weresh

MANUSCRIPT REVIEWERS

Isabeau Iqbal, Amanda Bradley, Brenda Collings, Ruth Levine, Laura Madson, Ernesto Ocampo, Caroline Willams, Michael Kramer, Ann Greenbaum, Liza Cope, Marie Thomas, Trudi Jacobson, Andreas Broscheid, Rick Goedde, Catherine Baillie, Renate Eberl, Chris Burns, Sarah Bongey-Bryans, Lindsay Davidson, Trent Tucker, Ron Carson, Herb Coleman, Maria Milazzo

COURSE MATERIAL EXAMPLES

Pete Ostafichuk, Paul Koles, Peter Balan, Sophie Sparrow, Margaret Sova McCabe, Sarah Leupen, Francis Jones, Marie Thomas

TRANSCRIPTION

Kirsten Starcher

COPYEDITING

Kirsten Starcher, Nicole Hirschman

PROOFREADING

Holly Fairbank

FIGURES AND GRAPHICS

Sophie Spiridonoff

STYLUS PUBLISHING

John von Knorring, McKinley Gillespie

PART ONE

Overview of TBL

CHAPTER 1

Introduction to Team-Based Learning

Team-Based Learning (TBL) is an extraordinary form of small-group learning—both effective and fun. TBL can and will transform you as a teacher, transform your students, and bring more fun, energy, and deep learning to your classroom than you may have ever thought possible. This chapter will introduce you to TBL.

Judy Currey had just joined the Critical Care Nursing faculty at Deakin University in Melbourne, Australia. As a first-time teacher, she was given the daunting task of redeveloping the lowest rated course at the university. She used a traditional course design model and turned it into the highest rated course in the university. Then, already at the top of her instructional game, she discovered TBL—and became so convinced about the value of TBL that she committed to redeveloping this highly rated course within the TBL framework. From the very start, she was glad she did:

> *The very first time we did TBL, we invited the ICU and Cardiac group students to a bit of an orientation to this new teaching method. With two colleagues, we met with the students at the end of the day, maybe 35 students. We gave them an advanced life support case put together in the TBL format. I assumed, with them having just completed the Advanced Life Support Assessment and Theory course, that they would have an easy time of it.*
>
> *I was facilitating, and we did a question where the patient's heart rhythm changes from normal to an abnormal rhythm. The point at which the rhythm changes is often the indicator of what that rhythm might be, and sometimes rhythms can look like each other, and it takes a fair amount of skill to discern between two or three possible rhythms. We gave them an ECG where the top half of the heart had stopped working and the bottom had come in as a support rhythm to keep the patient alive, but because it's from the bottom of the*

heart, it's wide and so it looks like it's a malignant rhythm. But it's a support rhythm. It's lifesaving.

Our question to the students was simply, should you defibrillate?

After some intrateam discussion and deliberation, the teams put up their voting cards. Every single team chose to defibrillate. Every single team had interpreted the rhythm as malignant. One of the other instructors came up and put her face in front of mine, her back to the students, and mouthed, "Oh my goodness, how could they have done this? Why haven't they learned?" I stayed calm and impassive and started asking,

"Okay, group six. You were going to defibrillate. Why were you going to do that?"

"Because it's ventricular tachycardia."

"Okay. Another group. You thought it was VT? So what are the characteristics of VT?"

"It's wide, and it's slow."

"Okay. Another group. So you all concur with that?"

"Yes."

"So how does VT start? Is that what happened here?"

And 35 heads went down, and it was just unbelievable. It was silent, and then there was a collective "Oh no!" as every one of them, at that moment, saw it was not VT and that they had in fact killed the patient. It was transforming. They thought they knew this, and they suddenly realized that they had not learned it properly, that they couldn't read the ECG accurately. Defibrillating the patient would have wiped out this ventricular rhythm that was keeping them alive. When you wipe that out, then they're dead. There was a collective professional embarrassment; we had shown them the power of TBL. It was an amazing moment. (Judy Currey, Critical Care Nursing, Deakin University)[1]

TBL is a unique and powerful form of small-group learning. It harnesses the power of teams and social learning combined with accountability structures and systematic instructional sequences to let you achieve powerful results. This book will be your guide, with practical advice, suggestions, and tips to help you succeed in the TBL classroom. This book will help you understand what TBL is and why it is so powerful. You will find what you need to plan, build, implement, and use TBL effectively. This book will appeal to both novice and expert TBL teachers. Each part will start with the basic principles to help the novice get started and then go deeper with concrete examples, practical advice, and nuances to help the more experienced TBL teachers understand their practice even better. Be forewarned that some TBL principles might challenge some of your beliefs about teaching.

Before we start, here are some ways you can use this book to improve your practice. You can learn

- the fundamental principles of TBL,
- how to effectively design a TBL experience,
- how to maximize the benefits and minimize the risks,
- how to prepare for the emotional journey, and
- to appreciate how TBL provides a reliable, coherent instructional framework to navigate the learning-centered classroom.

As you explore more about TBL, it will become apparent that fidelity to the essential elements of TBL will be your guiding touchstone. This fidelity goes a long way toward ensuring instructional effectiveness and a positive outcome. Experienced TBL teachers often comment on their growing understanding of the fundamental importance of certain essential elements, and their commitment to those elements is actually key to successful implementation of TBL.

Implementing TBL requires a commitment to examine your own beliefs about what good teaching is. You may find you need a shift in your beliefs as a teacher and a change in your thinking to be able to design and implement a TBL course well. Part of examining your beliefs and realigning them for success in the student-centered classroom is convincing yourself of the value of TBL. A good place to start is Sisk's (2011) or Haidet, Kubitz, and McCormack's (in press) systematic review of the TBL literature. In chapter 4, "The Evidence, Please," we will examine in detail the literature and educational rationales for using TBL. Objectives must evolve from the traditional "What do I want my students to know?" to "What do I want them to be able to do?" Considering deeply how our students will use what they learn motivates us to build course experiences focused more on doing than on knowing. Using the course concepts to solve significant, real-world problems is the instructional heart of TBL.

It can sometimes be difficult to reimagine our content-rich courses. TBL forces us to more accurately develop instructional objectives and really take those objectives to heart as we develop our courses. We need not only to know what we want the students to be able to do but also to design opportunities for our students to show us what they know.

Your shifting role as a teacher can be unsettling initially as your role morphs from a traditional teacher to a designer of high-quality learning experiences and a coach, facilitator, mentor, and guide. You may have relied in the past on your content expertise and "teaching by telling," but TBL will require a different set of skills. Some skills you will certainly have from your past teaching experience, and some may be new.

You may experience student resistance as well. Students who have been told all their lives what to know, when to know it, and when to give it back do not always appreciate being pulled from their passive role in the didactic classroom to the active role in the learner-centered classroom, but the results can be stunning when TBL is implemented well. By carefully orienting our students and convincing them of our rationales for using TBL, we can acknowledge possible student apprehension and lessen any resistance. The orientation process is described in detail in chapter 3, "The Whole Course Experience."

HOW TBL IS DIFFERENT

The TBL methodology is different from other forms of collaborative or cooperative learning, because it provides a whole coherent framework for building an entire course experience. Michael Sweet (2010) described TBL as

> a special form of small group learning using a specific sequence of individual work, group work, and immediate feedback to create a motivational framework in which students increasingly hold each other accountable for coming to class prepared and contributing to discussion.

TBL isn't a method that you sprinkle over your existing lecture course. It requires a complete rethinking of your overall course goals, a focused redevelopment of your course materials, and a commitment to take that adventuresome plunge into learning-centered teaching. There are powerful and important synergies between the components of TBL; although it is possible to selectively implement some components of the model, considerable instructional power is lost. Many experienced TBL teachers think it is best to commit to the entire model to get the largest benefits and effects. Preparing for TBL is very different from preparing for a traditional course. In a traditional course, you may be able to dash off a lecture at the last minute, but with TBL's requirement for thoughtful integration of reading, getting your student ready using the Readiness Assurance, and engaging in classroom Application Activities, last-minute prep will not work.

The TBL model can help you achieve two important things: having your students come to class prepared, and having them deeply learn the material by learning how to apply the course concepts to solve interesting, authentic, real-world problems. Using TBL's ingenious Readiness Assurance Process (RAP) ensures that students come to class prepared (more on the RAP in chapter 6). Next, students learn how to apply course concepts to solve problems by making complex decisions in teams, then publicly reporting their decisions; in this sense, TBL could easily be called decision-based learning. The public reporting and ability to compare answers naturally leads to teams defending their own decisions and critiquing the decisions of other teams. It is in this intense give-and-take reporting dialog that students deeply learn the material.

A useful analogy is to think of the work of a courtroom jury that sifts through large amounts of evidence, statements, and transcripts to come up with a simple decision: guilty or not guilty. The jury members ultimately need to consider the evidence presented to them, apply the law to the case, and arrive at a reasonable interpretation. TBL sets up a similar dynamic by requiring teams to arrive at a simple decision after interpreting complex and often conflicting data and selecting and applying appropriate criteria for decision making. TBL adds an important social learning step during the reporting. Now again imagine the jury; the foreman rises to state the jury's verdict, but another foreman rises from a different jury team in the same courtroom and states a different verdict. They naturally want to talk to each other; they naturally want to ask, Why? This simple comparability between decisions, and the natural tendency to ask the question *why*, is at the heart of TBL. This *why* motivation provides the instructional fuel to power insightful debates between student teams.

HOW TBL GOT STARTED

In January 1979, Larry Michaelsen was a junior faculty member teaching an organizational behavior course at the University of Oklahoma. Budget cuts had tripled his class size from 40 to 120 students. He had been advised by senior colleagues to give up on his case-based, Socratic dialogue approach and switch to lecturing. But he was unwilling to let go of working with cases and facilitating deep disciplinary problem-solving discussions. He felt strongly that these discussions really were at the heart of deep and enduring learning. He had an idea. He tried something different. He called it Team-Based Learning. It was an invention that preserved what he so valued in his teaching: engagement, decision making, deep discussions, and feedback. His method actually made positive use of the larger class size to improve the quality of the discourse.

He realized he needed to overcome two challenges. First, how could he engage large classes in effective problem solving when the teacher is a scarce resource and class size encourages anonymity rather than accountability? Second, how could he induce his students to come to class prepared?

Right from the start, he developed something very close to the structure that TBL classrooms still use today.

Student preparation was ensured by using the ingenious RAP. During an early Readiness Assurance Test, he listened to the students' discussions as they were answering the questions, and he realized that the students were actually discussing the very material that he would have been forced to cover if he had to lecture. He knew he was on to something.

Once Michaelsen knew his students were ready, he was in a position to help them begin problem solving. The overarching course goal of helping students learn how to apply course concepts was successfully structured using the "3 S" framework (now the "4 S" framework: Significant Problem–Same Problem–Specific Choice–Simultaneous Report). The 4 S framework encourages students to make difficult, data-rich decisions that can be quickly reported to the entire class. Much to his relief, he found that the decision-making and problem-solving aspects of the course that he valued so highly were in fact very possible, even in large classes. Using this structured problem-solving method, students engaged deeply with the content and were learning more than he had thought would be possible.

The elements of TBL have evolved slightly over the years, but these two original pieces that ensure preparation and guided problem solving are still the heart and soul of TBL. Over 30 years later, TBL is used with great success all over the world, in virtually all disciplines, and in classes as large as 400 students.

ESSENTIAL ELEMENTS OF TBL: AN OVERVIEW

There are four essential elements of TBL. These elements have evolved over the years. In the original TBL book (Michaelsen, Knight, & Fink, 2004), the four essential principles were (a) groups must be properly formed and managed, (b) students must be accountable for their individual and group work, (c) group assignments must promote both learning and team development, and (d) students must have frequent and timely performance feedback. These principles continue to be essential and will naturally happen when we adhere to the practices and guidance that are provided by the revised four essential elements of TBL. We will be using the revised four essential elements (see Figure 1.1) that were described in

FIGURE 1.1
The four essential elements of Team-Based Learning

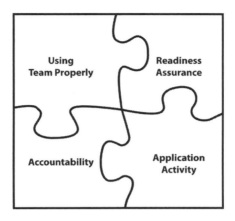

Sweet and Michaelsen's (2012a) book *Team-Based Learning in the Social Sciences and Humanities.*

The following sections introduce each of the four essential elements of TBL. Each of the essential elements will be discussed in greater detail in its own chapter (see chapters 5–8). The four essential elements of TBL are as follows:

1. Teams must be properly formed and managed.
2. Students must be motivated to come to class prepared.
3. Students must learn to use course concepts to solve problems.
4. Students must be truly accountable.

Element 1: Properly Formed and Managed Teams

TBL teachers recommend large, teacher-created, diverse teams. The importance of using teacher-created and diverse teams is consistent with recommendations in the educational literature. The recommendation for large teams (five to seven students) is unique to TBL. The large teams work well because of TBL's accountability structures and the complex nature of classroom activities. The literature on team formation is very clear on the importance of using teacher-created, criterion-based teams to ensure the best educational results. Teacher-formed teams outperform randomly and student-selected teams (Brickell, Porter, Reynolds, & Cosgrove, 1994). Students will often plead to be placed on teams with their friends, but the research shows that student-selected teams consistently underperform other team formation strategies. To paraphrase from Brickell et al. (1994), student-selected teams are often "social entities" where existing relationships and cliques can make team cohesion difficult.

Feichtner and Davis (1984) found

> that students are more likely to have positive experiences in classes where groups
> are either formed by the instructor or by a combination of methods (e.g., one
> instructor collected data on students' research interests and then grouped those
> with similar preferences). Specifically, in recording information concerning their
> worst group experience, 40 percent of the respondents noted that the groups were
> formed by the students themselves, while in the best group experience, only 22
> percent reported that the students were responsible for forming the groups. Thus,
> by nearly a 2 to 1 margin, if students formed their own groups they were also likely
> to list the group as being a worst group experience. (p. 60)

You must acknowledge and resist the request for self-selection by some students
by carefully explaining your rationale and standing your ground.

It is recommended that TBL teams have five to seven students. TBL teams need
to be larger than is suggested in most cooperative or collaborative learning literature
because of the complexity of problems to be solved. This may be contrary to your
intuition. Many people's first reaction to this recommendation for the large team size is
disbelief: Won't larger teams let some people hide and not contribute? The structure of
TBL alleviates this concern. The teams need to be large enough to have the intellectual
horsepower to solve very complex problems, individuals need to have accountability
to the instructor for their preparation, and individuals need to have accountability to
their teammates for the quality of their contribution to the team's success.

Peer evaluation lets us give the grading scheme the teeth to motivate every student to contribute and be fairly rewarded (or not) for his or her level of contribution. Because team scores are higher than individual scores, peer evaluation tempers
the effect of the high team score on a student's final grade. Contribute well to your
team, and you benefit from the high team score. When you don't contribute to your
team's success, you will not receive that benefit. The thoughtful design of activities to leverage the diversity of the teams can help ensure that all students remain
engaged in the activities. TBL is actually better with diverse teams, which is great
news for our increasingly diverse classrooms.

New TBL teachers often initially underestimate teams' abilities to learn how
to solve difficult problems and need to ratchet up the problem difficulty as the
semester progresses. This is because the teams, with time and practice, naturally get
better at problem solving.

Team members must stay consistent for the duration of the course. Groups take
time to gel into teams as they progress through Tuckman's (1965) stages of team
formation: forming, storming, norming, and finally performing. Students' shared
activities, shared goals, and accountability to the team all aid in the development
of an important factor known as team cohesion. Teams need to remain together
for this cohesion to occur. The sequence of TBL activities and its accountability
structures all synergistically aid the development of team cohesion.

There was a remarkable study that highlights the amazing development of team cohesion in TBL (Michaelsen, Watson, & Black, 1989). The study found that in early Readiness Assurance testing, student teams often used simple votes on split decisions and let the majority rule. But as team members found their social feet within the team and team cohesion began to increase with each testing cycle, the decision-making process progressively became more consensus based. It showed that in as few as four Readiness Assurance cycles, teams had switched strategy from majority rule to consensus-based decision making.

Element 2: Readiness Assurance to Ensure Preclass Preparation

The second essential element is using the RAP to get students prepared. Most teachers have had the bad experience of the class discussion where no one has read the preparatory material. These can be painful, disappointing events. Larry Michaelsen realized that motivating his students to come to class prepared was key to their being able to engage in the deeper, richer, and more interesting problem-solving Application Activities. In an attempt to induce preclass preparation, many teachers have used reading quizzes to promote some level of preparation. Unfortunately, these kinds of quizzes at best can provide some individual accountability and at worst may not effectively measure whether students have genuine understanding of the preparatory materials. A student can choose not to complete or do poorly on the reading quizzes, which can leave the instructor with the conundrum of either moving on and potentially leaving unprepared students behind or backing up and reviewing the material that the students were supposed to read. The problem with using class time to review the preparatory materials is that it eliminates the incentive to prepare, because the students know the teacher will go over it in class.

Michaelsen's RAP was an important discovery that solves this conundrum. The RAP has some similarities to traditional reading quizzes, because it does get at some individual accountability, but it goes further and builds on that preparation and accountability in the individual test by unleashing the power of social learning and immediate focused feedback during the team test. The magic of the RAP is that it actually builds on initial student preparation and turns it into genuine student readiness for the learning activities that follow in the Application Activity phase.

To build on students' out-of-class preparation, each module begins with the same structured RAP (see Figure 1.2). The RAP begins by assigning preparatory materials (e.g., newspaper articles, journal articles, textbook readings, PowerPoint slides, videos, or podcasts). The students come to the first class of each module having completed the assigned preparatory materials. Simply put, the in-class portion of the RAP is the administration of a series of multiple-choice tests. These multiple-choice tests are based on the preparatory materials. Students first complete the test individually (known as the iRAT, or Individual Readiness Assurance Test) and then retake the exact same test in their teams (tRAT, or Team Readiness Assurance

FIGURE 1.2
The Readiness Assurance Process stages

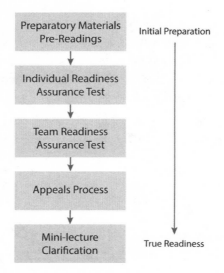

Test). Following the team test, teams are encouraged to appeal any questions that they disagree with, using a structured written process known as the Appeals Process where they can identify ambiguity in the reading or the question. To close out the RAP, the instructor provides a short mini-lecture or clarification on any specific troublesome topics that still remain.

The entire RAP will be discussed in greater detail in chapter 6.

Element 3: Learning How to Apply Course Concepts

The main goal of any TBL course is to help students use the course concepts to solve significant, relevant problems. TBL uses something known as the 4 S framework for designing and implementing effective problem solving in the classroom (see Figure 1.3).

This structured problem-solving model is used to create classroom events that require students to make complex decisions that can be reported simply, and then the public reporting discussion provides them with rich and specific feedback on the quality of their team's decision. Teams publicly report their decisions, and this leads to a give-and-take conversation between teams that is a powerful tool to help students develop a deep understanding of the course material.

Application Activities directly build on the students' individual preparation and their subsequent learning during the RAP. In each Application Activity, all teams are given the same significant problems to solve. Your use of the 4 S framework to carefully structure and design and implement your Application Activities allows you to consistently create successful activities that result in deep, meaningful reporting discussions.

FIGURE 1.3
The 4 S framework

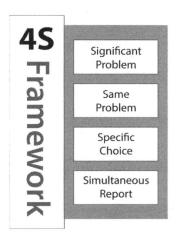

Remember the analogy of the two courtroom juries reporting at the same time, prompting that natural motivation to ask *why*? The team-reporting discussion is the students' opportunity to scrutinize the decision of other teams and, at the same time, defend their own decision. During this powerful give-and-take discussion, a social consensus begins to emerge on what constitutes a reasonable position and what reasonable evidence supports that position. In contrast to a simple jury decision, consider a fact-finding commission that generates long written documents that are often difficult to compare and therefore often lead to poor discussion. In long documents, the decision points that really let us compare our thinking are hard to find, and the readers will be in different states of overall readiness. The explicit comparability of a jurylike decision, based on analyzing a complex problem, drives these rich discussions.

The 4 S framework's Application Activities will be the focus of chapter 7.

Element 4: The Importance of Accountability

The final essential element is accountability. Every student and every teacher has likely had a bad team experience at some point. When you announce to your class that you will be using teams in your course, you may not be met with cheers. The students may have been burned by noncontributing team members or experienced dominating and bullying behaviors in previous group work. Helping your students understand the rationales for using TBL and its unique accountability structures that prevent most dysfunction is critical to selling TBL to them. Students may even have been subjected to poorly designed group work that was called "team-based learning" but did not use the TBL framework; therefore, you need to show them that genuine TBL is truly different.

There are multiple levels of accountability in a TBL course. There is individual accountability to the instructor from the iRAT (more on this in chapter 6), but what is truly motivating is accountability to one's teammates, and a formal peer evaluation process is also key. We can try to motivate our students through extrinsic motivators such as grades, but intrinsic motivation activated by accountability to peers is even more powerful and effective and is often reflected in student feedback like "I didn't want to let my teammates down."

The peer evaluation process should compensate students fairly for their contributions to the success of the team. Team grades are often higher than individual grades, and peer evaluation allows us to make sure that students are truly rewarded for their contributions to their team's success or else held accountable for their lack of contribution.

Accountability, peer evaluation, and grading will be discussed in greater detail in chapter 8.

THE RHYTHM OF A TYPICAL TBL COURSE

A prototypical TBL course is divided into roughly five to seven modules, arranged according to logical groupings of the content A timeline of a typical module is illustrated in Figure 1.4.

Before the course begins, you need to complete all your course design preparations (more on designing your course materials in chapter 2). When the first day of class arrives, you spend the first portion of the class with your students introducing TBL and convincing them of the value of TBL by carefully and thoughtfully explaining your rationales for using TBL (more on understanding the educational rationales in chapter 4). After that first class, you send students a reminder to complete the preparatory reading before the start of the first TBL module. Students

FIGURE 1.4
Team-Based Learning module timeline

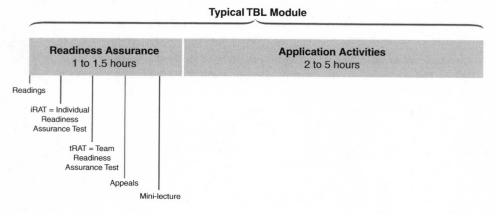

come to the first class of the module and then complete the RAP. Once the students are ready, you launch into a series of Application Activities (more on Application Activities in chapter 7). A few classes later, as the module is completed, you provide some closure and reinforcement for all that has been learned. As the next module begins, the familiar TBL rhythm starts to build: out-of-class preparation by the students, the RAP, and Application Activities. Partway through the course, we give the students the opportunity to give each other feedback on how well they are contributing to their team's success (more on grading and peer evaluation in chapter 8). More TBL modules follow. Finally, the course starts to draw to a close, and you help students consolidate all that they have learned (more on finishing well in chapter 3). The course completes with a final peer evaluation.

We have learned many things over the past decade helping teachers take TBL to their classroom. This book is based on our current and ever-evolving understanding. If you are new to TBL, this book can help you get started and successfully bring TBL to your classroom. If you already use TBL, this book can help you excel.

Let's get started.

NOTE

1. J. Currey, personal communication, January 22, 2013.

CHAPTER 2

Getting Your Course Ready for Team-Based Learning

Bill Roberson and Billie Franchini

In the next two chapters, we will guide you through the "big-picture" view of designing and implementing a great Team-Based Learning (TBL) course. This chapter will focus specifically on the course design process and the unique approach we recommend to using backward design. The next chapter will build on this by looking at the whole course experience. Don't worry if you have more questions about the four essential elements—they will each be examined in greater detail in Part Two (chapters 5–8). But for now let's examine the big-picture questions around designing a course experience and then successfully implementing it.

DESIGNING A SUCCESSFUL TBL IMPLEMENTATION

Course design, like most complex projects, is an iterative, nonlinear process, with the big course-level ideas and goals informing and affecting smaller daily tasks and vice versa. The implication for building a successful course is that you need to think simultaneously and dialectically about the overarching goals of your course and the steps students will take to reach those goals. Next, we sketch out one strategy for handling this back-and-forth between the big picture and the day-to-day of your course that we have found to be highly successful in our work with faculty. Dee Fink's (2003) *Creating Significant Learning Experiences* has deeply influenced our thinking about course design.

We encourage TBL adopters to start this process with the proverbial paper shredder. Run your syllabus through it and start from scratch, before you think about integrating TBL with previous versions of your course. Overlaying a traditional syllabus with assorted TBL elements is unlikely to be successful, as will become clearer in the following paragraphs.

Begin by Identifying Key Actions

We have found through several years of experience in working with university instructors that starting with big goals (e.g., "think critically," "develop a global perspective," "understand how to apply the scientific method") and trying to work down toward concrete activities for the classroom is less successful and less intuitive than starting with something concrete and representative then working back to the broader goals. We have seen many syllabi with beautifully written, lofty goals but with no evidence that those goals are operationalized in the daily work of students in the classroom. To avoid this, begin by recording what students need to do concretely to learn how to use your course content. These will become the basis for your team tasks (Application Activities) in class.

Why start with team tasks? Team tasks (Application Activities) are where most of the learning takes place because they translate knowledge and thinking (analysis, integration of information) into collective action. Actions, particularly decisions, are the embodiment of and visible evidence for thinking. These are the moments when students take what they are newly familiar with and experiment with using it in new situations. Team tasks also validate and reward students' preparation and performance on the Readiness Assurance Tests (RATs) by putting them into the role of autonomous agents whose decisions actually carry value within the marketplace of ideas in the classroom. We therefore advocate starting course design with a concrete description of what students specifically will be *doing* in your course on a daily basis, in order to practice using disciplinary content.

Start by writing down a set of concrete actions that someone needs to do in order to be successful in your discipline (as represented by your specific course content area). Write these in clear language that students can understand. Here are some sample actions from various disciplines:

- *History*: Interpret primary sources; evaluate arguments and evidence.
- *Biology*: Detect patterns of permutation in DNA; assess the impact of a given environment on a given species.
- *Economics*: Compare explanations for data; make judgments about the impact of a phenomenon on a given market.
- *Nursing*: Conduct diagnoses; make determinations about the accuracy of a given diagnosis.
- *Chemistry*: Evaluate hypotheses that attempt to explain variations in molecular configurations.
- *Business*: Evaluate; make a judgment about a given market's potential reaction to a given event.

The actions you identify as characteristic of expert work in your field will provide you with a concrete core around which to begin constructing the new version of your course. Your list of actions will point you directly to selecting or writing relevant RAT questions; creating engaging, relevant, and challenging tasks; and designing graded assignments that authentically measure student learning.

Draft a Single, Complete Learning Module Focusing on Student Actions

The reason for focusing next on a single activity sequence at the outset of course design is to give yourself early awareness of what learning looks and feels like in a TBL course. This exercise will give you a sense of how student experience in the course will need to be structured and paced overall.

Beginning in this way—in the middle and working outward—is counterintuitive for many of us in academe. The more common approach is to work deductively and hierarchically, from broad, dominant conceptual goals to specific content and activities. But here is the rationale for inverting the process: Without a core of action-driven team tasks (Application Activities) that embody disciplinary thinking, and without coherent sequencing of those tasks as a driver of student learning, TBL can (and often does, based on our observations of classrooms) quickly devolve into a series of RATs interspersed with too much accidental lecturing and unfocused, ad hoc, small-group conversations. The active, student-centered learning module is the backbone of the successful TBL course. It provides the logic and coherence of students' experience in the course and ensures that the broader course goals are visibly measurable and actually met.

DESIGNING A LEARNING MODULE

A note about language: We have purposely used the terms *module* and *learning sequence* instead of *unit* in order to avoid confusion with textbook "units," which typically refer to how authors and publishers organize content for publication. We recommend that TBL adopters think first in terms of a student action and thinking sequence, then consider how "units of content" can be used to drive those actions.

1. Identify a discipline-specific action or decision that students will need to practice, based on the kind of thinking you want them to develop in your course. Refer to the examples in the previous section.

2. Now think ahead to the end of the module. Construct an assignment or comprehensive task (written assignment, higher level test question, complex case analysis, problem set, etc.) that would make visible to you and to your students whether they are able to think and act the way you described in #1. This will be a draft of the final assessment for the module. It should be conceived at least in substantial part as an individual assignment, so that you will be able to monitor the progress of all students. Keep in mind that you've had students practicing application throughout the module, so it is essential that this final assessment be

appropriately challenging (i.e., don't just ask students to recall information or demonstrate basic understanding through low-level applications—ask them to make real decisions that simulate the actions of experts).

3. Now look at the content sources you are planning to use for the course. Ignore the sequence of chapters if you are using a textbook. Instead, select a set of readings (wherever they appear) that will be useful to students in providing the information they will need en route to executing the types of thinking and actions you have targeted in your final assessment for the module. Think first about the fundamental concepts students need to understand in order to be ready to do application tasks based on the readings and choose only readings that address these core concepts. This can lead to some very difficult choices, and it's easy to fall into the trap of assigning certain readings just because they are "important" generally or "really interesting" in themselves. It may be necessary to make selections that do not break with whole chapters because the concept you want students to use appears piecemeal in three different places. Keep in mind that you can assign additional, more focused follow-up readings later in a module, after students have mastered the larger concepts.

4. Develop a RAT on these readings. The RAT will be a multiple-choice test of understanding of key concepts (not small details). Bloom's taxonomy is a good guide to consider for distribution of questions of varying difficulty. Most of the questions will fall toward the lower end of the taxonomy (comprehension of concepts, simple application), but even these questions should be challenging enough that they force students to do more than simply recognize key terms or phrases. It will also be important to include a few questions at the higher end as well (analysis, synthesis, evaluation) to ensure good discussion within the teams. Most important, think of how you will use RAT questions to point students to the kinds of thinking you want them to practice in this learning sequence. We recommend keeping RATs fairly short (10–20 questions) so that both the Individual Readiness Assurance Test (iRAT) and the Team Readiness Assurance Test (tRAT) can be administered in one class meeting, but disciplinary needs and customs will affect your decision. Above all, it is important to keep in mind that the RAT should not be designed as a comprehensive assessment of mastery: It is a sampling of preliminary understanding and a learning tool. It is designed to bring students to a common point of awareness of key ideas so that they can begin working toward the real goal—learning how to use these ideas.

5. Now comes the hard part: Develop a series of team tasks (Application Activities) that scale from clarification of concepts to more complex, more ambiguous, and more difficult uses of those concepts. The most effective tasks take the form of actions that require students to use their knowledge to make a judgment resulting in a decision. Early in the sequence tasks can be short (3–10 minutes) and serve to clarify understanding of the content through simple applications or analyses that begin to push students beyond what they learned in the RAT. Later tasks

should require more analytical and integrative thinking, asking students to work with complex situations, cases, and scenarios that require knowledge and reasoning as well as judgment. In the more complex scenarios, students might need as much as a half hour to reach a decision. If there is a product (e.g., poster explanation or graphic) associated with the task, still more time might be needed. Designing tasks that conform to the 4 S principles will ensure that you are focusing on critical thinking and decision making. We recommend that you use PowerPoint or another presentation tool to project, step-by-step in concrete language, what students will do to complete these tasks. This will also help you prepare, by requiring you to envision in detail how the task will play out. Chapter 6 will explore application task design more completely.

6. Consider how you want students to continue processing on their own (i.e., as individuals) between class meetings. Some options: You can plan for students to work alone, outside of class, through some tasks on their own, so as to prepare them for more complex in-class team tasks (Application Activities); you can also assign supplemental readings to further their understanding within the sequence.

7. Finally, consider the pacing of the whole module. How much time will be needed for students to work through all the components of the sequence? Typically the iRAT and the tRAT together will take an hour or more to complete, which for most university class schedules takes most or all of one class meeting, especially if you have planned for appeals and for instructor clarification. If you teach in an extended class meeting format of 3 or more hours, the RAT typically takes up the first half, followed by a first round of team tasks (Application Activities). A typical module will be built around 5–9 hours of class meeting time distributed over 2–4 days, culminating in a substantive, graded individual or team assignment that caps the sequence.

FROM MODULE DESIGN TO WHOLE-COURSE DESIGN

Now that you have thought through the learning sequence for a complete module, it should be possible for you to envision how overall course design will support and provide context for this core structure. Having created a module, you are also now better prepared to produce a rhetorically effective syllabus. It's now time to extrapolate from your module draft back to the big picture of whole-course conceptualization. Designing a whole TBL course requires creating a limited number of similar modules (four to seven for a 15-week semester) that repeatedly put students through the protocols of reading, RATs, appeals, team tasks (Application Activities), and individual assessment. Each module should be designed to make clear to students—by way of active, concrete experience—how the conceptual understanding gained from course content feeds into their ability to think and act more and more "like experts" in the discipline.

Effective course design begins with your candid responses to two questions:

1. *How do you want students to be permanently different at the end of your course, compared to how they were at the beginning?* If we are serious about our teaching, we should aim for nothing less than having a lifelong impact on our students.

2. *How will you (and they) know if they are?* Assessment of learning is central to effective teaching. Without assessment there can be no feedback by which to help students learn.

Your answer to the first of these two questions is the basis for every element of course design and can be expressed in various dimensions:

1A. What can your students now do that they could not do before? For example,

- What are the anticipated deep changes in students' ways of acting in given situations when confronted with challenges?
- What kinds of judgments and decisions will they be more effective at making as a result of your course?
- What new skills, processes, and procedures will they have mastered as a result of your course?

1B. What ideas, concepts, and other key information will now inform all of your students' thinking and actions? For example, what are the big ideas from your discipline that will become a permanent part of your students' intellect and behavior? We have collected several highly evocative examples of "big ideas" from our colleagues and provide them here as food for reflection:

- *Psychology:* There is no such thing as YOU.
- *Business:* Business is not possible without trust.
- *Nursing:* Health care can kill you.
- *Literature:* All meaning is constructed from patterns.

1C. What attitudes, perspectives, and values will now be visible in all of your students' thinking and actions? Some examples from this category include healthy skepticism, empathy toward someone, passion about something, self-questioning, and a sense of humor about something.

Whatever the nature of the permanent changes you hope and plan to see in students, these should appear in your declared course goals. Setting and communicating high expectations will help students realize that your course is going to have a permanent impact on them. This can be highly motivating.

Your answer to the second question, "How will you (and they) know if they are permanently different?" is a statement of your assessment plan for the course. By answering this question at the beginning of the course design process, you will more easily identify the function of your course modules. Each module should reinforce the thinking and the ability of students to act in the ways outlined in your response to the first question. Students should also have opportunities in each module to practice thinking and acting in the ways you have targeted and to see evidence of their progress toward the permanent changes you envision through your feedback.

EMBEDDING YOUR COURSE CONTENT

Now that you have begun designing your whole course around the permanent changes you plan to foster in your students, it will become increasingly clear that the function of course content will need to evolve in order to reinforce the new dynamic. Although the specific content itself may not be substantively or quantitatively different from what you might use in a traditionally taught course, its selection and placement now serve the higher goals of changes in how students think and act using that content. By sketching out an initial learning sequence, you have begun to formulate this new relationship between student action and course content. As you continue the process of sequence design, you will need to continue thinking about how the content you choose will promote student practice in thinking along the lines of the course goal(s), keeping in mind that every learning sequence should specifically (and explicitly) support one or more of your goals. To this end we provide here a few examples of effective strategies for organization of content in a TBL environment:

- By principles that guide disciplinary thinking
- By types of thinking on the subject matter
- By questions or modes of inquiry within the discipline
- By perspectives that shape disciplinary thinking
- By themes that overlay the content
- By skills (professional, academic, critical thinking)
- By various contexts (audiences, clients, roles, agents)

This approach to organization can present a challenge for instructors who may have relied in the past on textbooks to help structure the presentation of content in their courses. We have found, however, that with time and familiarity, this way of thinking about content is liberating for instructors. It provides an escape from the tyrannical myth that "coverage" of content is the ultimate goal of a course.

Following are two examples of successful course design schemes that we have seen from our instructors at the University at Albany.

Political Science: "The [American] Presidency"

The conventional way to teach this course is chronological: from Washington to Obama. When our colleague converted this course to TBL, he decided to focus instead on key issues that surround the presidency and organized his course into six learning sequences (example supplied by Tim Lindberg, University of Minnesota, Morris):

1. Creating the Presidency
2. Presidential Growth and the Party System
3. Presidential War Powers and Backlash
4. Progressive Politics and the Conservative Backlash
5. Creation of the Modern Presidency
6. Dilemmas of the Modern Presidency

Education: "Human Exceptionality"

The typical organization of this course (which reflects the organization of text-books on the subject) is topical, with each day or week of class focusing on a different disability so that the syllabus is a list of potential disabilities an educator may encounter. There is no overarching sense of a conceptual relationship among the various disabilities. Our colleague in this case decided that she would focus on the principles that underlie the education system's (and a teacher's) approach to handling disabilities. She therefore organized her course into four learning sequences (example supplied by Tammy Ellis-Robinson, instructor in education at the University at Albany):

1. Justice: Legality, Equity, and Collaboration
2. Diagnostics: Ability Versus Disability
3. Communication and Equitable Experience
4. Culture and Adaptations

ALIGNING COURSE POLICIES WITH TBL PRINCIPLES

The legacy of the traditional, professor-centric classroom is the pervasive notion that perfecting student behavior will lead to more learning. Control the behaviors (e.g., pressure students to come to class, take good notes, turn off cell phones), the thinking goes, and you might control the learning. Implementing TBL upends the traditional teacher-student power paradigm. A TBL course, when optimally designed, uses the student learning process itself to drive changes in student behavior. To that end, TBL places a great deal of responsibility on students, in exchange for the benefit of becoming adult participants in working with you and with their peers in mastering the knowledge and practices of your discipline.

We caution first-time TBL adopters that the attitudinal shift required of students, although broadly supported by TBL protocols and processes, is not automatic when the TBL switch is turned on. Vestiges of traditional classroom management characterized by control and coercion can undermine an otherwise well-conceived course design and implementation plan. Problems emerge for students when they experience cognitive dissonance, for example, when the instructor asks students to assume greater responsibility, but the classroom remains a tightly controlled environment where the instructor authoritatively intervenes to judge behavior, mete out punishment, and bestow rewards. The inevitable distrust and pushback that results will place you back into the role of policeman, with students failing to take responsibility for the classroom and working instead to game the system.

We advocate taking the time to rethink how you promote a new dynamic by tending to some of the subtleties of course policies and syllabus rhetoric. A successful syllabus will communicate the changed expectations for students by framing policies in terms of choices and consequences, not mandates and punishments. In many cases, this means completely recasting course policies to reflect this new paradigm. Early in the adoption process we often see syllabi that read like a litany of behavioral prescriptions: You must come to class or be penalized! You must do your homework or be penalized! You must not open your laptop during lecture! You must turn off your cell phone when in class! Although we may do this with the best of intentions, the result is that we infantilize our students, thereby making *their* behavior *our* problem.

In TBL, focusing each individual class meeting on meaningful and challenging team tasks (Application Activities) means that students will simply be too busy to engage in disruptive behaviors. Furthermore, when students see evidence that they are learning (in the form of immediate feedback on tasks), their investment and sense of ownership will motivate increasingly productive behavior. If you find students frequently distracted or disengaged, this is a signal that you may need to rethink the design, timing, and/or management of team tasks. In addition, because a TBL course is structured around frequent feedback, students will have multiple opportunities to get the message that their behaviors are or are not working to help them succeed. Instituting a system for multiple instances of peer review and evaluation (see chapter 7) is also essential to ensure that students have the opportunity to receive formative feedback from their peers. Being accountable to peers will be a novel experience for many of them, and you will find that this is a powerful tool for encouraging the behaviors that lead to greater learning.

PRACTICAL POLICY IDEAS

We want to foster a classroom culture that casts students in the role of agents in control of their own destinies. To this end, ask students on day one, after they have been sorted into teams, to develop the criteria that they will use in conducting the peer evaluation part of the final grade. We recommend showing a slide with a sampling of three or four criteria (arrive on time, prepare for class, be respectful of each other's ideas, etc.), then asking the teams to create their own lists, including or discarding the presented examples as desired. Teams send a representative to a central committee, which makes the final selection that will serve the entire class. This practice ensures that all students are fully aware of what their teammates expect from them. It also gives students, themselves, the explicit responsibility to conduct their own policing if they see the need for it—or ignore a problem if they are willing to live with the consequences. If they ignore the problem, it is not up to the instructor to intervene; this is a choice the students have made. The opportunity for peer evaluation is an essential tool in TBL, as it gives students the power to influence behavior for themselves, rather than have to rely on the authority of the instructor.

In a well-run TBL course, attendance and participation typically do not need to be closely monitored or graded. We advocate eliminating grade components not tied to real student outputs and products. Attendance grades and grades for general participation can unintentionally project to students the instructor's arbitrary, parentlike influence over them. Anytime we, as persons of authority, evaluate behaviors rather than actual products, we send the message that grades reflect not the quality of student work but rather the students' relationship with us. In any case, behavior-based grade components are redundant, as the teams will hold their members accountable—or suffer the consequences.

The same logic supports the argument for eliminating punitive grade components that are directly attached to "bad behavior" (missing class, using a laptop, talking during lecture, etc.). A TBL course should transform the way policies and grades interact in your course: Rather than being wielded as a weapon, grades should become just one more vehicle for students to get feedback on their performance.

Finally, changing the classroom culture can be a simple matter of rhetoric, even if the policies themselves are not substantially changed. Here is an example of a typical course policy framed by the instructor's authority:

> Late papers will be penalized a letter grade for each day they are late.

Note how in this instance the student's decision to submit a paper late is framed as a crime, with punishment to be exacted by the instructor. The policy as written masks the poor choice the student has made. Compare this example with a version that is not different in substance but radically different in how it casts the student's behavior and responsibility:

> For this paper, students may choose their submission date. Papers that are turned in on April 3 are eligible for 100 points. Papers turned in on April 5 are eligible for 80 points. Papers that arrive after April 5 are accepted and will receive feedback but are eligible for 0 points.

The resulting grade for an assignment handed in 2 days late remains exactly the same, but in this case student choice explicitly drives the process.

We have emphasized careful attention to the language of your policies and syllabus because these will help to set the tone for the relationship between you and your students. Whether you are communicating the content of your course, describing your teaching method, or designing and enforcing policies regarding student behavior, every encounter students have with you and your course (in person or in writing) should demonstrate their agency and validate their ownership of the learning experience.

You are now ready to develop a schedule for your course. Once you have constructed a syllabus with a projected number of modules and identified specific dates for graded assignments and tests, we encourage you to focus your work on developing the first one or two modules, without spending much time on the later ones. Most of the work you do on the later modules will inevitably have to be revised in light of what you learn in modules one and two. As you get a feel for the rhythm of the course and for the time needed for individual components, you will find that this early experience transfers directly to the quality and efficiency of design for the later learning sequences.

TBL is a journey, not a set of techniques that succeed or fail on their own. If you can maintain this perspective as you plan and experience your course, you will avoid disappointment and frustration. Stay in the moment. Watch your students as they respond to your design. The most successful TBL instructors learn to design well, launch the process, then stand back, observe students, and listen while the design plays out. You have created a community of learners, and now you are one of them.

CHAPTER 3

The Whole Course Experience

It's one thing to read about how Team-Based Learning (TBL) should be done, but it's another to hear it directly from those who are doing it. This chapter will reveal what an actual TBL experience is really like for the teacher, so you can better understand how to begin a TBL course well, how to successfully work your way through TBL modules in the middle of the course, and, finally, how to close the learning experience in the most effective way. Figure 3.1 shows the typical course structure that is outlined in this chapter.

BEGINNING A TBL COURSE

How you begin, how you orient your students, and how you respond to students' questions can have a dramatic effect on how positive or negative the TBL experience will be for both you and your students.

Getting Your Students Ready

Thoughtfully preparing your students can go a long way toward helping both your students and you have a smoother and more enjoyable TBL experience. How you start—specifically, the tone you set and how you orient your students— can determine student acceptance and satisfaction with TBL. Before getting to the classroom, you should spend some time getting your own rationales and understanding of TBL well organized. Make sure you can answer the deceptively simple student question, "Why are you using TBL?" When you truly understand your own reasons, you are in a much better position to communicate to your students how the TBL classroom works and how TBL will greatly benefit them and their learning. If you fail to properly orient your students or fail to convince them of the value of using TBL, then you are at risk of increased student resistance.

FIGURE 3.1
Prototypical Team-Based Learning course structure

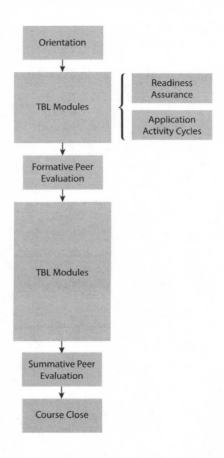

I do a lot of explaining at the beginning, because I know that most of them have had a lot of bad group experiences. First of all, I'm quite up front with it. "Group learning can be a very ineffective and miserable experience. I've experienced it myself." I say, "What are the problems with group learning?" and I will actually, on a whiteboard, make a list of all the pitfalls that they have experienced in group learning. And then one by one, I will go through those and say, "We can take care of that one in this way" or "TBL addresses the freeloading problem this way" or "You don't have to worry about doing outside work and the related scheduling problem, because in TBL all the teamwork is in class." (Brent MacLaine, Literature, University of Prince Edward Island)[1]

To get students started well, there are three goals you must achieve:

1. Students must be convinced of the educational value of TBL.
2. Students must be convinced that the structure of TBL addresses many of their legitimate concerns about group work.
3. Students must be introduced to the specific classroom processes associated with TBL.

Completing the following three tasks in the first session of any TBL course will help you achieve these goals:

1. *Introduce TBL*: Introduce the TBL method, state why you think students will be well served by TBL, and address any of their concerns about teamwork.
2. *Form teams*: In a small class, you can do the team formation process right in class. In larger classes, explain to students how and when you will be forming teams (typically using an online survey).
3. *Try TBL*: Run a mock Readiness Assurance Process (RAP) and Application Activity.

I give them an article that's in some way connected with information in today's world and that I think will engage them. So they're reading that as the other students are filing into the room. I introduce myself. We talk about the article for a bit. They're expected to start contributing immediately. Then we form the teams, so it happens really very quickly, and they have to pick the team name, and I don't give them a lot of time to do that. Then they have 10 minutes to read the syllabus, after which they have their first iRAT [Individual Readiness Assurance Test] and tRAT [Team Readiness Assurance Test]. They get thrown into it immediately. (Trudi Jacobson, Information Literacy, University at Albany)[2]

I introduced it by making the case that TBL is a bridge from the classroom to the world of practice. The first time I did this, I gave too much detail, because when we came to do it, people looked blank or forgot significant pieces of it. What I've learned to do is to introduce an overview and then revisit it in pieces. I talk about how the team typically outperforms the individual, and I address explicitly people's concerns about not doing as well because of their team. I address that very explicitly right at the front end, in the interests of informed consent and, shall we say, full disclosure. When we do that first group readiness assurance, it doesn't have a grade attached to it. I'll say, "Okay, I want you to think about in how many cases your group performance might have been better than an individual's performance." And most will say,

"Oh, yeah, we did much better as a group." Then I feed that back to them a couple of times. (Liz Winter, Social Work, University of Pittsburgh)[3]

I send out a message to all of my registered students a few days before the semester, warning them that I actually teach on the first day of class. I spend a few minutes telling them what Team-Based Learning is and why I'm doing it, and introducing them to terms like "higher-order learning skills" and "critical thinking," things that they may have heard of but they don't really know what that means. And then I spend the rest of the class actually doing an exercise. I find if I have a good activity on that first day, that's what sells it. That's what engages them. (Janet Stamatel, Sociology, University of Kentucky)[4]

Task One: Introduce TBL

It is extremely important to start off on the right foot. Students who have been told for years what to know, when to know it, and when to give it back to us on tests and exams won't always appreciate the transition from passive to active learner or the shift from "the instructor is responsible for my learning" to "I am responsible for my own learning." Some students will not be happy when you announce that your course will be using teams extensively. Missteps in the first days of class can be costly, giving unhappy or skeptical students cause to complain. Some preplanning and introductory activities can help ensure that students will support, or at least quietly tolerate, the switch to TBL. Teachers in any class will often have a very small subset of unhappy students, no matter which teaching method they use. TBL is no different. The good news is that most students by the end of the course see the value of TBL, and many students are clearly enthusiastic about it.

You need to be very clear in your own understanding, convictions, and beliefs about why you are using TBL. Students can quickly see through teachers who are not absolutely convinced of the underlying rationales for using any teaching approach that strays from the usual passive lecture model. You need to spend time with the TBL literature to gain a sufficient understanding of how the various components of TBL work both on their own and together and what each step of the TBL process is designed to achieve educationally. If you don't have clarity in your own mind, the students may sense it. This can lead to unhappy students gaining motivational fuel to voice their arguments for maintaining the status quo and resisting change.

During the transition to TBL, there is a lot going on for students, as well as teachers. Some students may not be strongly convinced of their own self-efficacy as learners. Some students view the teacher as the ultimate authority and view conversations with possibly less-capable peers as a waste of time. Some students have succeeded all their lives in traditional teacher-centered classrooms, often becoming very proficient in a "cram-and-flush" approach to learning, and they can resent this change in the rules of the "game." You need to take care of your students when they are new to the learning-centered classroom, where suddenly they are responsible for their own learning and, even more radically, partially responsible for their teammates' learning.

So the first time I taught TBL, it was new to me, and I told the students that this semester was going to be very different, that I was going to use Team-Based Learning. I went through the process of Team-Based Learning as comprehensively as I thought I could without overwhelming them with too much information, because it's almost just a lived experience. I decided not to try to overly sell Team-Based Learning as being this great phenomenon. I told them why I was doing it, that I thought it was better for them, that it fit well with my teaching strategy, and that I thought it'd make them better clinicians in the process. I got a lot of negative feedback from the first cohort. I responded to that by changing the level at which I wrote the iRAT questions. I had a cadre of students that cornered me in my office complaining "too much reading," "test questions suck," "we are teaching ourselves." But I stuck to my guns. With the second cohort of students, I had no resistance. They loved Team-Based Learning. They were disappointed that I would not be using Team-Based Learning this semester for the particular class that I'm teaching. So that was the second cohort. The first cohort of students was very different.

I also strongly agree that TBL is not for every teacher. It does require a teacher that's willing to let go, a teacher that's willing to be challenging at times, but the results are worth it. (Ron Carson, Occupational Therapy, Adventist University of Health Sciences)[5]

Showing Readiness Assurance Test (RAT) scores (like those in Table 3.1) can be very effective, particularly if the data are drawn from previous offerings of the same course. The particular data shown in Table 3.1 are drawn from a second-year mechanical engineering design course[6] and are based on the average scores over six RATs. As shown, the lowest scoring team (93%) still outperforms the highest scoring individual from the entire class (91%). Over the 4 years for which data from this course were analyzed (501 students in 80 teams), there was only one single student who outperformed the *lowest* team in the class, and no student ever outperformed his or her own team.[7] The average margin by which teams outperformed their *highest* scoring member was 14% (and the minimum margin, averaged over the 4 years of data, was 5.7%). These impressive results demonstrate the power of teams, and they are the norm in TBL. In addition to showing these results at the beginning of a course in order to sell TBL, some teachers will also show the results near the end of the term to reinforce the positive outcomes associated with the method.

TABLE 3.1
Comparison of Typical Individual and Team Readiness Assurance Test Scores Showing Lowest Scoring Team Outperforms Highest Scoring Student

Team	Individual Member Scores (%)			Team Score (%)
	Low	Mid	High	
1	62	73	87	97
2	66	78	86	97
3	65	70	85	94
4	74	77	83	98
5	56	74	85	97
6	64	79	83	98
7	68	77	79	94
8	71	79	85	98
9	55	75	81	94
10	54	70	**91**	97
11	70	77	88	96
12	55	72	78	**93**
13	54	70	75	96
14	66	82	88	98
15	64	78	85	97
16	68	80	88	98
17	55	75	84	95
18	59	80	89	95
19	57	73	82	96
20	60	78	83	97
Average	62	76	84	96

Peter Balan at the University of South Australia tells the story of how he uses data similar to those shown in Table 3.1:

> *In my introduction session to Team-Based Learning, I get students to actually do it. They go through all the stages and use all of the material, I then show them the complete RAP results of an earlier course, and I say to the students, "Okay, what does this information tell us?" It doesn't take long for someone to say that team scores are always higher than the individual scores.* (Peter Balan, Business, University of South Australia)[8]

With the first TBL course at the University of British Columbia, we made an early mistake by not repeating and reinforcing our rationales for using TBL often enough as the first semester progressed. We didn't realize we were giving too much room for students to express their unhappiness about change. Listening to the student voice is essential, but resistance needs to be anticipated and proactively addressed. We did orient the students on the first day to our rationales and to the mechanics of the TBL classroom, but we did not revisit our rationales as the semester progressed. This seemed to give argumentative fuel to the small subset of students who were unhappy. We now frequently revisit our rationales and often analyze activities after they have been completed in order to explicitly point out all the learning that has occurred.

Some Preparation Can Really Help

You should be well organized for every day in the classroom, but the first day is by far the most important. It can set the tone, good or bad, for the entire course. Be careful and thorough. For that first day, have all your materials printed and collated early; complete a detailed lesson plan; and, if you can, visit the classroom before your first class to get a sense of the layout. You need to plan how and when you will form teams and how you will facilitate the orientation activities. Demonstrate that you are organized and that TBL is well structured. Students in any class delivered in a nontraditional way, including TBL courses, can be much less tolerant of poor teacher preparation than they are in conventional lecture-based methods.

Even in well-prepared course offerings, at the beginning of any problem-solving activity, students usually experience a moment of mental discomfort as they really begin to grapple with the problem. The source of the discomfort can easily be refocused to the instructor's lack of preparation, and they may blame you for their frustrations. I work with one faculty member who consistently gets a few comments each year from students wishing that he were more organized. This intrigues me, because he is the most organized teacher I have ever met. I suspect the comments come from an uncomfortable student looking for someone else to blame. Isn't it the instructor's job to make learning easy, efficient, and painless? Any time we change the rules of engagement, we can give students cause to complain.

Plan the first class carefully. Practice your approach. Speak with passion about the learning possibilities that TBL offers and how it relates to professional practice and the workplace. You should acknowledge that most of us, students and teachers, have had bad team experiences and make sure to explain that TBL, by design, reduces or eliminates many of those difficulties.

Task Two: Form Teams

It is essential to build diverse teams. When the class roster is in a high state of flux, some TBL teachers will delay team formation until after the add/drop date. Having your teams closer to seven students per team can give you a bit of a cushion as people come and go at the start of the semester. Hopefully, teams will shrink only by a few students, but if teams fall below five students, you will likely have to do some adjustments. Team formation will be discussed more fully in chapter 5.

Task Three: Let Students Try TBL

On the first day, we also want to introduce students to the mechanics of TBL, because this may be their first TBL experience. We need to show them that TBL is going to be truly different. We should describe not only how the process works but also the educational value of each stage. It is good to point out how the entire TBL process feeds the main course objective of helping students learn how to use course content to solve relevant problems. It is often helpful to make a case for problem solving as an essential workplace skill and that the TBL classroom is a chance to acquire that skill in a more supportive setting.

Many teachers include a mock RAP and Application Activity on the first day. The mock RAP is sometimes based on the course syllabus, a short handout about TBL, or a short course-related article. Using a course-related article gets students to dive straight into the course material, which really announces that this course is going to be different! Often students are given a short amount of class time to read and review the reading material before taking the mock test. We make it very clear that these orientation activities are not for marks. Just like a regular RAP, students first take the test individually and then retake the same test in their teams.

Before and after the mock RAP, you should clearly explain what the RAP is designed to help students accomplish. Specifically, explain that the RAP is getting them ready for the Application Activities that follow. We can highlight how the RAP works, especially how students' conversations with their peers can take limited individual understanding and extend and deepen it naturally through dialogue.

Following the RAP, you can introduce the mock Application Activity. There are two common ways to do this. Some teachers will give the students a pithy article on a course-related issue and do activities based on that, but many TBL teachers use Gary Smith's (2008) activity from the *National Teaching and Learning Forum* newsletter article "First-Day Questions for the Learner-Centered Classroom."

For this activity, ask students, "Thinking of what you want to get out of your college education and this course, which of the following is most important to you?"

1. Acquiring information (facts, principles, concepts)
2. Learning how to use information and knowledge in new situations
3. Developing lifelong learning skills

In our own courses, we typically give teams 3–5 minutes to try to arrive at a team consensus of the best answer. The teachers will pass out the TBL voting cards. We then ask the teams to simultaneously report by holding up the card that corresponds to their team's decision. We then facilitate a full class discussion contrasting the various team decisions. We like this activity, because it shows the students the mechanics of the Application Activity process and clearly surfaces differing student beliefs on what good classroom learning should look like. There is a wonderful way to extend this activity (Smith, 2013). At the end of the activity, students are asked to revisit the items on the list and consider which of the items would be better achieved in class and which items could be achieved through individual study. They will quickly zero in on "acquiring information" as something they could do on their own. You can then revisit the format of TBL and show them that is exactly how TBL is structured: They acquire some information on their own and then come to class where they can work on higher order goals like application and lifelong learning skills.

Expect Some Resistance

Because most students have had miserable teamwork experiences at one time or another, you will need to take time to address their concerns and reassure them that they will not suffer the same problems while using TBL. You must clearly communicate how the accountability structures in the TBL classroom are designed to control dysfunctional team behavior. Nevertheless, the question is not "Will there be student resistance?" but "When will it start and how much will there be?" The transition to learner-centered teaching can be uncomfortable for students as they assume the responsibility for their own learning. When students are uncomfortable, they often will complain and may, intentionally or unintentionally, also make life uncomfortable for the instructor. Because you are transitioning to a new role as a facilitator of student learning, a guide, or a mentor, it can be hard to find balance at first. Although you may feel compelled to make the students feel at ease, always remember your primary goal is to help them learn. It is worth taking some time to consider how you may handle these challenges *before* you get to the classroom. Plan well and trust the method.

In my experience, the majority of students come into class with a history of being burned by group work. As a result, many students are resistant to the idea of TBL. I approach this challenge by first surfacing student concerns. We develop a two-column chart of pros and cons interactively. Students always come up with a great list: "slackers on my team," "I did all the work and nobody else contributed," "we couldn't find time when everyone could meet outside of class," "some members were too aggressive, and other members were too passive." Then the list of positives start to emerge: "teams come up with better solutions," "students learn how to work together," "it's more fun and more engaging," "students learn to communicate," "employers want team skills," "great to develop life skills," etc. Once their concerns and the benefits about group work have been surfaced, I make sure to address their concerns and talk about how TBL is different than their previous experience with small-group work, how TBL is designed to maximize the pros and minimize the cons. (Holly Bender, Veterinary Clinical Pathology, Iowa State University)[9]

I have great resistance for the first couple of weeks, until they realize how much they're learning. (Mary Hadley, Chemistry and Geology, Minnesota State University–Mankato)[10]

I was able to preempt the sense that they might feel they were doing all the work and we [the teachers] *weren't doing anything by really emphasizing how different our role was going to be compared to the traditional role and what our responsibility was. So I didn't get any resistance.* (Jenny Morris, Health Education, Plymouth University)[11]

If you thoughtfully develop a good orientation session by (a) effectively introducing TBL, (b) fairly and transparently forming teams, and (c) giving students an opportunity to try out TBL, you take the important first steps toward ensuring student buy-in and success with your TBL course.

MIDDLE OF THE COURSE

The structure of a TBL course (Readiness Assurance, Application Activities, and peer evaluation) results in a building or rolling rhythm as successive modules unfold. Early in your TBL experience, careful planning is an important ally. As the course rhythm starts to build, and as your experience grows, you will find more time to relax and enjoy all the learning that will be taking place around you.

Fink's (2003) castletop diagram can be useful to imagine the rhythm of learning events as they build across an entire module. In a typical course, the castletop visualization encourages the teacher to think about an integrated experience where in-class and out-of-class activities are synergistically linked to create a significant learning experience. The castletop diagram for a typical TBL course (see Figure 3.2) is slightly different from the usual diagram for two reasons: The complexity of activities in TBL builds as the module progresses, and the difficult work of solving significant, relevant problems is primarily undertaken by teams working *in* class.

The following sections will describe a prototypical TBL module with a series of class meetings over a 2-week period. For this example, we will imagine a course that meets twice a week for 90 minutes (total of four class meetings over 2 weeks). Course formats do vary widely, and in your course you may have 3-hour classes once a week or a single stand-alone session, but the underlying preparation principles are the same. For this prototypical 2-week module, we would schedule the RAP

FIGURE 3.2
Team-Based Learning cycle castletop diagram

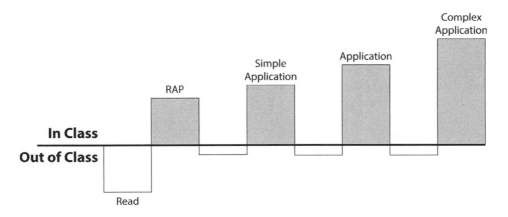

on day 1, carry out Application Activities on days 2 and 3, and end the module with a capstone activity with proper closure for the module on day 4. Every module should end by priming the students for the next module.

Module Start

The goal of the first class meeting of a module is to complete the RAP. (The specific classroom logistics for the RAP will be discussed in chapter 6.) In preparation for class, you will need to print a RAT for every student, prepare an iRAT answer form for each student (either a paper-and-pencil form or a Scantron form), prepare Immediate Feedback Assessment Technique (IF-AT) forms for each team, print appeal forms for each team, and then load them into the team folders.

It is important to do a last-minute check of folders and check that the IF-AT key matches the test key. Nothing is worse than finding out the hard way that the test and the IF-AT key do not match. I have done this—it is *very* uncomfortable. Don't let it happen to you!

Now you are ready to go to class.

Module Middle

In the class meetings following the RAP, you will typically spend the bulk of class time on Application Activities. Most of this time will be devoted to having the teams work on the activities. Your role in class will largely involve introducing the activities, facilitating the reporting and discussion, and closing the activities. Just like the first day, preparation is key. In preparation for each class, you will need to print out any student materials, such as problems and worksheets. Ready your PowerPoint slide deck, if you present Application Activities to students this way. You will also need to organize the supplies you will need to let the students report their Application Activity results, whether it is voting cards, whiteboards, flipcharts, worksheets, or whatever you use. You will need to review your lesson plan and any notes you might have taken if you have used the activity before.

There is a famous Dwight D. Eisenhower quote: "Plans are worthless; planning is everything." This pretty much captures the idea that you need to carefully plan events but realize that it is impossible to script out how they will actually unfold. The students are in control of their own learning. Your job is to provide the optimal conditions for that learning to take place. You can use the Set, Body, Close lesson-planning model (see chapter 7) to great effect to structure everything from single activities to whole classes.

It is worth remembering that TBL does not mean you never lecture. It is okay to lecture in small amounts, some of the time, for the right reasons. When your students become aware of a gap in their knowledge that may be preventing teams from moving forward, they will naturally look to you for help. This is a perfect time to give a mini-lecture to help the students progress. This is not a license to lecture for hours and hours but an invitation to provide a short, targeted clarification in response to students' questions or important gaps in their understanding.

Module End

Near the end of the module, there is often a penultimate or capstone activity that takes the problem solving students have been doing to a whole new level. As the module winds down, there are a few things you should strive to do: Help the students reflect on all they have learned; help them understand how what they have learned integrates into both the rest of the course and their discipline; and, finally, prime them for the next module. You can highlight how students can prepare successfully and preview the exciting activities ahead.

END OF COURSE

At the end of any learning experience, learners need to be reminded of all they have learned, but this is even more true with TBL. Students might feel shortchanged without a huge pile of lecture notes as a written record of their "learning." Their concerns about what exactly they have learned and what they will need to study for the exam can generate anxiety. We can add substantial value to any learning experience by providing effective closure and reinforcement.

An effective closure needs to achieve four things:

1. Provide a summary of all that has been learned.
2. Remind students of how they will use what they have learned.
3. Acknowledge their progress and effort.
4. Resist the temptation to introduce new material.

Closures can be used at the end of a single activity, a module, or an entire course. Closures at ends of modules and courses require more elaborate planning and implementation. The closure should help students pull together, integrate, and appreciate how much they have learned. Let's examine the components of a closure in more detail.

Summarize

You can start the closure with a recap of what has been learned. Try to integrate what has been learned into meaningful thematic chunks. Reinforce the major takeaway points. You can ask students to reflect on what they have learned and identify the two or three most important points.

I do a closing reflection at the end of the day. Before class ends, I say, "Okay, I want to hear from each team the three most important things you feel like you learned today." And sometimes they have a hard time doing this. They have to consolidate their knowledge. They're a little bit surprised by this. I won't let them out of the room before they can reflect on what they have learned. (Ruth Levine, Medicine, University of Texas Medical Branch)[12]

Useful Knowledge

You should always try to help students see the value in what they have learned. Often, the value of learning something is first introduced in the opening for the activity. The closure is your opportunity to revisit and reinforce the value of what has been learned. These common questions can be used during the closure: How will students use what they have learned? What will it let them do? What is it getting them ready for?

Acknowledging Progress and Effort

Students work hard during TBL classes. They are challenged to make hard decisions and commit to publicly defending their thinking. Not every team always gets an opportunity to speak. Let them know you appreciate their efforts by acknowledging them with "Thanks for your work today," "That was a great discussion; well done," or "I really enjoyed class today." Encourage their continued commitment and effort.

No New Material

You may have finished an Application Activity, and the students have had a terrific discussion that hit on almost all the main points. A few points weren't covered that well. You now have a difficult decision to make. Do you fill in the details and risk losing the big picture, main points, or important takeaways? There is no right answer to this question. What is important to keep asking yourself is, What is most important for student learning?

Consider an activity where you are hoping that students have three major takeaways. Introducing a new piece of missed detail during the closure can distract them from the three more important points you are hoping they remember. This is a conversation you need to have with yourself: Will introducing a missed point from the discussion strengthen students' overall learning or distract them from retaining the main takeaway points? Sometimes we should make the point, and sometimes we shouldn't. It can leave you unsatisfied when something was missed, but again, we must do what is best for student learning. Sometimes the point is so important we need to make it. Use your judgment.

Ending Activities Well

At the end of an activity sequence, you should help the students review and reflect on the activities to highlight all they have learned. Many teachers simply use 1-minute papers (Angelo & Cross, 1993) to help students reflect on what they have learned. Teachers will collect written student responses to the prompts "What are the three most important points you learned today?" or "What did you learn that surprised you?" Having students reflect on what they have learned can help make learning stick. We should make sure that our activity closure not only reinforces what has been learned but also clearly situates the learning in the larger course and disciplinary context.

Ending the Course Well

The following is a simple activity to alleviate many students' concerns about wondering how much they have learned. You can do a brainstorming activity, review the whole course and all the activities, and have students help build a long list of everything you have learned together.

Using Board Plans to Record Discussions

We can borrow a great idea from the case-based teaching world. During the reporting discussions, case teachers will often have preconceived a board plan to record the students' comments and contributions. The instructor, in planning for the session, will generate a concept map or infographic that captures the important points and shows their relationship to each other. By knowing what the final infographic will look like, the instructor can cluster and list items during the reporting discussion. It might not be clear to students at first why the teacher is recording their comments in this seemingly haphazard way, but as a final step, the teacher adds the final circles, arrows, and other emphasis, and the value becomes very apparent (see Figure 3.3). This can be effectively used during any closure to reinforce main points and show important relationships between concepts. When you start with a board plan, you end up building a complete infographic that can later be distributed to students. You could transcribe it or have a student take a picture and share it with the students at the next class or via e-mail. You can do a board plan to close any TBL activity, module, or whole course. These strategies can reassure students that they have learned a lot and reduce their anxiety levels.

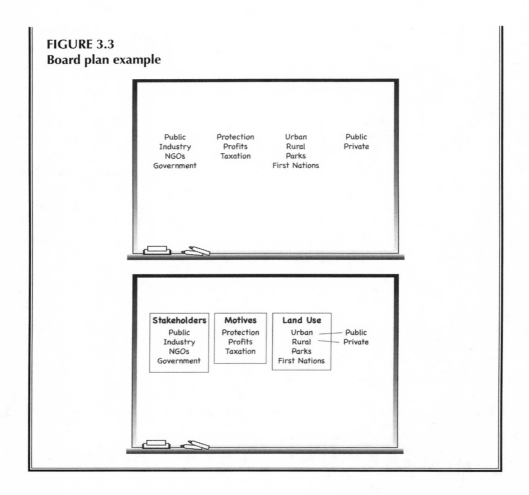

FIGURE 3.3
Board plan example

Integrating With the Big Picture

We should always take the opportunity at the end of any learning experience to help learners situate what they have learned in the larger course and disciplinary context. The traditional part-to-whole curriculum model, where teachers taught all the details then revealed at the end how these details integrated with the big picture, turns out to be ineffective (Bransford & Schwartz, 1998). It is ineffective because learners don't yet have a big-picture understanding in which to organize all the details they are learning during the activities. The part-to-whole approach forces students into rote memorization strategies, because they don't have enough context information to organize what they are learning into more powerful structures that better support retrieval and problem solving.

The curriculum model known as "whole-part-whole" is much more effective. In this approach, students are first introduced to the big-picture organization of the course concepts, then to the details, and then finally the details are reintegrated into the big picture. Because students have a sense of the big picture at the start, they can more efficiently store the details as they learn them.

Helping Students Reflect on Team Dynamics

By asking teams to do what teams are good at and having proper accountability structures in place, it eliminates the need to teach students about team dynamics. Most TBL teachers don't spend any time on the topic. But there is an interesting opportunity at the end of a TBL course to ask the question "Why did this work so well?" When we help the students reflect on what has transpired in a TBL course, we can help students see the value of the method.

Gathering Information to Improve for Next Year

Many TBL teachers end their course with a student survey that gives them feedback on the course and their learning experience. Validated tools have been developed that can be used for these surveys (Mennenga, 2012). Most of the tools use a list of questions to try to help us understand students' attitudes, beliefs, and understanding of their course experience.

Some examples are as follows:

- Do you prefer TBL or lectures? Why?
- Do you believe that TBL helped or hindered your learning? How?
- I would suggest the following to improve the course . . .
- When were you most engaged? What activities resulted in the best learning?
- When were you least engaged in your learning?

Reflecting on Your Experience and Planning for Next Year

The end-of-course survey results, the item analyses (described in chapter 6), and your reflective notes from the RATs and the Application Activities will give you what you need to improve your course. As the course progressed, you should have been taking reflective notes during and after tests and activities on what was working, what wasn't working, timing issues, and any other feedback you want to remember. At the end of a course, take a little time to complete this reflective process to improve your course for next year.

NOTES

1. B. MacLaine, personal communication, January 8, 2013.
2. T. Jacobson, personal communication, January 4, 2013.
3. L. Winter, personal communication, January 4, 2013.
4. J. Stamatel, personal communication, January 3, 2013.
5. R. Carson, personal communication, January 7, 2013.
6. MECH 223, Mechanical Design, University of British Columbia, 2012.
7. In fairness, the IF-AT process (discussed on p. 38 and further in chapter 6) allows teams multiple attempts for diminishing the score with each question, but even if this is accounted for and each tRAT is rescored with 1 point for the correct answer on the first scratch and 0 points otherwise, the results are still very convincing. For the data in Table 3.1, only 5 individuals in a class of 130 outperform the lowest team in the class, and no individual outperforms his or her own team. In considering 4 years of data from this course from 2009 to 2012 with over 500 students and 80 teams, there was only a single isolated instance where an individual outperformed his or her team (when the RAP scoring is based only on the first scratch).
8. P. Balan, personal communication, January 7, 2013.
9. H. Bender, personal communication, January 9, 2013.
10. M. Hadley, personal communication, January 9, 2013.
11. J. Morris, personal communication, January 9, 2013.
12. R. Levine, personal communication, January 3, 2013.

CHAPTER 4

The Evidence, Please

Karla A. Kubitz

If you still need convincing of the power and benefits of Team-Based Learning (TBL), or if you need to convince others, this chapter is for you. A wealth of information already exists on the efficacy of TBL, and this chapter draws from that educational literature to outline the evidence for how and why TBL works. The chapter also looks to the literature to summarize typical reactions of teachers and students new to the TBL classroom, as well as strategies for minimizing negative reactions.

With TBL we are told that students will prepare ahead of time, that there is no need to lecture, and that class time will be freed up for problem solving. But is all this really possible? I pondered that question myself when I first read about TBL. Through my own experience and from consulting the educational literature, I've decided that these lofty outcomes are not only possible but in fact very normal.

However, to achieve these outcomes, you need to do your homework first! You need to gather evidence, build your rationales, and be able to convince yourself, your colleagues, and, most important, your students about the benefits of using TBL. This chapter will help you gain some understanding of how and why TBL works and what to expect when you get to the classroom. We are going to base our understanding and expectations of TBL in the educational literature.

Some familiarity with the various theories of learning will also provide you with powerful and defensible explanations for why TBL works so well. Simply put, having some understanding of Chickering and Gamson's (1987) principles for good practice or Vygotsky's, Bruner's, Perry's, and Zull's theories of learning will make you a better TBL teacher.

There are three fundamental questions about TBL that teachers should be able to answer:

- Why do we switch to TBL?
- Does TBL really work?
- Why does TBL work?

We will also want to understand what to expect in the TBL classroom, including the following:

- What reactions do teachers have to TBL?
- What reactions do students have to TBL?
- If there are negative reactions, can they be minimized?

Let's start with our first fundamental question: Why do we switch to TBL?

WHY DO WE SWITCH TO TBL?

I switched to TBL almost 8 years ago to get a livelier, more interactive classroom. TBL sounded like it could be a good way to achieve this, and in fact it was. The educational literature provides a number of insights into why teachers switch to TBL, including dissatisfaction with lecturing, dissatisfaction with group projects, and a desire to develop critical thinking skills.

Dissatisfaction With Lecturing

It's probably no surprise that teachers reported switching to TBL because of dissatisfaction with lecturing (Clark, Nguyen, Bray, & Levine, 2008; Dana, 2007; Letassy, Fugate, Medina, Stroup, & Britton, 2008). I, too, was dissatisfied with the lack of student engagement during lectures. Clark et al. (2008) expressed it nicely when they said, "Despite efforts to make lectures livelier or to use more audiovisual material, students often remained passive and uninvolved" (p. 112). It was the same for me. I'd tried a variety of techniques to engage students (including case studies, "fishbowl" discussions, and discussion questions) with little success. In the same vein, Letassy et al. (2008) cited "varying degrees of [student] preparation and participation in class discussions and activities; inconsistent opportunities for application of material; [and] difficulty in keeping students engaged in the material during lectures" (p. 2) as their main motivators. Many teachers find that lecturing, with its emphasis on "covering information," leaves little time for learning to apply information. This is echoed in a comment by Dana (2007): "[My] dissatisfaction [with lecturing] arose from the fact that much of class time was spent reviewing the basic concepts contained in the textbook rather than exploring the implications and applications [of the course material]" (p. 63).

Dissatisfaction With Group Projects

Prior to implementing TBL, when I used group projects, I did so with the expectation that group projects would provide students with a much-needed opportunity to engage with one another and practice using the course material to solve problems. However, I was not getting high levels of engagement, and the student groups didn't seem that effective in solving problems. Given this, I was not surprised to find that many teachers switched to TBL because they were dissatisfied with their current use of groups and group projects (Dana, 2007; Nieder, Parmelee, Stolfi, & Hudes, 2005). Dana (2007) recalled, "I was dissatisfied with my attempts to use ad hoc groups to engage students and help them explore concepts in more depth" and that "groups tended to be ineffective, because only a few students would have done the reading carefully enough to be able to discuss the question at anything more than a superficial level" (p. 63). Along the same lines, Nieder et al. (2005) noted, "The small group sessions designed to review anatomical content via case problems had [historically] suffered from poor attendance, variable student preparation, and inconsistent group problem-solving achievement" (p. 56). As these quotes illustrate, my experiences with group projects prior to TBL were not atypical, and these experiences have also led other teachers to switch to TBL.

Desire to Develop Critical Thinking Skills

Teachers and employers alike want students to learn to think critically (Andersen, Strumpel, Fensom, & Andrews, 2011; Clark et al., 2008; Dana, 2007; Letassy et al., 2008). Andersen et al. (2011) switched because they were looking for enhanced team discussion and a higher level of critical thinking. Clark et al. (2008) pointed out that "recent trends in nursing education demand that exit goals for graduating seniors include critical thinking skills and problem solving skills" (p. 112). Dana (2007), likewise, emphasized the need for critical thinking when she said, "The most important reason for switching to TBL was a realization that my teaching method did not adequately allow students to develop and practice their critical thinking and decision-making skills" (p. 63). Last, from the medical school arena, Letassy et al. (2008) also noted, "We became dissatisfied with the students' ability to think critically and apply information to patient cases during class and to live patient interactions during their advanced pharmacy practice experiences" (pp. 1–2).

When we listen to these voices of experience, it seems clear that the most common reasons teachers switch to TBL are

- dissatisfaction with current teaching practices;
- dissatisfaction with lecturing to unprepared, passive students;
- dissatisfaction with outcomes of traditional group work; and
- a desire to help students develop critical thinking and problem-solving skills.

Now that we know what can lead teachers to switch to TBL, let's see what the educational literature says about how well TBL works.

DOES TBL WORK?

The outcomes of TBL have been shown to be equal to or better than those of other teaching strategies. This has been shown when researchers compared Individual Readiness Assurance Test (iRAT) and Team Readiness Assurance Test (tRAT) scores (Chung, Rhee, Baik, & Oh-Sun, 2009; Grady, 2011; Nicoll-Senft, 2009; Nieder et al., 2005) and examination scores between TBL and non-TBL courses (Grady, 2011; Koles, Nelson, Stolfi, Parmelee, & DeStephen, 2005; Koles, Stolfi, Borges, Nelson, & Parmelee, 2010; Letassy et al., 2008; Levine et al., 2004; Persky, 2012; P. A. Thomas & Bowen, 2011; Vasan, DeFouw, & Compton, 2011; Zingone et al., 2010). Let's look specifically at how well TBL fares in each of these comparisons.

tRAT Scores

TBL produces tRAT scores that are higher than iRAT scores, demonstrating the power of teams. Although the magnitude of the difference varies, most studies reported statistically significant differences between tRAT and iRAT scores. For example, Chung et al. (2009) compared iRAT and tRAT scores in students taking TBL sessions on medical ethics and found statistically significant differences between iRAT and tRAT scores (i.e., tRAT > iRAT by 1 point on a 5-point scale). Similarly, Nieder et al. (2005) transitioned the small-group component of a medical anatomy course from case-based discussion sessions to TBL sessions and found a statistically significant difference between iRAT and tRAT scores (tRAT > iRAT by an average of 16%). Finally, Nicoll-Senft (2009) reported that for her graduate-level special education students tRAT scores were also significantly higher than iRAT scores (by an average of 7.26 points on a 100-point scale). As was discussed in chapter 3, even the team with the lowest tRAT score in the class typically outperforms the individual with the highest iRAT score.

Exam Scores

TBL produces equal or better performance on final and standardized exams in comparison with non-TBL classes. This finding is consistent across different types of studies that have examined the effects of TBL on final exam scores, including historical comparisons (Grady, 2011; Letassy et al., 2008; Persky, 2012), quasi-experimental studies (Zingone et al., 2010), and experimental studies (Koles et al., 2005, 2010; P. A. Thomas & Bowen, 2011). Most of the historical and quasi-experimental studies listed here found that TBL maintains performance on final exams. The standout, Persky (2012), observed a statistically significant increase in final exam scores between pre-TBL-taught and TBL-taught formats. These results are extremely interesting. Students perform as well as they normally do, and sometimes better than that, on final exams with relatively little lecturing!

Koles et al. (2005) used a crossover design to compare case-based group discussion and TBL formats and found that average final exam scores were the same regardless of format. TBL student performance equaled non-TBL student performance. In an interesting follow-up, Koles et al. (2010) compared performance on final exam questions taught via TBL with performance on questions taught via other instructional strategies and found that performance on TBL-taught pathology concepts was significantly higher than for non-TBL-taught pathology concepts. P. A. Thomas and Bowen (2011) compared TBL and traditional small-group formats and found that students got significantly more final exam questions correct when the information was taught with TBL than when it was taught with the small-group format. These two studies (Koles et al., 2010; P. A. Thomas & Bowen, 2011) indicate that students learn information taught with TBL better than they do information taught via other instructional strategies.

TBL improves performance on standardized exams. This is particularly exciting, especially for those of you in settings where your students are required to take standardized exams. Levine et al. (2004) replaced 8 out of 16 lectures in a psychiatry clerkship with TBL sessions and compared student performance on the National Board of Medical Examiners (NBME) psychiatry subject test and found a significant increase in scores from lecture to TBL formats. Likewise, Vasan et al. (2011) transitioned a medical anatomy course from lecture to TBL, emphasizing the Readiness Assurance Process (RAP) aspect of TBL, and found a statistically significant increase in NBME Subject Examination scores from lecture to TBL formats.

With good evidence that TBL does work, let's now take a look at the fit between TBL and current thinking about how students learn best. That is, let's look at *why* TBL works.

WHY DOES TBL WORK?

Over the years, I've learned that I'm most effective when I'm able to interact with smaller groups of students and that my students learn best when they are actively involved with the course material. This notion is supported by the seven principles of good practice in undergraduate education proposed by Chickering and Gamson (1987), which stress the importance of contact between teachers and students as well as the importance of active learning. Chickering and Gamson's other principles, including developing reciprocity, cooperation among students, time on task, high expectations, and respecting diverse talents, also apply to TBL, as do several theories of learning. Let's start by looking at the implications of Vygotsky's theory for our understanding of why TBL works so well.

Vygotsky's Theory

Vygotsky's theory of learning (Bigge & Shermis, 1999; Shabani, Khatib, & Ebadi, 2010; van de Pol, Volman, & Beishuizen, 2010) includes two important ideas. He believed that both social interaction and the use of language are essential for learning. Vygotsky believed that students need to interact with other people in order to deepen their understanding of their experiences. They need to put their thoughts into words, share their thinking with others, and receive feedback from others on the quality of their thinking. TBL fits nicely with Vygotsky's theory, as students are routinely required to put their thoughts into words to discuss and develop a team consensus. This occurs both during tRATs and during Application Activities. This aligns nicely with Vygotsky's emphasis on social interaction and on the use of language.

Vygotsky's theory of learning (Bigge & Shermis, 1999; Shabani et al., 2010; van de Pol et al., 2010) also looks at learning as a process that can be facilitated by the right kind of learning activities. Students begin the learning process using the skills that they currently possess. The learning activities that follow should focus on tasks that are just slightly more difficult. When students are working in this slightly advanced area, they are in what Vygotsky refers to as their *zone of proximal development* (ZPD), and it is in the ZPD where the best learning takes place. It is important to remember that students in their ZPD are working on skills that are too difficult for them to do independently but not too difficult for them to do with help. In TBL, at least some of the Readiness Assurance Test (RAT) questions and all Application Activities should place most of the students in their ZPDs.

In Vygotsky's learning theory (Bigge & Shermis, 1999; Shabani et al., 2010; van de Pol et al., 2010), the learning process is facilitated through interaction with "more knowledgeable others." Both teachers and peers can serve as more knowledgeable others. However, peers work best as more knowledgeable others if they are at slightly different skill levels from one another. TBL takes advantage of this because TBL teams are, by design, heterogeneous in many different ways, and different students will have the opportunity to serve as the "more knowledgeable other" at different times.

According to Vygotsky, interaction with peers is particularly beneficial because it exposes students to different yet fairly close understandings of course concepts, and it asks them to merge these different, individual understandings into a single, shared understanding. The intellectual effort involved in aligning individual thinking into one common understanding facilitates learning. In the RAP, students share their individual answers to RAT questions; discuss their differences; select a team answer; and, as a result, end up with a shared understanding of the course content.

Vygotsky also says that interacting with teachers facilitates the learning process because teachers can "scaffold" learning. Scaffolding (van de Pol et al., 2010) occurs when a teacher helps a student by providing a special kind of temporary support that facilitates the completion of a task that the "student otherwise might not be able to complete" (p. 272). Scaffolding is providing the right kind of help at just the right time and in just the right amount. It requires a finely tuned sense of the type of support that a student needs and an ability to choose the right moment to provide that support. Examples of scaffolding include providing a timely demonstration (e.g., do it like this), providing specific or clarifying instructions (e.g., start by examining the outcomes of the study), or asking appropriate and timely questions. In TBL, teachers design Application Activities that put students in their ZPDs and provide sufficient scaffolding to allow them to be successful. For example, a teacher might pose a question to a team that appears to be struggling during an Application Activity or provide a worksheet that helps structure students' thinking in a step-by-step manner during an Application Activity.

Vygotsky said that scaffolding benefits both teacher and student: "Scaffolding is . . . a fluid, interpersonal process in which both participants . . . actively build common understanding through communicative exchanges" (van de Pol et al., 2010, p. 272). Vygotsky said that student and teacher learn from one another by the question-and-answer exchanges involved in scaffolding. This is one of my favorite parts of TBL. As I listen to my teams' deliberations during the tRAT and Application Activities, I get a much better understanding than ever before about the aspects of the course content that are difficult for my students and why they are difficult. I can "hear" or "overhear" their thinking! Quite often, I am surprised at the different interpretations (theirs and mine) of the same sentences in the textbook.

Vygotsky's theory applies to many aspects of TBL and can help us understand why TBL works. The tRAT and Application Activities provide numerous opportunities for social interaction and language use, the Application Activities are designed to occur within the students' ZPDs, and the tRAT and Application Activities provide excellent opportunities to scaffold learning. When I think of helping my students learn how to effectively use language, I need to both model and demand the correct use of the language. For example, in psychology, students quite often refer to personality characteristics as "traits." I need to model the correct use of this language and use it only when I am referring to a behavioral tendency that someone exhibits across different situations. I also need to require that all students use the word correctly during TBL Application Activity reporting.

Bruner's Theory

Bruner's theory of learning (Bigge & Shermis, 1999) can not only help us understand why TBL works but also help us implement it effectively. For Bruner, the best learning occurs when students are challenged to put thoughts into words, express them to someone else, and solve problems. Sounds exactly like the TBL classroom! Bruner said that when students do these things, they "construct" knowledge. In

Bruner's theory, knowledge consists of experiences that learners have had and have "processed." Learners have decided what those experiences mean, how they fit with what they already know, and what they are able to do with what they have learned.

For Bruner, "learning" is representing knowledge mentally (i.e., getting it off the page and into the head), and as students become more cognitively sophisticated, they should be encouraged to move from concrete to increasingly abstract representations of knowledge. For example, college students initially "learn" by copying notes word for word off PowerPoint slides and memorizing them. Bruner said that teachers should help students to, instead, represent knowledge by talking about it, thinking critically about it, and applying it in problem-solving activities. In TBL, students begin knowledge construction as they prepare for the iRAT and continue it throughout the tRAT and Application Activities.

Bruner also said that knowledge involves learning rules, known as coding schemes, which can be used for organizing new experiences and information. Learners use the coding schemes that they have developed to integrate what they know and what they are learning. For example, in my classes, students learn to distinguish theories of motivation from theories of group development. They know that each of the different kinds of theories has a different, unique purpose. So, if I tell them that self-determination theory is a theory of motivation, they know that it can be used to help change the behavior of sedentary individuals considering starting an exercise regimen. According to Bruner, the teacher's purpose is to teach the student how to learn and how to construct knowledge and apply coding schemes. Bruner (1966) said, "We teach a subject not to produce little living libraries on that subject, but rather to get a student to think mathematically for himself, to consider matters as an historian does, to take part in the process of knowledge-getting. Knowing is a process, not a product" (p. 72).

Bruner's theory clearly applies to TBL. TBL works because it allows students to actively construct their own knowledge and exposes students to multiple problem-solving opportunities using tRAT and Application Activities. If we use Bruner's theory to guide us, we will want to create data-rich Application Activities that challenge students to use figures, models, and data to make decisions. This is because they require students to use complex data sets to make specific decisions, creating excellent opportunities for knowledge construction and problem solving.

Let's switch perspectives once again and look at why TBL works so well through the lens of Perry's framework for cognitive development.

Perry's Theory

Perry's framework of cognitive development (Perry, 1999; Thoma, 1993) also has the potential to help us understand and implement TBL. It describes four stages of cognitive development that students progress through. The stages start with *Dualism*, move on through *Multiplicity* and *Relativity*, and finish with *Commitment*.

Students with a dualistic view conceive of knowledge as absolute (i.e., right or wrong) and the teacher as the expert whose primary purpose is to deliver the "correct" answer. Once students enter the Multiplicity stage, they acknowledge that diversity of opinion exists, but they have no ability to judge between different opinions. They view knowledge as subjective and their opinion as just as valid as anyone else's (i.e., all opinions are considered equal). When students enter the Relativity stage, they begin to be able to use discipline-specific criteria to judge among different perspectives. However, they are not yet able to apply their newly developed critical thinking skills outside the disciplinary context. Once students reach the Commitment stage (typically not until after college), they are able to apply critical thinking skills in a variety of contexts to judge among different perspectives and arrive at difficult but reasonable decisions based on reasonable evidence.

For Perry, the teacher's goal is to facilitate the transitions between stages (Nelson, 1996). Students facing the transition between Dualism and Multiplicity need help recognizing and accepting that there are different perspectives and that they must become comfortable with uncertainty and ambiguity. Kloss (1994) cautioned teachers to "nudge" rather than "shove" students into transitioning between stages. To move students out of Dualism, Kloss (p. 152) suggested

- "using subject matter that provides possibilities for ambiguity, varied interpretations, and multiple perspectives";
- "reinforcing for students that alternative points of view may be legitimate";
- "requiring students to explain concretely the reasons for any point that they reject"; and
- "reinforcing the legitimacy of students' personal views and experiences."

Students facing the transition between Multiplicity and Relativity need practice judging different perspectives. To move students out of Multiplicity, Kloss (1994) suggested

- using small-group work frequently,
- using guided discussion frequently, and
- keeping expectations high that students can be taught to substantiate opinions, ideas, and hypotheses with evidence.

Students facing the transition between Relativity and Commitment need practice applying discipline-specific criteria for judging different perspectives in a variety of different situations or contexts. To move students out of Relativity, Kloss (1994) suggested

- helping students see that they must make choices and commitments and
- providing opportunities for students to articulate personal worldviews.

Perry's theory suggests that TBL works because it facilitates the transitions between stages. For example, both the tRAT and the Application Activities expose students in Dualism to multiple perspectives. Over time, they come to see that alternative points of view may be legitimate and that it is important to listen to their peers' reasons for their points of view. TBL also exposes students in Multiplicity to the use of discipline-specific criteria to evaluate alternative points of view. During tRAT and Application Activities, individuals and teams are expected to substantiate opinions and ideas with evidence.

In addition, a number of TBL teachers have noted that the sequence of activities during the Application Activities mimics the sequence through Perry's stages and have wondered whether this is also one of the reasons that TBL works so well. Figure 4.1 illustrates the relationship between Perry's stages and the activities that go on during a typical conversation as students work on an Application Activity. In the beginning, teams are tasked with a question that requires them to make a specific choice. Individual students make pronouncements about their preferred choices. This is normally in a very Dualistic (i.e., right vs. wrong) way. Next, teammates share their choices, and a multiplicity of opinions often emerges (Multiplicity stage). This is where diversity during team formation can greatly enhance the

FIGURE 4.1
Perry's framework of cognitive development

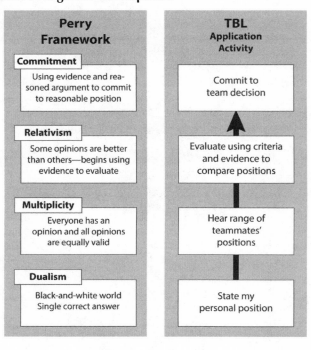

quality of the discussion. The teams are then forced into Relativism to sort through the opinions in search of the "best" choice. This is where the evidence and criteria of the discipline must be used to sort stronger from weaker opinions. Students must accept that there *is* a single best answer and that they must use the evidence to identify it. As the time approaches to report their choices to the whole class, teams must come together and make a final commitment to one best choice (Commitment stage). Teams work with this commitment as they publicly present their decisions to the other teams and participate in a whole-class discussion examining the decisions of all the teams.

I really appreciate Perry's theory because it helps me understand why some of my students don't like TBL. Students in the Dualism stage can be very uncomfortable when we deemphasize lecturing, emphasize teamwork and peer teaching, and focus on developing critical thinking skills. To them, teaching is lecturing, and peers are not valid sources of knowledge. Given that many undergraduates are in the Dualism stage for a good portion of their undergraduate career, Perry's theory implies that I should, if I want to be a good TBL teacher, take the students' stage of cognitive development into account and provide scaffolding that helps them move into and through the stages. For example, one of my learning objectives is that students learn to use the language of psychology correctly. I could scaffold them in this by beginning the semester by asking teams to choose the best from several already-written answers (i.e., answers presented as written by other students) and, over the course of the semester, progressing to asking teams to use the language of psychology to develop their own answers and be able to correctly explain or defend them.

Let's shift viewpoints one last time and use Zull's learning theory as a way to understand why TBL works so well and how to implement it effectively.

Zull's Theory

Zull's learning theory (Zull, 2004) includes five key ideas about teaching and learning that can give us important insight into why TBL works. The first is the idea that the brain is malleable and learning creates connections between neurons, creating neural networks. The second is that students benefit from using neural networks during their learning. Neural networks will change and grow when those areas of the brain are actively engaged in the learning process. The third is the idea that students benefit from becoming emotionally involved in their learning. As Zull said, "To create and change this buzzing network [the neural networks in the brain] we need more than just activity, we need emotion" (p. 70). TBL clearly gets emotional when teams argue, sometimes quite intensely, about which option to choose during the tRAT and cheer when they uncover the "star" on the Immediate Feedback Assessment Technique form that indicates a correct answer. The fourth is the idea that teachers should seek out and learn from student errors. Zull said, "It was futile to imagine that I could eliminate students' existing neuronal networks with a shake of my head or a red marker. Instead I [decided to view] . . . student errors as clues for teaching. Errors help identify gaps in student networks and provide ideas for how to build on those networks" (p. 71). TBL brings errors in thinking to light during the tRAT, appeals, and the Application Activities by allowing teams (intrateam or interteam) to compare their thinking and get focused feedback. The fifth idea is that teachers should involve peers in teaching one another. "When I began to understand knowledge as consisting of networks of neurons, it dawned on me that my students' knowledge was actually physically different from my own" (p. 70). Instead, Zull recommended asking students to explain concepts to one another, "reasoning that their networks will be a better match with those of their peers" (p. 70). TBL is consistent with Zull's recommendation that students explain concepts to one another using their own "student" neural networks. This most notably happens during the tRAT and during the Application Activities.

The implication is that TBL works because it gets students emotionally involved and engages their neural networks. TBL also includes a strong focus on eliciting and challenging errors in students' thinking. Zull's theory suggests that to be good TBL teachers, we need to design both RAT questions and Application Activities carefully. We need to design at least some RAT questions so they reveal common errors in thinking, and we need to design Application Activities so they are significant and emotionally engaging for students.

Next we will consider what kinds of reactions students and teachers have to TBL.

WHAT REACTIONS DO TEACHERS HAVE TO TBL?

Three common faculty reactions to TBL are increased excitement about teaching, a perception that one's role as a teacher has changed, and increased stress associated with the demands of switching to TBL. Insights to better understand these teacher reactions can be found in studies based on self-report instruments and narrative studies accompanying various "how TBL works" experiences.

Increased Excitement

In numerous studies, TBL teachers reported increased excitement about teaching and about what was occurring in their classrooms (Andersen et al., 2011; Dana, 2007; Jacobson, 2011; Letassy et al., 2008; Nicoll-Senft, 2009). I definitely felt this way when I first started using TBL. Jacobson (2011) observed, "There is nothing more gratifying than walking around the classroom while teams engage in discussion, hearing them analyze fine points about the course material and defend their positions with evidence" (p. 97). I agree. Andersen et al. (2011, p. 10) echoed this, saying, "Once student teams are engaged in an activity . . . the classrooms become virtual beehives of activity." Dana (2007) noted that using TBL "was an extraordinary experience . . . to hear students argue vigorously over a point of law using correct legal terminology that just three days before they had never even heard of" (p. 72).

Perception of a Changed Role as a Teacher

TBL teachers reported thinking differently about their courses and about their roles in the classroom (Andersen et al., 2011; Dana, 2007; M. D. Thomas & McPherson, 2011). Andersen et al. (2011) noted that creating reading guides for the RAP encouraged faculty to be more critical in their reading of the textbook and more selective in their assigning of readings (p. 6). Echoing the increased focus on selectivity, Dana (2007) said that switching to TBL made her realize that her course focus would be to give students the tools they need and teach them how to logically think through a problem to make a good decision rather than to cover as much content as possible (p. 65). She added that using TBL allowed more time to delve into more interesting applications than lecturing would permit (p. 82). M. D. Thomas and McPherson (2011) summed up saying, "Because students were more likely to come to class prepared, we were freed from the need to lecture about the assigned material. Instead, we spent class time on interesting activities . . . and real-world application of the research literature" (p. 488).

Increased Stress

In addition to having these positive reactions, TBL teachers also reported that making the switch to TBL was sometimes very time-consuming (Andersen et al., 2011; Dana, 2007; Drummond, 2012; Fujikura et al., 2013; Walters, 2012). When I first switched to TBL, I revamped just one of my courses at a time as a way of managing the time commitment involved. The perception that switching to TBL can be time-consuming was supported by the survey that Fujikura et al. (2013) conducted of their TBL instructors. They found a high level of instructor agreement (4.44/5.00) with the question "Did you find preparing for each session was hard work?" In addition, Walters (2012) noted, "TBL took at least as much effort as I would have spent preparing new lectures" (p. 3). Drummond (2012), similarly concerned, warned, "Each TBL session requires considerable preparatory time (offline) by the instructor and [an] extensive amount of grading to be performed after the TBL" (p. 60). Finally, Dana (2007) advised, "TBL should not be attempted without investing the time in advance to make it work" (p. 86).

Switching to TBL can be both exciting and time-consuming. Teachers were excited about seeing students deeply engaged with one another and with the course material. Teachers moved away from being simple deliverers of content and toward becoming facilitators of student problem solving and designers of high-quality learning experiences. Some teachers struggled with the time required to revamp classes and experienced stress and anxiety as a result.

Teachers are excited and changed by TBL. What about the students? What are their reactions? Let's take a look at student reactions to TBL.

WHAT REACTIONS DO STUDENTS HAVE TO TBL?

Some students have positive reactions and others have negative reactions to TBL. This range of reaction has been true from my experience, as well as in the educational literature. I have had some students write letters to my department head raving about the wonders of TBL, and I have had other students write scathing comments about it on my evaluations at the end of the semester. Let's look closer.

Increased Engagement

Among the positive reactions, students are more engaged in TBL courses than in lecture-based courses (Chung et al., 2009; Clark et al., 2008; Kelly et al., 2005; Levine et al., 2004). When students were surveyed about their level of engagement, they reported higher levels during TBL. For example, Chung et al. (2009) assessed student engagement using a single "engagement-related" question during TBL sessions on medical ethics and found a high level (4.26/5.00) of student engagement. In addition, Levine et al. (2004) assessed student engagement using the Classroom Engagement Survey and found significantly higher student engagement in TBL compared to lecture classes, with mean scores of 4.24/5.00 for TBL and 3.46/5.00 for lecture. Similarly, Clark et al. (2008) assessed student engagement using the Classroom Engagement Survey and found significantly higher student engagement (in the Learner Participation subscale specifically) in TBL compared to lecture classes.

In addition, when students were observed directly, higher levels of student engagement were evident. Kelly et al. (2005) compared student engagement in TBL and lecture classes using the STROBE. The STROBE is a classroom observation tool, and STROBE data are collected during "live" class sessions by trained observers. Using the STROBE, student behavior is coded as learner-to-learner interaction, learner-to-teacher interaction, or learner self-engaged. STROBE data were collected during seven of Kelly et al.'s lecture classes and three TBL classes, and engagement was significantly higher during TBL classes. TBL classes had less learner-to-instructor interaction than lecture (21% for TBL vs. 58% for lecture) and more learner-to-learner interaction than lecture (51% for TBL vs. 9% for lecture).

Improved Attitude Toward Teams and Teamwork

Also among the positive reactions, student attitudes toward teamwork are sometimes improved after TBL. For example, Levine et al. (2004) administered the Value of Teams Survey before and after a series of TBL sessions and found an improved attitude toward teams and teamwork in the Working With Peers and Value of Group Work subscales. Likewise, Grant-Vallone (2010) asked students in a TBL and in a cooperative learning class to respond to the statement "We could have done a better job working alone." Grant-Vallone found that students in the TBL class were less likely to agree with the statement than students in the cooperative learning class. That is, the TBL students valued their team experiences and didn't think that they could have done a better job working alone. In the one conflicting study, Clark et al. (2008) administered the Value of Teams Survey before and after an 8-week TBL-taught class and found no significant pretest to posttest differences in attitude toward teams and teamwork.

Increased Frustration

TBL students reported three main areas of frustration: missing being lectured to, being uncomfortable with uncertainty and ambiguity, and disliking the peer evaluation requirements.

Some students were frustrated that they were missing what they saw as valuable opportunities to "learn" from lectures. Persky (2012) noted, "Twenty-eight percent of students agreed that they missed out on instructor contact because of the TBL format" (p. 4). P. A. Thomas and Bowen (2011) said, "Students perceive the absence of didactics [lectures] to be withholding faculty expertise at the expense of 'active learning' strategies" (p. 35). Andersen et al. (2011) reported that students asked "why they were expected to learn the content themselves" (p. 7).

Some students were frustrated by the ambiguous nature of the 4 S Application Activities. Specifically, they found it difficult that there could be more than one correct answer (depending on the rationale provided for it) to a multiple-choice question. Andersen et al. (2011) noted that students "wanted and expected the faculty to provide a single 'correct' answer after their team discussions [and] . . . were very uncomfortable with having more than one option for patient care dependent on the situation" (p. 9). P. A. Thomas and Bowen (2011) noted, "TBL relies on ambiguity in the Application Activities to stimulate team discussions, and medical students may especially find this aspect disconcerting" (p. 35).

Some students were frustrated and annoyed by the peer evaluation requirements of TBL. Nieder et al. (2005) said, "The most contention was over the peer
evaluation system that required at least some discrimination between team members. Students were very reluctant to do this and several students admitted that their
team 'fixed' the scores so that everyone would receive a 10-point average score" (p.
59). P. A. Thomas and Bowen (2011) found peer evaluations were not appreciated,
even if the TBL sessions were (p. 35). Andersen et al. (2011) reported, "Students
who have never had the experience of evaluating their peers . . . may not understand
this process, or even accept that it is appropriate for them" (p. 12).

Students react both positively and negatively to TBL. The positives are increased
engagement and an improved attitude toward teams and teamwork. The negative
reactions are related to lack of lecturing by faculty, difficulty dealing with ambiguity, and not liking the peer evaluation requirements. Negative student reactions
are always worrisome. One of the things that I did in response to negative reactions from students was to spend additional time at the beginning of the following
semester helping students understand why I teach using TBL. G. A. Smith's (2008)
"First-Day Questions for the Learner-Centered Classroom" is particularly helpful
in getting student "buy-in" to TBL. Smith's "First-Day Questions" is discussed in
greater detail in chapter 3, in the section on orienting your students.

I wondered whether there might be other ways to minimize negative student
reactions. I found a couple of strategies that I'll share with you.

IF THERE ARE NEGATIVE REACTIONS TO TBL, CAN THEY BE MINIMIZED?

There are several strategies to consider for minimizing teacher stress and anxiety
during the transition to TBL. First, faculty should seek out support or build a personal support network. This can involve direct support from a local teaching and
learning center or finding another like-minded colleague to talk with. Andersen et
al. (2011) reported that, in their case, "faculty met informally to discuss successes
and challenges, as well as formally to debrief and capture initial perceptions of
TBL" (p. 7). Likewise, Freeman (2012) noted, "An important aspect of support
is academic development on 'nitty-gritty' matters, such as devising suitable [RAT]
questions" (p. 165). Parmelee, Michaelsen, Cook, and Hudes (2012) suggested
that it is helpful if leadership supports the idea that "classroom time needs to be
used for solving problems and not just transmittal of information" (p. 283) and
Sibley and Parmelee (2008) observed, "The institutional culture, including the students, must support instructional innovation and understand that a new strategy
has a trial-and-error [or piloting] period" (p. 47).

In addition, it can be helpful if new teachers can see TBL in action. As
Freeman (2012) said, "TBL needs to be seen in action because observation enables

demystification, and the 'hum of students engaging' is persuasive to would-be adopters" (p. 164). Similarly, Andersen et al. (2011) described a faculty orientation that included "TBL theory and a mini TBL experience (teachers read the same information, wrote an iRAT, and then completed a tRAT using scratch cards)" and in which "the benefits of TBL such as enhanced team discussion, critical thinking, and competitiveness, were illuminated by the orientation. Additionally, the mini TBL experience resulted in increased faculty understanding and 'buy in'" (p. 3).

Students also benefit from receiving an orientation to TBL. Andersen et al. (2011) described a mandatory student orientation that is conducted on the first day of class (p. 6). As part of this orientation, teachers are ready to respond to student concerns with sound rationales and prepared presentation materials highlighting benefits of TBL. Similarly, Levine et al. (2004) use several introductory orientation activities to familiarize students to the TBL approach (p. 271), and Masters (2012) gives an orientation where the students run through the TBL process twice (p. 345). Thoroughly and persuasively orienting students to TBL may prevent some of the frustration they sometimes experience.

In addition, TBL can be adapted to accommodate the students' stages of cognitive development. In fact, Kloss (1994) advised teachers to "determine at the outset of the semester the level of cognitive development upon which students are functioning," because doing so "suggests which supports and which challenges one should offer to the group or to select individuals" (p. 153). He recommended that "instructors should have students in the first class write a short diagnostic essay on one of two topics: 'The Best Class I Ever Had' or 'How I Learn Best,'" because "either of these topics will enable the teacher to see that students will fairly readily fall into the categories of the Perry Scheme with the vast majority responding as dualists and the others scattered among the remaining levels" (p. 153). Learning activities can then be adjusted so that students are gently "nudged" into and through the transitions between stages and consequently experience less frustration than they would otherwise.

Both faculty and students can experience both positive and negative reactions to TBL. Combining ideas from the TBL literature with some understanding of learning theory can help you maximize positive reactions and minimize negative reactions to TBL.

The evidence is clear: TBL works!

Now that you are armed with an understanding of how and why TBL works, why faculty and students can have both positive and negative reactions to TBL (or any learner-centered shift in classroom teaching), and the things you can do to make sure your experience is the best it can be for both your students and yourself, we are ready to head back to the classroom.

PART TWO

Essential Elements of TBL

CHAPTER 5

Using Teams Effectively

Proper team formation and management is the first essential element of Team-Based Learning (TBL). This chapter will help you understand the principles of forming the balanced, diverse teams you will need to make your TBL course a success.

We have all had team experiences—undoubtedly, some of these experiences were bad and some were good. If we are lucky, we have also had team experiences that we could say were phenomenal. So what makes for the truly great team experiences? Usually, it involves having teammates with whom you share mutual trust and respect, can communicate openly with, and are able to work with toward a shared goal or vision in a way that feels as much like fun as work. Whether this seems to come naturally or takes effort, one thing is clear: Building a strong team takes time. The principles of TBL and the structure of the TBL activities support the development of these ideal team elements, but they do not guarantee every team experience will be a good one. To maximize the opportunity for each student to have a truly great team experience, we must also have a sound understanding of how teams function and develop, and we must pay careful attention to forming appropriate teams. Although some of these approaches to fostering strong teams in TBL are very similar to what you might expect in other areas, there are some differences that might surprise you.

As Trudi Jacobson, David Raeker-Jordan, and Liz Winter note in the following, the larger team size needed in TBL may be contrary to your intuition, and how the teams are formed will have a big impact on how the class runs.

One of the things that I railed against was the size of the teams. But I am finding that the larger teams are important. (Trudi Jacobson, Information Literacy, University at Albany)[1]

The first thing I learned was that I had too many teams. I had two teams of five and one team of four, and looking back on it, if I had problems, it was

*in the team of four. I actually need more people to do TBL. The other profes-
sors think I am crazy to want more students.* (David Raeker-Jordan, Law
Widener University)[2]

*When you stratify the teams correctly, then a richness comes out of that in
terms of what students learn from each other and contribute to each other
and to the process, which I think is fabulous!* (Liz Winter, Social Work,
University of Pittsburgh)[3]

WHAT NEEDS TO BE IN A TBL TEAM?

TBL Teams Need to Be Balanced

The whole range of student strengths and weaknesses must be fairly distributed
across all teams. Does every team need to have a member with prior work experience, someone who has lived overseas, or someone with a previous degree? Whatever important student assets and liabilities you can identify should be fairly
distributed to create balanced teams.

TBL Teams Need to Be Diverse

We want to have heterogeneity in every team to ensure that a wide range of skills,
opinions, and personal experiences can come into play during team deliberations.
This is great news, because efforts to increase enrollment of underrepresented
groups and to recruit larger numbers of international students are increasing diversity in our classrooms year after year. TBL actually gets better with more diverse
teams if we craft our activities to leverage that diversity. Student-selected teams
are often very homogeneous, and this can easily lead to "group think" behaviors,
because teammates on a student-selected team are often very similar in cultural,
educational, and life experiences. These student-selected teams may not have the
diverse range of talent and experiences they need to be successful in the TBL classroom.

To get these balanced and diverse teams, we always form the teams for the students. Student-selected teams are a very bad idea. The educational literature is very
clear about the importance of not letting students create their own teams (Brickell,
Porter, Reynolds, & Cosgrove, 1994; Feichtner & Davis, 1984). Student-selected
teams consistently underperform other team formation strategies. We paraphrased
from Brickell et al. (1994) in the opening chapter, but it is worth repeating here:
Student-selected teams are often "social entities" where existing relationships and
cliques can make team cohesion difficult.

Use teacher-created, criterion-based team formation, which ensures the best educational results. Teacher-formed teams have been shown to outperform randomly and student-selected teams (Brickell et al., 1994). Feichtner and Davis (1984) found by a 2-to-1 margin that students are more likely to have better experiences when the teacher forms the groups.

Handling Student Insistence on Self-Selection

Occasionally, you will get very determined students who adamantly insist that self-selection would be better for them. Even after carefully explaining your rationales and repeated attempts to stand your ground, they persist. Here are two helpful ways to handle this.

I handle it by inviting students to write a one-page critique of Brickell et al.'s (1994) paper "Assigning Students to Groups for Engineering Design Projects: A Comparison of Five Methods." I explain that if I accept their arguments in their *written* critique, I will allow self-selection. No student has ever taken me up on it.

Laura Madson,[4] a teacher in psychology at New Mexico State University, suggests another method. She uses a fictitious scenario to great effect during these debates with students. She has students imagine being on a team that has a boyfriend and girlfriend who break up midsemester, and she asks, "Do you really want to be on that team?"

TBL Teams Need to Be Large

Teams should be composed of five to seven students. TBL teams need to be big enough to solve the wonderful, complex, messy, real-world problems that are at the heart of every TBL course experience. The larger team size gives the teams the intellectual horsepower to solve these problems. TBL teams need to be larger than is suggested in most cooperative or collaborative learning literature because of the complexity of the problems.

The recommended size of five to seven students may be contrary to your intuition and experience. But again and again, new TBL teachers who try smaller team sizes are disappointed with the results. TBL has structures and processes that effectively manage student teaming behaviors and control "social loafing." Every individual has accountability to the teacher for his or her preparation (Individual Readiness Assurance Test [iRAT]), and all individuals have accountability to their teammates for the quality of their contribution to their team's success (Team Readiness Assurance Test [tRAT] and peer evaluation). Peer evaluation lets us give the grading scheme the teeth to motivate students to contribute and be fairly rewarded (or penalized) for their level of contribution to their team.

TBL Teams Need to Be Permanent

TBL teachers often talk of initially underestimating teams' abilities to solve difficult problems and needing to ratchet up the problem difficulty as the semester progresses. This is because the teams naturally, with time and practice, get better at problem solving. For the teams to "gel," the members must work together consistently. For this to happen, teams must be permanent for the duration of the course. This "gelling" process, known as team cohesion in the literature, can be seen in the classroom. With time, groups of students become high-performance learning teams.

MANAGING TBL TEAMS

A remarkable aspect of TBL is that teams often don't need to be managed at all. Unlike other forms of cooperative learning, lecturing on group dynamics and assigning specific roles to team members is simply unnecessary. The combination of thoughtfully created teams and the focus on decision-making activities eliminates the need for team management. This is because shared activities and goals, the sequence of TBL activities, and accountability to one's team all synergistically aid in the development of team cohesion. There was a remarkable study that highlights the amazingly rapid development of team cohesion in TBL (Michaelsen, Watson, & Black, 1989). The study found that in early Readiness Assurance testing, student teams often used simple votes on split decisions and let the majority rule. But as team members found their social feet within the team, and team cohesion began to increase with each testing cycle, the decision-making process progressively switched to a more consensus-based one. It showed that in as few as four Readiness Assurance cycles, teams had switched strategy from majority rules to consensus-based decision making.

There is more on designing and implementing the Readiness Assurance Process in chapter 6 and more on designing Application Activities in chapter 7.

There are a number of useful theoretical frameworks to help you understand the progression that your student teams will typically move through in their development.

Tuckman's Stages of Team Development

One such framework is Tuckman's (1965) original stages of team development:

- *FORMING stage:* Teammates meet for the first time, share personal background information, and generate first impressions.

- *STORMING stage:* Task-focused work begins, but considerable team energy is used learning how to function effectively as a team. Some conflict is normal at this stage. Individuals are finding their place in the group. This stage closes when the team learns how to work together for the good of the task.
- *NORMING stage:* This stage is focused on developing the best way of working together. There is a more complete shift from individual goals to team goals.
- *PERFORMING stage:* Student teams are working at a very high level. Team members know each other well enough that they naturally rely on each other's skills and contributions to succeed. Teams can solve problems quickly and efficiently. When team members disagree, they have the social capital, motivation, and skills to address and work through the conflict for the good of the project.

Wheelan's Cycle of Group Development

Wheelan's (1994) integrative life cycle model of group development can also be useful to help you understand the processes that you will see unfold in your classroom. Early in a team's development, a large amount of effort will be expended navigating the social space: Teammates are unsure of each other's strengths and weaknesses, communication styles can conflict, approaches can vary, and teammates may be uncomfortable with directly challenging each other. At this point, a democratic vote may be used to navigate an intellectual impasse. As the team develops and the teammates' understanding of each other's styles and strengths increases, task-focused energy and consensus-based decision making begin to predominate.

THE NUTS AND BOLTS OF TEAM FORMATION

There are a number of team formation approaches to creating those balanced, diverse teams that you need. The approach you use will depend on the size of the class and the layout of the classroom.

Forming Teams in Small Classes

In smaller classes with reasonable classroom space, you can simply line the students up. You can use various prompts to quickly order a line, for example:

1. I want everyone with work experience at the front of the line.
2. With the remaining students not yet lined up, who has a previous degree? Please line up behind them.

3. With the remaining students not yet lined up, who has lived overseas? Please line up behind them.
4. Everyone else line up at the end of the line.

Students will often fit into multiple categories, but you will begin the line with the categories that are most important for team success. This is not an exact process, and it doesn't need to be. You are creating diverse teams with a range of talents. The questions and criteria you choose to use to order the line depends on who your students are and what assets and liability you want to distribute across all teams. Once the students are in the line, you do the simple math of how big the class is and how many teams you can have with five to seven students on each team. Once you know the number of teams you want, you simply count off the teams.

For example, in a class with 42 students, you have decided to have 7 teams with 6 students on each team. Now you would count off from the start of the line: 1, 2, 3, 4, 5, 6, 7 . . . 1, 2, 3, 4, 5, 6, 7 . . . until you run out of students. Don't worry about being exact. The literature shows that randomly formed teams perform almost as well as teacher-formed teams. So there's no need to obsess over every last student getting into the exact right group. You might keep track of your most important sort criteria and do a few last-minute shuffles that might be necessary to get teams of equal strength. As an example, in a foundation engineering course, we might shuffle a few people at the end of the team formation process to ensure that each team has both a geological engineer and someone who is good with math.

This simple procedure has been used with great success in TBL classrooms for over 30 years. It might feel like it takes up valuable class time, but students really seem to enjoy the team formation process, and it is important that students know the teams were formed fairly and transparently. Once teams are formed, students will sit back down with their team, and we will give them a few minutes to do introductions inside their teams. Some teachers will at this point also ask the teams to come up with a team name.

Forming Teams in Large Classes

In large classes, it is often impractical or impossible to line the students up around the room. We then use an online survey to gather some student information that is used to order students in an Excel file, for example. We often use online survey tools in a learning management system (LMS), such as Blackboard, Canvas, or Moodle, to gather the information. This must be set up as a quiz, because with a survey we cannot trace specific responses to specific students. (I will use the word *survey* with the students to stress the nongraded nature of the quiz.) We decide on the assets and liabilities that need to be distributed across the teams. We ask a series of questions to find out more about these assets and liabilities in our students.

For instance: What is your major? Do you have work experience? Have you lived overseas? We ask whatever questions we feel are necessary to get the information needed to build balanced and diverse teams. Sometimes we want to make sure each team has someone with work experience, someone who is good at stats, or someone who has a laptop he or she can bring to class. Once we have the student responses, we perform nested sorts in Excel to order the list, and then we simply count off the teams.

For example, I download the survey results for the 180 students in my course. Then I build a sort based on the column order that I feel is the most important, first sorting on most important criteria, then on second most important, then on third, and so on. This kind of sorting is extremely simple in Excel. You can sort by multiple columns by simply using the + control on the Excel sort dialog box and adding columns in the order from most to least important. Figure 5.1 is an image of the sorting dialog box from Excel. In this example, I first sort on work experience, then previous degree, and finally gender. This lets you in one simple step do a sort that is similar to ordering the line of students in the classroom.

Once sorting is complete, I simply count off on the Excel table. In the case of this course of 180 students, I may decide to do 30 teams of 6 students. Next, I would count down the sorted Excel results, numbering the students 1, 2, 3, and up to 30 and then repeating the 1 to 30 numbering as needed for the entire class list. The list is then sorted into alphabetical order by student name, and the resulting roster of teams 1–30 is posted to the LMS.

When using any team formation method that isn't done in front of the students, you should inform them of the procedure you used to form the teams. Students need to feel that the teams were fairly created.

FIGURE 5.1
Nested sort in Excel

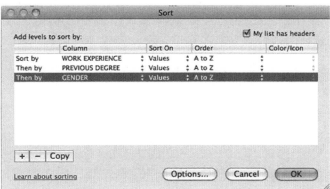

FIGURE 5.2
Large classroom map

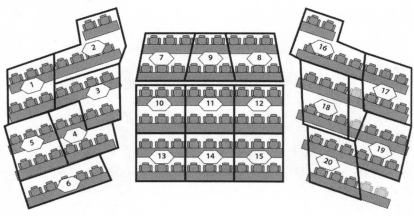

Students will need to know where to find their team in large classrooms. To help with this, we create classroom maps that show exactly where each team should sit (see Figure 5.2). We post this along with the team assignments on the course website or LMS before the first RAT. We also display this map on the classroom screen when students are arriving at the first RAT, so they can find the correct place to sit. In large classes, we have students sit with their teams right from the start. This prevents any disruption from students changing seats at the end of the iRAT.

Tip: Optimal Team Size in Lecture Halls

The nature of the classroom affects the optimal size for teams in TBL. It is important that all team members can see each other and that no one is left as a straggler at the end of the group, cut off from the conversation. In large classes, especially in tiered lecture theaters with fixed seating, we usually use teams of six so all team members can easily see each other. Teams with odd numbers have a person who is left uncomfortably dangling at the end of the team. A team of six is about the best we can do to ensure that everyone can see each other in a large lecture theater.

You might worry that TBL is impossible in larger classes, but rest assured, it has been used in difficult rooms and large classes with great success. Give students something exciting and compelling to do, and they will hang off the lights to do it! When an activity is really engaging, concerns about the room seem to vanish. No doubt larger classes are more challenging to facilitate, but our experience shows it is entirely possible.

FIGURE 5.3
Team formation checklist

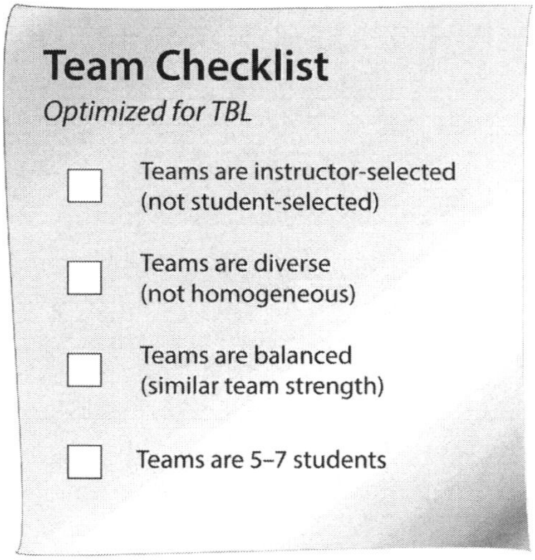

Team Checklist
Optimized for TBL

☐ Teams are instructor-selected
(not student-selected)

☐ Teams are diverse
(not homogeneous)

☐ Teams are balanced
(similar team strength)

☐ Teams are 5–7 students

NOTES

1. T. Jacobson, personal communication, January 4, 2013.
2. D. Raeker-Jordan, personal communication, January 4, 2013.
3. L. Winter, personal communication, January 4, 2013.
4. L. Madson, personal communication, January 2012.

CHAPTER 6

Readiness Assurance Process

Having students come to class prepared is the next essential step in Team-Based Learning (TBL), and making this happen is what the Readiness Assurance Process (RAP) is all about. This chapter describes the RAP in detail. It reviews the individual components of the RAP, how to construct effective Readiness Assurance Tests (RATs), and finally the scheduling, administrating, and grading logistics associated with the process.

Classroom discussions have long been heralded as a way to get your students to really learn the material. But most of us have had the difficult, uncomfortable experience of trying to lead a discussion in a classroom full of unprepared students. In smaller classes, teachers can coerce some readiness by their physical presence and a more familiar relationship with individual students. However, as class sizes increase, many teachers find it more and more difficult to hold their students accountable for completing out-of-class reading assignments designed to prepare them for class discussions and activities.

Having students come to class prepared is critical in order to have any possibility of deeper classroom conversations and meaningful problem-solving activities. Students not only need to be accountable for their initial preparation but also actually need to be ready for the activities. Larry Michaelsen, looking for a solution to his problem, conceived of the RAP, a structured process that holds students accountable for their initial preparation and builds on this preparation to generate genuine readiness. The original process he developed is very similar to the five-stage process that is still used today (Figure 6.1).

OVERVIEW OF THE RAP

The RAP is designed to get your students ready for the upcoming instructional sequence. The RAP is a five-stage process that is used at the beginning of each module in your course. The purpose of the RAP is to ensure that students understand the fundamental concepts, definitions, and foundational knowledge they need to begin problem solving. The RAP centers on administering two short multiple-choice tests. The first test is taken individually, and then the students in their teams take the same test again. It sounds simple, but it has powerful results.

The RAP prepares students for the activities that follow. It is *not* about testing. Students will become very upset if the RAP is presented as just another assessment strategy rather than as preparation for the activities that follow. If the RAP is not carefully integrated with the activities that follow, you can expect the unhappy student cry of "Testing before teaching makes no sense!" It's the synergy among the crystal-clear objectives of the instructional sequence, the RAP, and the Application Activities that follow that gives TBL much of its instructional power.

The prototypical RAP occurs at the beginning of each 2-week instructional sequence or module. The RAP centers on the administration of a 10- to 20-multiple-choice question test based on the preparatory material. Module lengths and course structures do vary, and there can be successful implementations with very different structures, such as the class that meets once a week for 6 hours and has a RAP at the start of each class, or the textbook that is so dense that shorter modules and more frequent RAPs make sense. Whatever the frequency you choose, you need to thoughtfully and proactively manage the students' reactions. You need to show students that the process is about getting them ready for the activities that follow and not simply about testing. There is no magic number for the correct module length, but overtesting the students is a very common mistake that new TBL teachers make. Issues like overtesting will be discussed more completely toward the end of this chapter, in the section "When Readiness Assurance Goes Wrong."

List of Important Terms

- *RAP:* Readiness Assurance Process
- *iRAT:* Individual Readiness Assurance Test (sometimes referred to as *iRAP test*)
- *tRAT:* Team Readiness Assurance Test (sometimes referred to as *tRAP test*; you also will sometimes see *gRAT* in the literature, but we prefer *tRAT* because we use teams, not groups)
- *MCQ:* multiple-choice question

Let's start by examining each of the five stages of the RAP:

- *Stage 1:* Student Preclass Preparation
- *Stage 2:* iRAT
- *Stage 3:* tRAT
- *Stage 4:* Appeals Process
- *Stage 5:* Mini-lecture/Clarification

FIGURE 6.1
Readiness Assurance Process stages

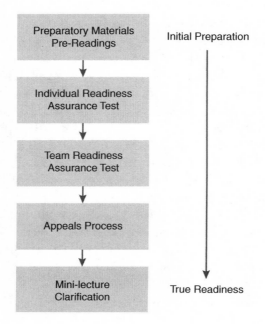

Preclass Preparation: Readings or Other Preparatory Materials

Prior to the beginning of each module, students are assigned readings or other preparatory materials such as newspaper articles, journal articles, textbook chapters, podcasts, PowerPoint slides, or instructional videos. They must study these materials to prepare for the module activities. We typically assign 30–60 pages in preparation for a 2-week module. The specific amount of preparatory materials will depend on the length of the module, the difficulty of the material, the discipline, and the institutional culture. In general, we have found that shorter and more focused readings are better.

TBL teachers find that the quality of the reading materials is even more important in TBL classes than it is in traditional courses, because the students will actually be required to read the course materials.

One final caution: Your campus bookstore will typically order fewer textbooks than the number of students in your course, assuming that not every student will buy a textbook. This is a problem for a TBL course where every student *must* have a textbook to get ready for the RATs. If some students don't have the textbook, this can seriously mess up early modules in a TBL course. Warn your bookstore that this course is different and that every student will need a textbook for the first day of class.

I quickly discovered that the quality of the text is key, because students will be spending time reading the text. They do invest themselves in the book, so if they're forced to read a book that is low quality, or not appropriate for the context of the class, it's not going to be a good experience. (Ron Carson, Occupational Therapy, Adventist University of Health Sciences)[1]

Student comment: "This is my fourth semester here. I've bought textbooks every year and never opened them, then returned them for full price at the end of the year. This is the only time I've ever had to read a textbook." (Mary Hadley, Chemistry and Geology, Minnesota State University–Mankato)[2]

One thing I really liked this past semester in my contract drafting class was that on the day when we'd have a RAT and I'd walk into class, every student had their book open, and they were reviewing their notes. Usually when I come into class, the students are just sitting around waiting for me to do something. But on the day of a RAT, they were all reading. It was a pleasant change. The students said that the RAT really motivated them to read more carefully. Instead of simply reading for some general purpose, they had a specific reason to be reading, because they knew that they were going to be responsible for the major ideas. (David Raeker-Jordan, Law, Widener University)[3]

It is important to get the length of the readings correct. We have learned over the years that less is more. We found that students seem to assign a fixed time to preparation, regardless of the density or length of the readings. When we have assigned shorter readings, students seem to try not only to complete them but also to actually understand them. If we assign readings that are too long or complicated, their eyes may have passed over the words, but they don't seem to retain much, or else they read until they are out of time and stop wherever they end up. Readings that are too long or too detailed can also erode student goodwill.

We also shouldn't make the assumption that our students know how to read effectively. We may need to help them with this. We will address this later in this chapter when we look at reading guides.

Teachers who have structured a TBL module around chapters of a book might assign only subsections of each of the chapters needed for the instructional objectives of the module. For example, if Module 1 covers chapters 1–4 of a textbook, then the students may be asked to read only two to three introductory pages in each chapter.

iRAT

After completing the preparatory materials, students come to the first class session of a TBL instructional sequence or module. They then individually complete a short 10- to 20-question multiple-choice test based on the readings. The RAP test is typically closed book, but some teachers do allow short summaries on index cards. However, teachers should be mindful that high-quality RAT questions are not based on rote memorization or recall.

At a very simple level, the iRAT is about individual accountability for pre-class preparation. Did students complete the preparatory materials? The test should focus only on giving students the vocabulary and important foundational concepts they need to successfully begin problem solving. Using the analogy of a book, the test should be constructed closer to the table of contents level than to the index level. It is recommended that you stay away from picky details and focus only on important major concepts. However, iRAT questions should still be fairly challenging. Overall, the average student score is typically 65%–75% on the iRAT and 85%–95% on the tRAT.

Improving iRAT With Confidence Testing

After I read the original TBL book (Michaelsen, Knight, & Fink, 2002), I soon invited Larry Michaelsen to come to my campus. During his workshop, he demonstrated something called confidence testing as part of the iRAT process, which he originally developed in response to students wanting partial credit for partial knowledge.

During the iRAT, students are given the opportunity to "wager" a fixed number of points across the different answers in a multiple-choice question. Instead of answering each question only once on the iRAT, students answer the same question multiple times with the opportunity to change their answer with each question instance. Because there is still only one correct answer, how they spread their responses depends on their confidence in their responses. This leads to an interesting metacognitive benefit of confidence testing; students are, in real time, assessing the quality of their current understanding. If students notice that they are consistently spreading out their points across multiple possible answers, they may realize that their preparation for the test was not adequate. Confidence testing is yet another powerful way to add feedback to the already feedback-rich RAP.

Confidence testing is phenomenal, and it is a strong teaching point. I tell my students that we are going to mark each answer three times, and each correct answer is worth 1 point. Most of them look at me like I have three heads. At that point, I ask them if they know what metacognition means. Then I delve into explaining how metacognition is kind of like knowing what you know. I use the example of a nurse not being sure of whether one drug interacts with another drug that she is supposed to administer to a patient. I explain that it is important for that nurse to be 100% sure about her decision. I explain to the students that knowing if you are correct is a critical skill you need on the job, and it is one you have to learn and practice. This allows me to lead into discussing how confidence testing and all aspects of TBL will provide the students with an applied setting to practice metacognition with their teammates throughout the semester. (Mary Gourley, Psychology, Gaston College)[4]

To use confidence testing, teachers may serially repeat the same question on the answer sheet, whether it is a pencil-and-paper form or a Scantron form (see Figure 6.2). For example, "For question one, please use rows 1–4. If you are confident of your answer, please fill out all four rows the same. If you are less confident of your answer, then you can wager points on different answers, based on your confidence that a particular answer is correct." The points to wager should be one less than the number of options in the question. If there are four options in the question, students should be given 3 points to wager. If there are five options, students should be given 4 points to wager. This eliminates wagering 1 point on every option and being rewarded for no knowledge.

When I first heard about confidence testing, I liked the idea, but I was concerned that repeating the same question on the form would confuse the students and get their answers out of sync. After my recent interviews with many TBL teachers using this kind of confidence testing, there were no major reports of student problems once the students had a chance to practice the strategy in their orientation class.

FIGURE 6.2
Confidence testing scanner form

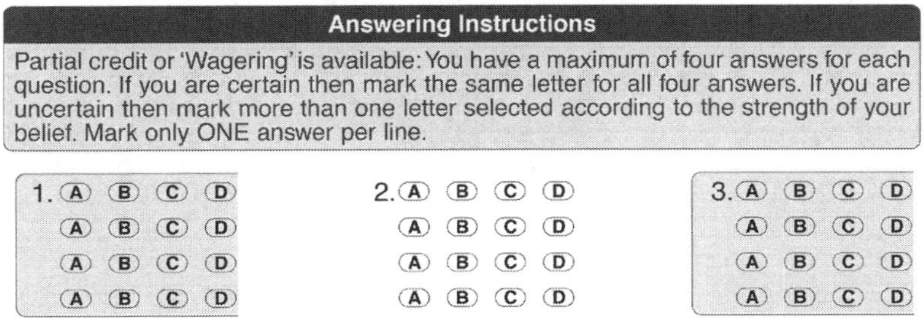
Answering Instructions

Partial credit or 'Wagering' is available: You have a maximum of four answers for each question. If you are certain then mark the same letter for all four answers. If you are uncertain then mark more than one letter selected according to the strength of your belief. Mark only ONE answer per line.

1. A B C D
A B C D
A B C D
A B C D

2. A B C D
A B C D
A B C D
A B C D

3. A B C D
A B C D
A B C D
A B C D

The University of Sydney created an Apperson form (A1699) that makes this kind of confidence testing easier. The form is compatible with Apperson's Datalink scanners.

Peter Balan from the University of South Australia created a very simple but effective pencil-and-paper form for confidence testing, illustrated in Figure 6.3. He prints a form for each student; then, using the same document, he prints one copy on a clear acetate transparency and blacks out the incorrect answers with a marker. By overlaying this clear marking form, he can very quickly and accurately mark the student iRAT forms.

Doing iRATs Online

Some TBL teachers have their students complete their iRATs online before coming to class. They use their course management system, such as Blackboard, Moodle, or Canvas, to administer the tests. This is an idea that has been hotly debated in the TBL community, and no consensus has been reached.

People who have adopted online iRATs seem extremely pleased with how they are working, and they report no shift in iRAT or tRAT performance or the vigor of classroom discussion during the tRATs. They also find that online iRATs allow students with special needs to have the time they need to complete the test.

FIGURE 6.3
Confidence testing pencil-and-paper form

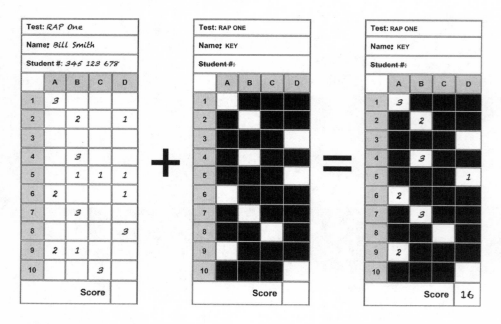

Left: The form is printed on paper then filled in by a student who wagers up to 3 points per question. Middle: The form is printed on transparency for the instructor to mark the template. Incorrect answers are blacked out with a marker. Right: The transparency is placed over the student's form, allowing the instructor to quickly mark and tally the student's score.

Those who don't like the idea of online iRATs worry that not doing the iRAT and tRAT at the same time will generate a host of problems, including less vigorous discussion during the tRAT, loss of the cohesive energy of the tRAT directly following the iRAT, and students cheating on their iRAT.

There are a couple common practices that are used with online iRATs. First, students are required to sign an honor code, and second, the online tests are available only for a short time, usually about 15–20 minutes. Send a query to the TBL LISTSERV (www.teambasedlearning.org/listserv) to get more information if you are considering using this iRAT method.

Using Clickers for iRATs

A number of schools use clickers to collect student responses to the iRAT questions. There are primarily two ways to implement this. With the simpler clickers, students complete the RAT using a pencil-and-paper form, and then when the designated time has expired, the teacher cycles through each question using PowerPoint slides and gives students 15–20 seconds to submit each response using the clickers. The fancier approach involves using clickers with a display that allows students to navigate question by question and answer as they complete the test.

There are some advantages to using the clickers. First, the software will automatically randomize the question options for each student to reduce cheating; this requires another handout of a standardized tRAT that is the same for all teams and matches the IF-AT. The other advantage is that test statistics are available immediately, which can help teachers know what to focus on in the mini-lecture.

tRAT

The team RAP test, or tRAT, begins immediately after the iRAT (except as discussed previously with the online iRAT, in which case the tRAT begins as soon as possible after the iRAT). In smaller classes, following the iRAT, the students move to their teams. In large classes, it is preferable to have students sit in their teams during the entire RAP to reduce disruption at the beginning of the team test. At the end of the iRAT, students keep their question sheet but must turn in their individual scanner cards or scoring sheets before beginning the tRAT. The exact same questions are used for both tests.

Team tests are high-energy, noisy, and often chaotic events as students discuss and negotiate their answers and deepen their understanding. Typically, we budget 25 minutes for a 20-question team test, although we let students know that when half of the teams are done, the remaining teams have 5 minutes to finish.

Although tRATs can be completed using either pencil-and-paper or Scantron forms, an extremely powerful alternative to energize the classroom is the IF-AT scratch cards, described in the next section.

Immediate Feedback Assessment Technique

A special kind of scoring sheet, known as an Immediate Feedback Assessment Technique (IF-AT) form, is typically used for the team tests. IF-ATs are "scratch-and-win"-style scoring sheets (see Figure 6.4). They dramatically increase the quality of discussion in the tRAT process and, more important, provide rich, immediate corrective feedback. Students absolutely love using these test cards! You can expect high fives and cheering as students complete the tRAT. We have even had some students thank us for the test! If you have not tried these, you must!

Students love them. I use them as part of the practice test on the first day, and students get all giggly. They just love the scratch-offs. They're fun and effective, not only as a means of giving instant feedback but also the students really take the scratching of each answer very seriously. It's fun to watch their reactions when they get it right. It's all "Yes!" "Go team," and all that kind of stuff, and when they get it wrong, it's "Ahh!" "Crap!" (Mark Stevens, Urban and Regional Planning, University of British Columbia)[5]

FIGURE 6.4
Immediate Feedback Assessment Technique cards

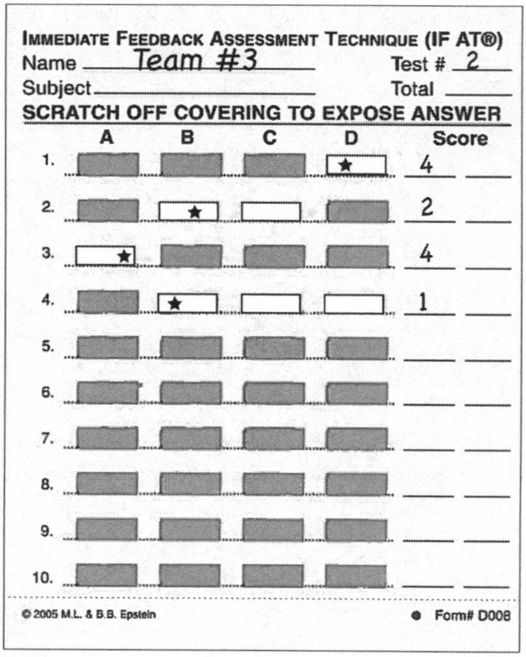

IMMEDIATE FEEDBACK ASSESSMENT TECHNIQUE (IF AT®)
Name Team #3 Test # 2
Subject Total
SCRATCH OFF COVERING TO EXPOSE ANSWER

	A	B	C	D	Score	
1.				★	4	
2.		★			2	
3.	★				4	
4.		★			1	
5.						
6.						
7.						
8.						
9.						
10.						

© 2005 M.L. & B.B. Epstein • Form# D008

These "scratch-and-win"-style answer sheets were developed by Mike Epstein at Rider University. On an IF-AT form, each question has a row of boxes that can be scratched like a lottery ticket. Students must scratch off the opaque coating one box at a time in hopes of finding the right answer, which is indicated by a small star icon. The power of these cards is in the conversation that students are forced into as they try to generate shared understanding and consensus before choosing which box to scratch. The other powerful feature of these cards is the immediate corrective feedback.

We also use decrementing scoring to induce teams to continue to discuss the questions after an incorrect scratch. One possible point-allocation system for an IF-AT card could be 4 points for the right answer on the first scratch, 2 points for the right answer on the second scratch, 1 point for the right answer on the third scratch, and 0 if they need to scratch off all four boxes to reveal the correct answer. This encourages teams to re-engage with a question and continue the conversation until they know the correct answer.

Teachers commonly report witnessing a transformation in the decision-making procedures used by teams through the course of a semester. In the beginning of the semester, extroverted individuals commonly dominate the decision-making process, the focus is on what answer everyone selected, and "majority-rules" voting techniques are frequently used to resolve controversy. However, as the semester progresses, many teachers report that no single individual is found to dominate the decision-making process. Rather, students are expected to explain and justify why they selected a given answer, and the most convincing argument is selected.

Teachers new to TBL often ask how to print IF-ATs to match their tests. In fact, each set of numbered cards already has the stars in a particular pattern, and teachers rearrange their answer choices on their test to match the selected card. Cards are available in many different answer patterns to give the teacher flexibility in arranging answer choices and to prevent the students from memorizing or predicting the answers. Each card has an identifying key number on a perforated tab at the bottom that the teacher can remove before handing the card out to students. The IF-AT cards are available in lengths of 10, 25, and 50 questions and with either four options (A–D) or five options (A–E). IF-AT forms are available at www. epsteineducation.com.

Appeals Process

The Appeals Process is a structured method that provokes teams into looking up answers they got wrong on the tRAT. Near the end of the tRAT process, the teacher circulates around the room and encourages teams that may have gotten an answer wrong on the tRAT to consider appealing the question. The teams use an appeals form that is included in their team folder. The form describes in detail how to make a successful written appeal (see Figure 6.5). Appeals are accepted only from teams, not individuals. To appeal a question successfully, teams need to build a written rationale that makes a case, supported with evidence, for why a particular question's answer might be wrong. They can declare ambiguity either in the question or in the readings. To support their case, they must make specific citations to the source of the ambiguity or reword the question to eliminate the ambiguity.

It is important to stress with students that appeals are accepted only from teams. One way to ensure that all members make a contribution to writing the appeal is to have each member sign a statement at the bottom of the form that reads something to the effect of "Every member of my team contributed to the work required to complete this appeal." When and how appeals are submitted does vary from teacher to teacher. In some classes, appeals are due immediately or by the end of class, whereas in other classes they are due by the end of the day. The teacher then reviews the appeals between classes and will announce the success or failure of an appeal at the next class meeting. If a team successfully appeals, the team test score will be adjusted, and any individuals on that team that selected the appealed response will have their individual test scores changed to correct. Only the teams that appealed a question receive the benefit of the appeal. Granting an appeal to a single team can send an important message to other teams that didn't appeal, motivating them to dive back into the reading material to check next time if they should appeal an incorrect response.

- *Argument:* "We feel that both A and C should be considered correct answers for Question 2."
- *Evidence:* "According to Sousa on page 121, 'the glycoprotein and ligand bind together using surface binding sites.' This would lead us to conclude that glycoproteins have binding sites on their surface."

FIGURE 6.5
Appeal form

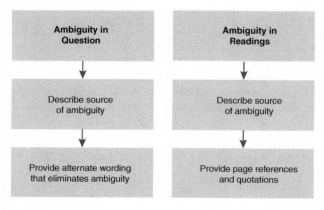

Mini-lecture/Clarification

Following the Appeals Process, the teacher can, if necessary, provide a short, targeted mini-lecture or clarification on the RAP concepts that the students are still having difficulty with. The teacher focuses just on what the students don't know, rather than on what they already know. Students are often anxious to begin the Application Activities. Going over every question or talking for too long can burn up student goodwill. A common mistake made by new TBL teachers is to sequentially review every question. Don't do it. This can quickly drain energy from the class.

Most of the time after the tRAT a mini-lecture isn't required. By the end of a tRAT, they've figured out why they were wrong and generally they're happy about it. (Peter Smith, Business and Economics, University of Auckland)[6]

ACCOUNTING FOR THE EDUCATIONAL POWER OF THE RAP

Remember, the purpose of the RAP is to get students ready for the activities that follow.

Preclass Preparation Outcomes

The preclass preparatory materials you select can significantly help focus student attention on the most salient course concepts. Using a reading guide can be of even further benefit and focus students' attention. It is important to remember this is not students' only opportunity to learn course content. During the problem-solving Application Activities, they will continue learning. The students are motivated by their own interest and the knowledge that their understanding will be on public display during the Application Activity reporting. This is a powerful motivator for students to take preparation seriously.

Individual Readiness Assurance Outcomes

The iRAT can accomplish a few different things. Its main purpose is to have individual accountability for each student's preclass preparation. Simply put, if you don't prepare, you probably won't do well on the iRAT. The focus of the RAP also cues students to the most important course concepts. If confidence testing is used, there is also an interesting metacognitive component, where students might admit to themselves that they really don't know something. This can be a powerful motivator to have them reconsider their preparation strategy for next time.

Team Readiness Assurance Outcomes

During the tRAT stage, some very interesting educational outcomes begin to emerge. First, through social dialogue and peer teaching, students generate a deeper shared understanding as they try to come to a consensus on the answer for a particular question. Second, if you are using IF-AT cards, the teams receive immediate corrective feedback on each question. Students leave the test knowing the answer to every question; you can't get more immediate than that!

Third, the IF-AT cards also help establish more positive group norms. The pushy student with the wrong answer may be a few scratches away from having the team stop listening. Similarly, a quiet student can be drawn into the conversation if the team recognizes that he or she often has the right answers and that listening to the quiet student will help the team. Finally, the chronically underprepared student is usually found out by his or her teammates, and peer pressure and peer evaluation can sometimes motivate these underprepared students to work harder.

Appeals Process Outcomes

The magic of the Appeals Process is that it pushes students back into the reading or other preparatory material, right where they are having the most difficulty. These difficulties are clearly identified by questions they got wrong on the tRAT. Teams must look up the concepts they still don't understand to successfully prepare an appeal. They may research the answer only to find that the teacher is correct, or they may unearth a genuine ambiguity. They need to build the appeal by reviewing both the preparatory material and the question and by building a case supported with evidence.

Mini-lecture/Clarification Outcomes

At the end of the first four stages of the RAP, both students and teachers have a clearer understanding of which course concepts continue to be difficult. The students have had extensive feedback during the tRAT process and an opportunity with the Appeals Process to clear up any lingering misconceptions. But some troublesome concepts can remain. These can be clarified during the short mini-lecture that closes out the RAP. The power is that the clarification focuses on what the students *know* they *don't know*. It doesn't waste class time on things they already understand.

But how do teachers know which concepts are still troublesome?

If teachers are using a classroom scanner, such as Scantron, they can review the tally report from the iRAT and see which questions students most often got wrong. The weakness of this approach is the students may have cleared up the misunderstanding during the team test and no longer need the teacher to review the question.

An elegant and simple solution is for the teacher to put the question numbers on the board and have a representative from each team put check marks beside the questions that need to be reviewed when teams return their IF-AT card. This results in something similar to a stem-and-leaf plot and quickly identifies which questions students are still struggling with (see Figure 6.9 later in this chapter).

A word of caution: Teachers new to TBL often fall in love with the structures and outcomes of the RAP and may think about implementing just the RAP and not the rest of the pieces of TBL. I believe this is a mistake, because the main power of TBL is to help students learn how to use course concepts to solve significant problems, which occurs during the Application Activities. The RAP is about getting your students ready. If you use only the RAP in your course, students can legitimately complain about testing before teaching. If you use only the RAP, what are you getting students ready for?

I've grown reluctant to talk about the RAP, because to some people that becomes the entire method, and it's really not. It's the least important part. It sets up your ability to do application exercises, but if you go into it thinking this is just about the RAPs, I think you miss the point. And I think a lot of people do miss the point. (Shawn Bushway, Criminology, University at Albany)[7]

RAP TEST DRAFTING

In this section we will examine strategies for developing RATs, how to write good multiple-choice questions, and finally how to use item analysis to improve the quality of your questions.

There'd be one warning: You have to learn how to write good multiple-choice questions, because you could really derail the whole thing. With bad questions, you get student resistance or, worse, student apathy, and they have to perceive the questions as being useful and fair and pointing in the direction of good learning. (Brent MacLaine, Literature, University of Prince Edward Island)[8]

For each module you will need to construct a RAT. As a reminder, this is a multiple-choice test that covers the important foundational knowledge from the preparatory materials that students will need to begin the Application Activities. The

RAP fits into the backward-design process. You need to first identify the problems you want students to be able to solve and the classroom situations that you need to create, so that students can both solve the problems and show you what they have learned. The RAP acts as the first step that introduces the foundational concepts in preparation for the Application Activities that follow.

One way to imagine the outcome of the process is to imagine a student's mental schema as an empty road map with just the major roads and towns marked. After the RAP, as student teams problem solve, they will fill in more detail into this road map or mental schema. Remember, the RAP is about generating readiness in your students, *not* about testing. Testing picky detail that is not necessary for the activities that follow, testing too often, or putting too large a grade component on the RAP can undermine students' acceptance of TBL.

Good RAP questions are based on two ideas. First, what can I truly expect students to learn from carefully studying the preparatory material? Second, what do students need to begin work on the Application Activities? When selecting topics for your questions, begin by reviewing the readings, activities, and objectives. You need to have absolute clarity on your outcomes and objectives to effectively design backward. Start with identifying the concepts that must be learned by the students to begin problem solving. Remember, this is not the only place they will be learning the content. They will continue to deepen their understanding and extend their knowledge as they problem solve in the Application Activities.

The advantage to acquiring knowledge while problem solving is twofold. First, learners can better organize what they learn if they are applying it while they learn it, thereby creating better mental structures that make retrieving what they know during problem solving easier (see Bruner's theory of learning in chapter 4 for more details on developing mental schemas). Second, their motivation for learning is enhanced when they need to know something to solve a significant, interesting problem.

There are a number of different strategies that TBL teachers use to identify topics for testing in the RAP.

First, identify the most important concepts from the readings. Then think about which of those concepts the students must really know to begin the Application Activities. A list of salient concepts can be constructed by reviewing the readings with the Application Activities in mind. When you encounter a concept that the students will likely need to understand to solve an Application Activity problem, write it down in the form of a question. Using this process, you can quickly develop 30–40 question stems that students should be able to answer. These question stems can later be repurposed into a reading guide and become the starting point for selecting a subset of the most important concepts that must be included in your RAT.

The next step is to take that list and ask yourself the question, "Do students *absolutely* need to know this to begin problem solving?" This will let you cut the list down to a few of the most foundational concepts. You may end up with a list of 10–15 concepts, terms, or important facts that you can use to focus the development of the questions. You need to ensure that the questions cover the minimum range of foundational concepts that will prepare students to successfully begin problem solving: not everything they need to solve the problem, but enough to get them started. If you test concepts that are not subsequently used or built on in the Application Activities, then students can legitimately complain that this process actually was about testing and not readiness.

At the beginning, you should draft out an overall plan for your RAT. This is a process of globally identifying the intention of the whole test, and this can help focus your selection and presentation of concepts to be tested during the RAP. When you look at a well-constructed RAP test, you should get the sense that the test is preparing the learner for what follows.

You will likely want to write your Readiness Assurance questions at different Bloom's taxonomy levels. When we describe levels of questions, we often refer to Benjamin Bloom's Taxonomy of Educational Objectives (Bloom, Engelhart, Furst, Hill, & Krathwohl, 1956). In Bloom's cognitive domain, the taxonomy has a series of levels: remembering; understanding; applying; evaluating; synthesizing; and, at the highest level, creating. A prototypical RAP mix is 30% simple recall (Did you do the readings?); 30% comprehension (Did you understand what you read?); and, finally, 40% simple application, often in the form of "Which concept applies to this situation?" (Are you ready to use what you have read?). It is often said to write the RAPs at the table of contents level and not the index level. More accurately, most TBL teachers write at a slightly deeper level than the table of contents, but remember, this is about the minimum students need to know to begin problem solving. Depth of understanding will come later.

Specific Suggestions From TBL Teachers

TBL teachers describe writing good RAP questions and Application Activity questions as the most difficult aspect of TBL. The quality of the questions is extremely important. Once you have created and refined your RAP questions and Application Activities, you have done all the heavy lifting, and it is time to go to the classroom and have fun. Do yourself the favor of spending the necessary time to writing good questions and, if possible, work with someone else to look over your questions, as this can give you valuable feedback before trying them out on your students. You can work with a peer, a colleague, your teaching assistant, or maybe your local teaching center. What is important is to have someone else with an impartial eye review your questions. Question flaws that are obvious to a reviewer may not be obvious to the writer. It is more comfortable to find question flaws in your office than in the classroom in front of your students.

A number of specific suggestions gathered from teacher interviews are included next. Not all suggestions will resonate with you, and they may not all apply to your course context, but they can give you a valuable window into a teacher's intention and actions when constructing RAP tests.

I say to myself as I'm writing, "Is this an important issue? Is it something they really need to know?" And if the answer's no, then I don't ask it. (Larry Michaelsen, Business, University of Central Missouri)[9]

I teach literature. I would read for about 30 pages in a novel, and then I would stop, and I would say, "What is the chief idea there that I can expect a student to have understood without my help, without any explanation, theory, context, or background? What would a reasonably intelligent university student reading this book have grasped without me, even when the student's reading strategies might be less than satisfactory?" That's my question. And then I'll stop at the next 30 pages. Do it again. That's how I generate my questions. (Brent MacLaine, Literature, University of Prince Edward Island)[10]

I try to do big-picture, broad-concept, lower level questions, but there are occasional detailed questions, if I feel that it's appropriate. I typically stay away from asking really detailed questions. I try to stay away from testing just rote memorization. I try to go with the big-picture-type questions but at a lower level. (Michael Nelson, School of Pharmacy, Regis University)[11]

I have some questions that are pretty basic. Did you do the reading, do you understand the definitions? And then I have some questions where I'm really trying to get them to think a little bit harder and to have some team discussions, and I tend to lean toward applications. (Janet Stamatel, Sociology, University of Kentucky)[12]

What are the important facts without which they really can't go on? (N. Kevin Krane, Medicine, Tulane University)[13]

Because my RATs are only five questions, I try to hit the five most important concepts. When I write a RAT, I'll skim the entire reading before I start writing to make sure I understand everything that is going to be a part of this assignment, and then I think in terms of what are the five most important concepts. I try to write it at the table of contents level, not the index level, but sometimes it's tempting to get a little more detailed. (Rick Goedde, Management Studies, St. Olaf College)[14]

We often include a few simpler questions that just provide simple accountability that the student has completed the readings. We also identify topics that students are likely to interpret incorrectly. We want to identify common misconceptions that might undermine students' ability to successfully begin problem solving. We can ask which concept applies to a given situation or scenario, corresponding to the Bloom's level of "light application." We can focus on the relationship between concepts; this is an efficient way to test two concepts at once. Why ask what A is, then what B is, when you can simply ask about their relationship, because the student must know A and B to understand their relationship? If an example was provided in the textbook or reading, consider reworking the example into a question based on a different scenario.

It's worth remembering that the RAP doesn't represent the simplified version of what students need to know but represents the first basic ideas embedded in a developing schema or road map that helps students organize all they will learn during the Application Activities.

WRITING GOOD MULTIPLE-CHOICE QUESTIONS

Well-constructed multiple-choice questions are not easy to create. But the quality of the multiple-choice questions you use in your RAT can make or break the tone of your class. Students who are not sure about TBL but willing to try the experiment with you can quickly become fierce opponents if you dash off some poorly constructed questions, inflict them on your students, and hope for the best. Nothing is more uncomfortable than rushing poor questions to the classroom and having to endure the inevitable student backlash. Good questions are absolutely essential to the success of TBL, and putting in the effort to write good questions is worth your time and attention.

In question-writing workshops, many teachers agree that it's not uncommon to spend 1 hour creating each question. With such a hefty time investment, teachers worry about question security and trying to ensure that the questions aren't leaked. Fortunately, the great thing about multiple-choice questions is that you can reuse them and improve them using the item analysis results (more on item analysis later).

Multiple-choice questions are often thought to be useful only for testing lower levels like knowledge and recall. Writing questions at a higher Bloom's level is difficult but not impossible. This does take additional effort and care.

Higher-Level Multiple-Choice Question Example

In your argument, you are citing a number of cases from different courts. This is the first time you cite any of these cases. What is the most accurate citation sentence (use your citation manual)? (This example question was developed by Sophie M. Sparrow and Margaret Sova McCabe, University of New Hampshire School of Law.)

1. Wyman v. Newhouse, 93 F.2d 313, 315 (2d Cir. 1937); Henkel Co. v. Degremont, 136 F.R.D. 88, 94 (E.D. Pa. 1991), Willametz v. Susi, 54. F.R.D. 363, 465 (D. Mass. 1972).
2. Henkel Co. v. Degremont, 136 F.R.D. 88, 94 (E.D. Pa. 1991); Willametz v. Susi, 54. F.R.D. 363, 465 (D. Mass. 1972); Wyman v. Newhouse, 93 F.2d 313, 315 (2d Cir. 1937).
3. Willametz v. Susi, 54. F.R.D. 363, 465 (D. Mass. 1972); Henkel Co. v. Degremont, 136 F.R.D. 88, 94 (E.D. Pa. 1991); Wyman v. Newhouse, 93 F.2d 313, 315 (2d Cir. 1937).
4. Wyman v. Newhouse, 93 F.2d 313, 315 (2d Cir. 1937), Willametz v. Susi, 54. F.R.D. 363, 465 (D. Mass. 1972), Henkel Co. v. Degremont, 136 F.R.D. 88, 94 (E.D. Pa. 1991).

As you can see from this example question, testing higher Bloom's levels is possible. In the example, students are asked to select the citation that is *most* accurate, not which citation is accurate. All the provided citations have errors, so the students are really being asked to hypothesize which errors will have the greatest impact on the citation's accuracy.

Some Important Terms

- *Stem:* sometimes called the question leader. Most of the time, it should be a stand-alone question that students can answer without seeing the answer options.
- *Distractor:* incorrect question answers.
- *Keyed response:* correct question answer.
- *Options:* distractors plus keyed response.
- *Item:* The question stem and options; the whole multiple-choice question.

Developing Question Stems

When beginning to construct a multiple-choice question, write the stem of the question first. A well-constructed stem is most often a stand-alone question that students can answer without examining the options. The wording of the stem and the verbs it contains determine the overall cognitive level tested by the question.

TABLE 6.1
Bloom's Taxonomy: Verbs

Remembering	Understanding	Applying	Analyzing	Creating
know	restate	translate	distinguish	compose
define	discuss	interpret	analyze	plan
memorize	describe	apply	differentiate	propose
list	recognize	employ	calculate	design
recall	explain	demonstrate	experiment	assemble
name	identify	dramatize	compare	construct
relate	locate	practice	contrast	create
		illustrate	criticize	design
		operate	solve	organize
			examine	manage
				judge
				appraise
				evaluate
				compare
				value
				select
				choose
				assess
				estimate
				measure

You can use Bloom's taxonomy to help you prepare the stems to test concepts at the appropriate cognitive level. Table 6.1 lists verbs that relate to different Bloom's levels, and in Table 6.2, the Bloom's levels are related to possible question stems. The list of question stem verbs was developed from Linda Barton's (2007) excellent *Quick Flip Questions for the Revised Bloom's Taxonomy*.

Rules for Question Stem Development

For good multiple-choice questions, consider following these rules for question stem development:

- When possible, stems should be worded as stand-alone questions.
- Stems should be grammatically complete.
- Use negative stems with caution.
- If a key word appears consistently in the options, try to move it to the stem.
- Word the stem such that one option is indisputably correct.

TABLE 6.2
Bloom's Taxonomy: Question Stems

Remembering recalling, defining, recognizing, listing, describing, retrieving, naming	What is . . . ? How is . . . ? Where is . . . ? When did . . . happen? How would you describe . . . ? Can you select . . . ? Why did . . . ?
Understanding explaining ideas or concepts, interpreting, summarizing, paraphrasing, classifying, explaining	How would you classify . . . ? What facts or ideas show . . . ? Interpret in your own words . . . . Which statement supports . . . ? How would you summarize . . . ? What is the main idea of . . . ?
Applying using information in another familiar situation, implementing, carrying out, using, executing	What is the best first step? What is the most significant problem? What would be the worst thing to do? Would it be a mistake to . . . ? What is the most common mistake? Which test would you order next? What is the most common diagnosis? How would you use . . . ? How would you solve? What is the most logical order? What approach would you use . . . ? What would result if . . . ? What facts would you select to show . . . ?
Analyzing breaking information into parts to explore understandings and relationships, comparing, organizing, deconstructing, interrogating, finding	Why is this the best first step? How is X related to Y? What is the theme of X? What are the parts of X? What inferences can you make . . . ? What conclusions can you draw . . . ? What is the relationship between X and Y? What is the function of X? What ideas justify X?
Creating designing; constructing; planning; producing; inventing; evaluating; justifying a decision or course of action; hypothesizing; critiquing; judging; generating new ideas, products, or ways of viewing things	What changes would you make to solve X? How would you improve X? How would you adapt X to create a different Y? What could be done to minimize X? Formulate a theory for X. What would be the outcome if X? How would you prove X? How would you prioritize X? How would you justify X?

Note. Adapted from Barton (2007).

Bury the Verb!

There is a rather simple way to write multiple-choice questions at higher levels. It does violate the stand-alone stem rule, but it can be very effective. First, identify the verb in the question, then switch the verb to a "-tion" noun form. For example, change "describe" to "select the best description" or "explain" to "select the best explanation." This clever twist raises a question from simple understanding to evaluation and discrimination. This puts students in the role of having to evaluate the possible answers against a specified criterion. For example, "Which description best exemplifies the basic tenets of social constructivism?"

Developing Options: Some Considerations

Once the stem has been constructed, you can begin to create the correct and incorrect options. Options should focus on testing the understanding of important concepts and testing common misconceptions. Creating plausible distractors is one of the most difficult aspects of creating good multiple-choice questions. Collins (2006) suggested that the best distractors are either accurate statements that do not meet the full requirements of the problem or incorrect statements that might seem right to the student. The following guidelines can help when preparing options:

- Make sure each incorrect option is plausible but clearly incorrect.
- Make sure that the correct answer (keyed response) is clearly the best.
- Avoid, if possible, using "all of the above."
- Use "none of the above" with caution.
- Try to keep options similar lengths, because test-wise students will pick the longest option if they are unsure of the answer ("too long to be wrong").
- Make sure options are grammatically consistent with the stem (question leader) and use parallelism.
- Make sure that numerical answers are placed in numerical order, either ascending or descending.

When developing the options, you will find it useful to map them on a continuum from correct to incorrect. This mapping will allow you to visualize the "correctness" of a given option. If all the distractors are clustered around the incorrect end of the spectrum, as in Figure 6.6, then the question will be unambiguous and will likely not stimulate team discussion or debate.

FIGURE 6.6
Question options clustered near incorrect response

C D	A	E		B
Incorrect				Correct

FIGURE 6.7
Question options clustered near correct response

A	D	C	E B
Incorrect			Correct

As the options begin to cluster at the correct end of the continuum, as in Figure 6.7, the stem will need to include superlatives like *most* or *best*. Which is *most* significant? What is *most* important? What would be the *best* solution? These kinds of questions will require finer discrimination by the students; they can lead to spirited discussion but can also lead to potentially unhappy students. Use this with caution.

The last step of the test construction phase is to rearrange the questions and options to match the pattern on the IF-AT card. Some questions require a specific order, such as numerical lists. We typically first find a place for these questions on the IF-AT, then rearrange the remaining questions. Poorly written questions are often difficult to rearrange.

Improving Your Questions Using Item Analysis

Most test scanners and test software automatically create test statistics. These are most commonly known as item analysis. It is a numerical process that analyzes each question, or "item," and relates how well students did on the question versus their overall test score. It is most often used to identify questions that are not working properly. For example, a difficult question that high-achieving students consistently get wrong and low-achieving students consistently get right might point at a question construction error. Item analysis lets you find these problems.

Table 6.3 is a typical item analysis chart. It consists of two major portions: an analysis section that shows the success frequency, and a tally. The success frequency displays the percentages (or sometimes the raw counts) of students with the correct answer when considering the entire class (whole group), the top quartile of the class (upper 25%), and the bottom quartile of the class (lower 25%). The tally frequency section indicates the number (or sometimes percentage) of all students selecting each option. The percentage correct across different subsets of students can be used to determine the discrimination of the question.

There are two useful ways to use the item analysis in your TBL course:

- In real time, after scanning the iRAT test sheets during the RAP, you can use the tally frequency portion of the item analysis to identify questions with which students had difficulty. Understanding where students are having difficulty can help the teacher provide appropriate and timely clarification on any troublesome concepts after the tRAT.

TABLE 6.3
Typical Item Analysis Chart

Q	Correct				Tally				
	Whole Group	Upper 25%	Lower 25%	Discrim	A	B	C	D	E
1	81	97	56	.46	8	6	79	1	3
2	55	53	59	−.06	1	27	9	54	7
3	99	100	96	.18	0	96	0	1	1
4	100	100	100	.00	98	0	0	0	0
5	89	87	74	.14	5	4	2	87	0
6	89	87	74	.20	18	42	9	13	16

- In the off season, you can use the item analysis results to revise and improve your questions. By reviewing the discrimination values of a particular question, you can understand how the question performed in the test. By reviewing the tally report frequency with which each option was chosen, you can identify options that may have never been chosen and need to be improved or made more attractive so some students might choose them.

Using Discrimination Value

Discrimination index ("Discrim" in Table 6.3) represents the ability of a question to differentiate between students with a good overall understanding of the test topics (i.e., those with a high overall test score) and those with a weaker overall understanding (i.e., those with lower overall test scores). The discrimination index value can range from −1.0 to +1.0. A large positive value indicates the performance on that individual question is strongly correlated to the overall test score. As the discrimination approaches zero, it indicates no relationship between the question and overall performance, and as it becomes negative, it indicates students who didn't prepare are more often answering the question correctly than students who did prepare! This is usually indicative of an issue with the question wording or topic. The aim is to create questions that have a higher, positive discrimination index, showing that we are discriminating between the well-prepared students who understand the material and those who did not prepare or do not understand the material.

In the example shown in Table 6.4, Question 2 has a low discrimination value, giving us the information that students who didn't prepare performed

TABLE 6.4

	Correct				Tally				
Q	Whole Group	Upper 25%	Lower 25%	Discrim	A	B	C	D	E
2	55	53	59	−.06	1	27	9	54	7

TABLE 6.5

	Correct				Tally				
Q	Whole Group	Upper 25%	Lower 25%	Discrim	A	B	C	D	E
1	81	97	56	.46	8	6	79	1	3

better on this question than students who did prepare. This question probably should be revised.

In the example shown in Table 6.5, Question 1 has a higher discrimination value. This indicates that students who prepared performed better than students who did not prepare. This question probably needs no revision.

Finally, in the example shown in Table 6.6, all 98 students correctly selected answer A in Question 4. The question has a discrimination value of 0, indicating it does not discriminate between those with strong overall test performance and those with weak performance. This question is a candidate for revision on the basis that it is likely too easy. It would be especially important to revise this question if you suspect some students were not well prepared for the test, and yet they still were able to answer the question correctly.

Typically, when questions discriminate poorly, the writers will reexamine the question and how it has performed to determine if revision is required. There isn't a discrimination value threshold that clearly delineates a good question from a bad one. Discrimination values give us useful inferences to determine if the question is doing what we want it to.

Using Tally Reports

By examining the tally section, teachers can identify answer options that were never selected. This might point to the need to rewrite some options to make them more attractive, forcing students to more accurately discriminate between options. One extreme case is the example in Table 6.6, where no student selected options B through E.

TABLE 6.6

Q	Correct				Tally				
	Whole Group	Upper 25%	Lower 25%	Discrim	A	B	C	D	E
4	100	100	100	.00	98	0	0	0	0

Using *p*-Values

Many test scanners will also provide question *p*-values. The *p*-value represents the difficulty of the question. For example, a *p*-value of .6 means 60% of students selected the correct answer. It is recommended that a test contain a range of *p*-values from .25 to .75. A difficult question would have a *p*-value approaching .25, and an easy question would have a *p*-value approaching .75. As previously mentioned, a prototypical RAP mix is 30% simple recall or remembering (Did you do the readings?); 30% understanding (Did you understand?); and finally 40% simple application, often in the form of "Which concept applies to this situation?" (Are you ready to use what you know?). Therefore, on a 10-question RAT, one possibility is to have 4 very difficult questions, 3 medium difficulty questions, and 3 easy questions.

COURSE LOGISTICS

The RAP is the gateway into each module. Remember, we want to prepare students; we don't want to upset or scare them. There should be no surprises for the students during the RAT. The trick is to manage students' expectations and give them the help they need to be successful.

Reselling the RAP

At the beginning of any TBL course, it is necessary and advisable to orient the students to the procedures in TBL, your rationales for using TBL, and what your expectations are for the students. Students need to know why and how they need to prepare—and you need to sell it. Before the first RAP test, you should revisit your rationales and remind students what the RAP is preparing them for. You can reinforce this in the reading guide. In class, you can sell it by talking about how fun, interesting, and useful it is going to be to be able to solve complex, real-world problems. Remember the RAP is about preparation, not difficult testing or quizzing exercises. I recommend not using the term *quiz*, because it sends the wrong message.

Helping Students Prepare for the RAP

At the beginning of each module, especially early in the course, you should remind students of how to successfully prepare for the upcoming RATs. Many TBL teachers provide reading guides.

Materials for helping students with the reading can be broadly broken into two categories: generic materials that address critical reading skills, and specific guides that highlight concepts, definitions, and other foundational knowledge that students should learn from the specific preparatory materials. In either case, students need to be reminded that critical reading is an active endeavor. They should be taking notes, recording important concepts, and periodically testing their understanding.

Generic Reading Guides

Generic reading support materials can introduce students to different strategies for critically reading texts. They often highlight the strategies that experts use in reading, such as cognitive maps, outlining, and other strategies. The expert approach is often very different from the average student approach.

Consider when experts read an article. They often start by reading the abstract, identifying the research question, then flipping through the article looking at the section headings and overall organization, maybe reading the results and discussion sections, looking at the figures, then going back and reading any sections they feel necessary to help their understanding.

Contrast this with a typical student approach. Students start at the beginning and inch through the text word by word, assuming that if their eyes pass over the

---

Tips on Critical Reading

Critical reading is focused on active, engaged, thoughtful reading. Our students may not be able to do it without our help. Here is a list of ideas to help get them started:

1. First skim quickly, studying organization, headings, illustrations.
2. Write key ideas and main points in margins.
3. Outline and summarize as you go.
4. Ask questions as you read: What does this mean? What's the main point?
5. Consider clarity, accuracy, importance, and relevance.
6. Look for connections and contrasts.
7. Identify the conclusion and determine if there are good reasons supporting it.

words, they will somehow learn it. If they get to the end and still don't understand, they may skip back to the beginning and reread the text, hoping it will sink in. Students need to be coached to use a more productive approach.

Specific Reading Guides

Specific reading guides can be a series of questions that students should be able to answer after reading the assigned text or other preparatory materials. Reading guides can take the form of a list of concepts and facts or a series of questions, such as "What are the three main causes?" "What is the definition of . . . ?" "What does . . . mean?"

For example, in a literature course, the teacher could suggest that students write one sentence to summarize each paragraph as they read. This gives them a simple, concrete way to read the text more effectively. The reading guide is your opportunity to focus students' attention on the important concepts that will be tested in the RAP and enable students to successfully begin problem solving.

Here are some specific examples of reading guides. The first excerpt is from Pete Ostafichuk's reading guide for a second-year mechanical engineering course, the second excerpt is from Sarah Leupen's reading guide for an undergraduate physiology course, and the third is a guide from Marie Thomas's advanced psychological statistics course.

Mechanical Engineering Reading Guide Example

Required: "Eggert—Failure Mode Effect Analysis.pdf" posted on WebCT. This gives a brief introduction to how you can assess risk in parts, devices, and processes using the failure mode effect analysis (FMEA) procedure. This is a common tool used in industry. After completing this reading, you should know what a failure mode is, the parameters that effect risk, and how we quantify risk. You do not need to memorize the steps in FMEA, but you should be familiar with them.

Required: Ulrich and Eppinger, Chapter 15, Appendix A (pp. 325–328). This gives you a quick overview of how an amount of money at one time has a different value at another time due to interest. After completing these readings, you should be familiar with how to calculate net present value (NPV) and the concept of sunk costs. It is recommended that you read this appendix before moving on to the next reading.

Required: Ulrich and Eppinger, Chapter 15, pp. 308–313. Focus on understanding what Exhibit 15-2 is describing and how NPV is used to evaluate all cash flows present and future.

Physiology Reading Guide: Goals Section

For all goal sheets, goals that are italicized are goals you should be able to do for the RAT (for this chapter, the RAT is in the 12th week of class, the 4th week after spring break). All goals will be assessed on the quiz or test that completes the unit.

I. Goals you should be able to accomplish without use of any resources except your wonderful brain (which these goals are all about!):

- Vocabulary: *autonomic nervous system, sympathetic nervous system, parasympathetic nervous system, cholinergic, adrenergic,* nicotinic receptor, muscarinic receptor, alpha adrenergic receptor, beta adrenergic receptor, *agonist, antagonist,* autonomic neuropathy, *vasodilation, vasoconstriction,* hypertension, Raynaud's disease.
- List several effects of sympathetic, and of parasympathetic, nervous system activation; *identify a major effect (e.g., increased heart rate) as being either sympathetic or parasympathetic.*
- *Predict the general effect of sympathetic nervous system activation or parasympathetic nervous system activation on any organ or organ system.*
- *Differentiate between the parasympathetic and the sympathetic nervous system in terms of (a) under what conditions they are activated* (fight or flight vs. rest and digest), (b) what effects they produce, (c) what neurotransmitters they use, and (d) where their fibers originate on the spinal cord.
- List or identify the organs and tissues that are innervated by the sympathetic but not the parasympathetic division.
- *Recognize that effects mediated by nicotinic acetylcholine receptors are always excitatory.*
- Give an example of a condition under which the sympathetic and parasympathetic divisions work cooperatively.

II. Goals you should be able to accomplish using the book and any notes you have (usually, but not always, also in collaboration with your team members):

- Predict the effect of a drug, identified as an antagonist or agonist for any ANS receptor subtype, on any organ (e.g., *How would an antagonist for adrenergic B1 receptors affect heart rate?*). . . .
- Choose a drug to treat a particular clinical problem and predict its side effects (e.g., *What kind of drug would you take to increase insulin secretion? Answer: A drug that blocks alpha-2 adrenergic receptors. What side effects would you predict for this drug?*)

Note. From "Chapter 14: Reading Guide and Goals," by Sarah Leupen (2011). Retrieved from http://www.teambasedlearning.org/misc. Adapted with permission.

Advanced Psychological Statistics Reading Guide

The reading assignment is chapter 6 in David Howell's (2013) *Statistical Methods for Psychology.*

- *I can describe the characteristics of the chi-square distribution.*
- *I can define the terms expected and observed frequencies.*
- *I can perform a chi-square goodness-of-fit test by hand* and using statistical software, *and can interpret the results.*
- *I can perform chi-square contingency table analysis (test of independence) by hand* and using statistical software, *and can interpret the results.*
- I can describe the problems associated with small expected frequencies.
- *I can describe the assumptions associated with chi-square.*
- I can describe one way to handle dependent or repeated measurements using chi-square.
- I can explain and demonstrate how to calculate *d*-family and *r*-family measures of effect size.
- I can explain and demonstrate how to calculate kappa.

"I don't expect my students to understand the entire chapter without some help. I highlight (bold) the outcomes that will be covered by RAT questions, but students understand that for the midterm/final they are responsible for understanding all of the listed concepts" (Marie Thomas, personal communication, December 27, 2013).

Showing students how to read effectively can be very helpful in both the short term and the long term. In the short term, it helps their preparation for the RAP, and in the long term, it develops important lifelong learning skills that can be valuable for other courses and ultimately their careers.

Reading isn't about passing their eyes over the text. It's about actually figuring out what it is that they are supposed to learn from the text and knowing what it is so that they can take the next step. And all of that happens prior to the class, and I love that about RAT and about TBL. I love the fact that it creates the right incentives such that the student has done a significant amount of work prior to coming into my class. (Shawn Bushway, Criminology, University at Albany)[15]

Managing Anxiety at the End of the RAP

At the end of the RAP tests, students can be disappointed at their individual scores, and you may need to manage their anxiety. Scores on iRATs are typically in the 60%–75% range, but this can be initially disconcerting to "always A" students. They need to know that this is a typical outcome and be reminded that when combined with the 85%–95% tRAT score, they in fact have done well on the test. You also can remind them of the small portion of the total course grade that each iRAT represents. If the RAP has prepared them well for the activities that follow, then it is a success.

CLASSROOM LOGISTICS

In this section, I will introduce you to the classroom logistics of the RAP. The RAP is like any other classroom activity, where preparation can help to make sure the process runs smoothly.

Teachers' Preclass Preparation

Many teachers use team folders to handle getting all the class materials to and from students. Team folders are preloaded with the test sheets, the answer forms (maybe Scantron in larger classes), and an appeals form, as shown in Figure 6.8. Folders let you simplify the handling of materials. In large classes, we ask team representatives

FIGURE 6.8
Team folder contents

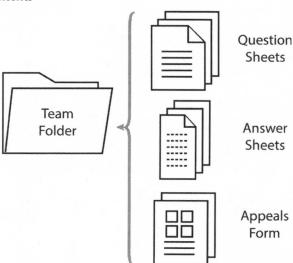

to come to the front of the class to pick up and drop off their team's folder, so the teacher remains at the front of the class. Creating these folders for each team not only simplifies getting materials to and from the teams but also sends the important message to your students that you have taken time to be organized.

Class Start

Before the start of the iRAT, some teachers give students a few minutes to ask any last-minute questions, but most go straight into the iRAT. We start the RAP class by announcing the events scheduled for the day and how much time students will be given for each segment of the process. A general rule of thumb is 3–5 minutes for distributing folders and getting names on forms, 1 minute per question on the iRAT, and slightly longer for the tRAT (1.5 minutes per question).

In class sessions that are only 50 minutes, teachers often reduce the RAP length to 10–12 questions, so the entire RAP can be more easily completed in one class period. An alternative method is to give the class 5 minutes after the first student or team has finished the iRAT or tRAT.

iRAT

To begin the iRAT, we ask students to put away any notes or other reading materials. We then ask one representative from each team to come to the front of the class to pick up the team's folder. Teams are not to open their folders until all teams are reseated. Next, we ask the teams to open their folders, distribute the tests, and begin. While the students are completing the iRAT, we circulate around the room and clarify any difficulties that students may have understanding the questions.

Once the allotted iRAT time has elapsed, students are asked to collect their team's individual answer sheets and send one representative to the front of the room to exchange the answer sheets for their IF-AT card. Students are reminded to hang on to their question sheets for the tRAT.

Students who are absent on the day of a RAP typically receive a zero for both the iRAT and the tRAT unless they have satisfied some other predetermined course requirements. These requirements could be to make plans with the teacher in advance to take the iRAT separately, to provide a medical note in order to be excused from the RAP and have the tests excluded from grading, or to require a signed note from their teammates with permission to share the team score. In the latter case, if a student has been a prepared and consistent contributor to the team, most teammates are happy to share their team score with the absent student.

tRAT

At the beginning of the tRAT, we announce how much time will be allowed for the tRAT process, then tell the students to begin. Before starting, we remind students of any decremental scoring scheme we might use with the IF-AT cards. On a four-option IF-AT card (A–D), we often award 4 points for a correct answer on the first scratch, 2 points for the second scratch, 1 point for the third scratch, and 0 points if they need to scratch all four possible answers. Different teachers use different decremental scales. Whatever scale you use, the important thing is that you are rewarding the students for continuing to discuss the question seriously. Otherwise, after one incorrect scratch, you would just rub off and reveal all the other answers, and a valuable learning opportunity would be lost.

During the tRAT, we circulate around the room monitoring the students' progress. If we notice that a large number of teams are finished before the allotted time is up, we will ask the whole class who needs more time. If only a few teams need more time, then we will often announce that there are perhaps 2 minutes left.

If you have a classroom test scanner, you can scan the individual tests during the tRAT. Remember, the iRAT is about accountability, so scanning the tests immediately in the classroom, although nice, is not essential. If you do scan them immediately, the tally report and item analysis can be used to help you identify topics with which students are still having difficulties, and you can clarify these difficulties in the last step of the RAP. The tally and item analysis information can be used to tailor your mini-lecture to be the most helpful. If you don't use a classroom scanner, you can simply write the question numbers on the board and ask teams to put check marks beside the question or questions they would like clarified (see Figure 6.9). This is actually a very good option, because some concepts are clarified enough during the tRAT that students do not need further clarification. If you work only from the tally report of the individual tests, you may end up talking about topics that were already resolved during the team test.

Teachers often record the teams' average iRAT scores and the range of tRAT scores on the chalkboard. This achieves two goals. First, it shows students the value of working as a team, as tRAT scores are usually 10%–20% higher than the average

FIGURE 6.9
Student feedback on which RAP questions to review

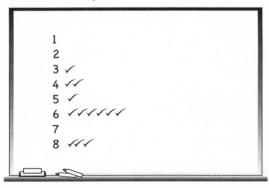

iRAT score. Second, it motivates teams to perform better than their peers by creating friendly competition.

The Appeal

At the end of the tRAT, teams are encouraged to appeal questions that they got wrong. Scholarly appeal arguments can be generated by any team and are written on the appeal form included in each team's folder. The teacher makes it clear that the appeals will be considered only outside of class time and that the results will be announced at the next class. Some students will try to open a conversation about why a particular answer should be considered correct; you can shut the conversation down by simply asking the team to complete that appeals form and you will look at it after class. You need to establish a rule of when appeals are due. Some teachers insist by end of class; other teachers insist by end of day, often submitted by e-mail. One way to ensure that all team members have contributed to the appeal is to have them sign a statement of collaboration at the bottom of the appeal form.

Teacher Clarification/Mini-Lecture

At the end of the testing and appeal phases, teachers respond to items identified in the RAP as still challenging to students. You must *not* review the test question by question but only review the questions and concepts that remain problematic for the students. Students like the mini-lecture because they know it won't be too long, and the teacher is talking about something they know they don't know.

Ending Class Well

Students are asked to place all question sheets and the IF-AT form in their team folder for collection. We often get team members to sign the back of the IF-AT card, as this can simplify requests made by absent students who still want credit. We remind students that all question sheets must be returned or the whole team will receive a penalty, usually a mark of zero. We mark the folders with the number of students in each team; this lets us easily check that all question sheets are returned. A team representative is then asked to bring the team folder to the front of the room.

Timing of the RAP

The typical RAP takes 50–70 minutes for a 20-question test. In shorter classes, teachers will often shorten the RAP test. For our 50-minute classes, we often give 12–15 questions in 50 minutes; this gives us time to complete the entire five-stage process.

One of the most helpful things we've done to improve faculty and student acceptance of TBL is to standardize the procedure across our curriculum so everyone knows what to expect. We use a standard PowerPoint slide show in every TBL session in the curriculum to guide the process. It does not include content. For example, on screen before the session starts, the first slide instructs students to collect their materials from the front of the room and assemble with their team. The second slide instructs them to open their folders and to complete the iRAT independently. There are reminders that this is a closed-book exam and that students must not copy the questions so faculty don't need to waste time reiterating this information. We give a fixed time of 15 minutes for the iRAT, after which their individual responses are collected by iClicker. There are a few "I had a problem with my iClicker" cards in the folders to reduce stress if students forgot their clicker, had a battery failure, etc. The PowerPoint then guides class through the tRAT including reminders that talking to teammates is now permitted but that using materials or the Internet is not. We monitor progress through the tRAT using "done" cards that teams put up when their team is done. When about half of the teams have finished, we announce that the other teams have a couple more minutes to finish up. Typically, all of this takes somewhere around 30–45 minutes, and we then give students a break while we review the collected IF-AT cards.

During break, faculty review the IF-AT cards to identify questions that many teams missed. We do not ask the students to explain problem questions to each other because it takes way too long and kills the momentum. Similarly, it's a waste of time to go through every item. Remember, because of the IF-AT cards, all the teams learned the correct answers and discussed them during the tRAT. Instead, a faculty member will take 5 minutes and go through the most troublesome topics, perhaps one or two items on a 10-item test. We complete the Readiness Assurance Process by collecting any written appeals from the teams. These are dealt with outside of class, because points are involved, and the session may devolve outside the scope of the class. Of course, if there's a major flaw with an item, we'll address that right away to keep the class moving forward into the Application Activities. This is where the real fun begins! (Chris Burns, Microbiology, University of Illinois)[16]

WHEN READINESS ASSURANCE GOES WRONG

There are many reasons why the RAP may go wrong. Students are often uncomfortable as they transition to their new roles and responsibilities in the TBL classroom. From experience, we know there are a few major things we may do wrong when we implement the process. We may unintentionally do things that can fuel student discontent. Remember, if students come to believe that the RAP is about testing, they will resist. If the tests seem disconnected from the activities that follow, they will resist. It is important to build and sell a RAP that helps students prepare for the activities that follow.

Giving TBL a Bad RAP

People sometimes see in my workshops that bad questions actually generate significant discussion. They will invariably ask if writing bad RAP questions is a good way to generate student discussion. It's not. We want to invest as much time as we can into writing the best questions possible. We want to be intentional here and have the questions generate the discussions we were planning, not unexpected tangents by upset students.

Discussion about bad questions can be uncomfortable for the teacher. We all will write some bad questions; the trick is to learn from the experience and handle the resulting classroom discussion in the most productive and helpful way. Some teacher humility is probably appropriate when we find we need to admit to our students, "That wasn't a very good question." Make sure to actively listen to students' discontent and, as much as possible, remain an active listener rather than the infallible teacher defending your work. The Appeals Process can take care of a few bad questions, but if bad questions are the norm, students will lose confidence in both the TBL process and the teacher.

When a bad question is identified, make sure to take notes so you can revise the RAP test for next time. Nothing is more deflating than taking the same test to the class next year and having that same unrevised question not work again. Sounds far-fetched? It's not! I've done it. The discomfort of standing in front of a room full of unhappy students should inspire you to do the work and expend the effort to improve the question, so you do not suffer the same fate again next year.

Types of Bad RAP Questions

Many starting TBL teachers either develop their RAP questions at too high a Bloom's level or focus on nitpicky details. Students will push back if overly difficult questions are the norm. We need to keep the purpose of the RAP in mind: the idea that we need to focus on the minimum foundational knowledge that will get the students ready to begin problem solving.

The first time using TBL, I was writing too specific, detailed questions that were not appropriate for what the RAP was trying to accomplish. The quality of the questions has changed significantly for me. When I began writing questions more at the outline level, rather than the specific detail, things improved. (Ron Carson, Occupational Therapy, Adventist University of Health Sciences)[17]

I started off writing questions that were a bit more complicated than I write now, and I did some case-based test questions. But I've really backed it up, and I really try to make questions much more foundational. If these are truly readiness assessment questions, they can't be the same level of complexity as your final exam questions. (Lindsay Davidson, Surgery, Queens University)[18]

I was probably making the questions a little too complicated in the beginning. (Mary Gilmartin, Geography, National University of Ireland–Maynooth)[19]

The biggest mistakes I made during my first TBL semester were that my RAT questions were too difficult and that I commented on all of the RAT questions after appeals were submitted. I've learned over time to err on the side of writing RATs that are too easy, rather than too hard. The benefit of easier RATs is that students then go into the applications with a positive attitude like "Yeah, we get this stuff! This isn't so hard!" Then I can really challenge them on the applications. I know I can use the applications to motivate them, showing them that the material is more challenging than they think. How RATs are used is especially important because if anything upsets students, RATs will, either having too many, [making them] too hard, or [making them] too high stakes. (Rick Goedde, Management Studies, St. Olaf College)[20]

Having Too Many RAPs

Another common mistake with first-time TBL teachers is to have too many RAP tests. More is always better, isn't it? Not in this case. Students have very negative reactions to overtesting.

I didn't realize how negative and difficult it becomes if you overassess by having too many questions and too many RAPs. Students begin to see the whole focus as all about testing instead of learning. (Mark Freeman, Business School, University of Sydney)[21]

Reacting Productively to Student Discomfort

TBL can uncomfortably thrust students into new roles in the classroom. They may question their self-efficacy as autonomous learners, because they are usually placed in a passive role, with the teacher expected to be responsible for their learning. Students grapple with issues around the need for social dialogue and discourse. All these issues can make students uncomfortable, and uncomfortable students may look for a convenient scapegoat. Teachers can easily become their target. A percentage of students will choose to complain, no matter what instructional strategy you choose. You should expect it and be ready for it. Even with well-thought-out courses in our 10th year, we typically have 10% or so of students who complain. Most students are extremely happy with TBL, but we, in a very human way, often tend to hear the unhappy students a little louder.

The challenge is figuring out how to pitch the course, and then managing the pushback, the resistance, and knowing in advance that the resistance is coming and there's nothing wrong with it—it takes you two or three rounds to get to the point where you say, yeah, that's okay. (Bill Roberson, Faculty Member and Faculty Developer, University at Albany)[22]

Complaints in the TBL classroom can be different from those you can receive when lecturing. You have organized the unhappy into teams, so they can complain more effectively! It is important to have your teaching rationales rock solid so you can endure and respond effectively to these complaints. We can often moderate these complaints by talking about them openly in the classroom. Most often, not all students will feel the same way. I have seen other students shut down the chronic complainer by saying, "What we are doing here is important, and you're not letting us get our work done." Have a plan, stick to the plan, and don't back down.

Eighty percent of my students like me when they walk in. They're probably going to like me when they leave. They are taking the course because they have to, they're going to try to make a good grade, and they will most likely walk away satisfied with my TBL course. And then I've got 10% who just dislike me, but they would have disliked me no matter what. And then I've got another 10% that really, really like me, and they would feel that way no matter what.

Overall, my course evaluations have improved; the comments are the only interesting difference. The comments referring to a TBL course are often more intense than I remember when I lectured. In a course of 30 students, I will get at least 15 intensely positive comments (e.g., the best college class I have ever had; TBL experience was awesome; more classes should be taught this way). I will also receive one or two intensely negative comments (e.g., I did not learn anything; I had to teach myself; I wish the teacher would have actually taught). When I lectured, I don't remember particularly intense negative comments. I do feel like I get at least two or three scathing comments per semester that are completely related to Team-Based Learning, but that is okay. (Mary Gourley, Psychology, Gaston College)[23]

It is important to keep remembering that some student discontent is absolutely normal. Unfortunately, as teachers, we have the normal human tendency to focus on the bad news. Those hurtful comments from unhappy students can be very difficult to accept. It doesn't seem to matter that the majority of students are happy with TBL; those complaints still sting. As you become more experienced with TBL, you come to expect this as a necessary stage in the students' learning process and the TBL process.

Now that the students have completed the RAP, they are ready to move on to the Application Activities.

FIGURE 6.10
Readiness Assurance Process checklist

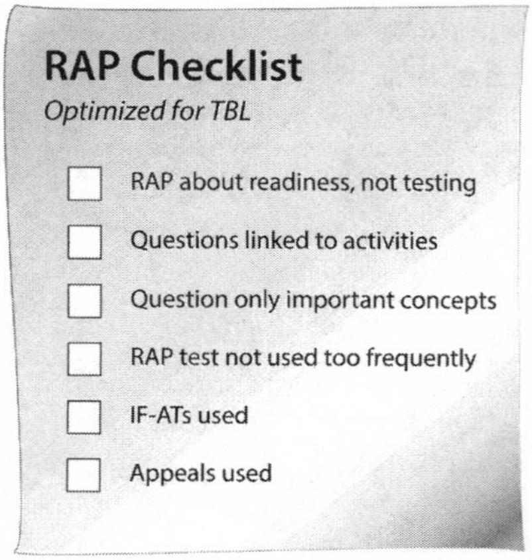

RAP Checklist
Optimized for TBL

☐ RAP about readiness, not testing

☐ Questions linked to activities

☐ Question only important concepts

☐ RAP test not used too frequently

☐ IF-ATs used

☐ Appeals used

NOTES

1. R. Carson, personal communication, January 7, 2013.
2. M. Hadley, personal communication, January 9, 2013.
3. D. Raeker-Jordan, personal communication, January 4, 2013.
4. M. Gourley, personal communication, January 2, 2013.
5. M. Stevens, personal communication, January 16, 2013.
6. P. Smith, personal communication, January 17, 2013.
7. S. Bushway, personal communication, January 18, 2013.
8. B. MacLaine, personal communication, January 8, 2013.
9. L. Michaelsen, personal communication, January 2, 2013.
10. B. MacLaine, personal communication, January 8, 2013.
11. M. Nelson, personal communication, January 8, 2013.
12. J. Stamatel, personal communication, January 3, 2013.
13. N. K. Krane, personal communication, January 18, 2013.
14. R. Goedde, personal communication, January 23, 2013.
15. S. Bushway, personal communication, January 18, 2013.
16. C. Burns, personal communication, January 7, 2013.
17. R. Carson, personal communication, January 7, 2013.
18. L. Davidson, personal communication, January 7, 2013.
19. M. Gilmartin, personal communication, January 9, 2013.
20. R. Goedde, personal communication, January 23, 2013.
21. M. Freeman, personal communication, January 15, 2013.
22. B. Roberson, personal communication, January 2012.
23. M. Gourley, personal communication, January 2, 2013.

CHAPTER 7

Application Activities

Application Activities are the heart of Team-Based Learning (TBL). It is during these activities that student learning dramatically deepens—first through dialog with one's teammates, then even further during the intrateam discussions that follow the simultaneous reporting. The magic of a discussion that results from decision making is that the conversation quickly switches from facts or "What is the correct answer?" to "Why?" "Why did you decide that way?" "What was your evidence that supports your decision?" "How did you arrive at your answer?"

Lecturing is comfortable. For the majority of us, lecturing is the style of teaching we were exposed to for most of our time as students. Chances are, most of your colleagues who teach rely on lectures too. Moving to something different, like facilitating TBL activities, can be unnerving and can feel like stepping into the unknown. But rest assured, there is a wealth of collective experience and proven techniques to draw from in order to help make the unknown known and to make that first step a smooth and confident one.

As a metaphor for the difference between lecturing and facilitating TBL activities, imagine you are an outdoor enthusiast and you want to teach a group of students how to river raft. In the lecture analogy, this might be an activity where you place yourself in a raft, anchored in a slow-moving section of a river, and gather your students on shore to watch and listen. You meticulously plan your demonstration in advance and prepare a scripted list of talking points to make sure your presentation covers everything. From your location on the river, you try to teach your students all there is to know about river rafting, and you enthusiastically expound how much fun it is. You are engaging and energetic throughout. You are the star of a show to which your students are the audience. You encourage your students to sometime try for themselves everything you have told them. For the next group of students, you do it all over again, polishing your script and your delivery along the way.

Now consider what this might look like as a TBL activity. The first change is that your students are not passive observers from shore but active participants in teams, in their own rafts, on the river. They are going to learn how to river raft by actually doing it. Of course, you still diligently plan the activity in advance, and you guide the students to acquire the basic skills they are going to need before they get to the river. You carefully choose a river location that is within the students' ability but still challenges them and requires they work together with the others in their raft. While rafting, you continue to give pointers and demonstrations, but these are now short, targeted teaching moments done ad hoc as needed. Your role has largely shifted to developing the activity and being there to jump in (pun acknowledged) if needed. Students are now much more responsible for their own learning, as well as the learning of everyone else in their raft. Every team will follow the path of the river, but beyond that you do not know exactly which route individual teams will take. Students will still look to you as the expert, although it is now the activity that is the star. When it comes time for the next group of students, it will be an entirely new journey, even though the river is the same.

Which of these two approaches is likely to lead to more competent and more confident river rafters? Which is going to be more fun and engaging for the students? Which is going to be more fun for you the teacher?

Among the many takeaways from this river-rafting metaphor, one of the most important is that TBL facilitation requires a mind-set and a skill set that are different from those used when lecturing. The teacher devises, organizes, and manages the activity, and the students learn by working together to apply the material. With this shift, you give up some control, but in the process, you are freed from the script and inject excitement into learning. It is also important to recognize that the students' roles change from passive observers to active participants.

Facilitation: A Different Skill Set

TBL requires a different set of skills than traditional teaching, and that's something that we're trying to develop in our faculty. Some people are better at facilitation than others, but really, I think it is a new skill we're all learning. (Simon Tweddell, Pharmacy, University of Bradford)[1]

This chapter is all about the core of TBL: the Application Activities. The structure of TBL provides the framework for effective team functioning, and the Readiness Assurance Process ensures that teams are ready to use the course content, but it is during the Application Activities where the high-level, impactful learning happens. The Application Activities are hands-on exercises that take place during class time. Students reach higher level learning outcomes (critical thinking, synthesis, evaluation, and so on) by applying their knowledge, skills, and judgment in an exercise—hence the term *Application Activity*.

FIGURE 7.1
The Fink Triad of objectives, activities, and assessments

A HIGH-LEVEL VIEW OF CLASS PLANNING

Whether you are thinking about a single class, an entire course, or a complete program, it is always helpful to keep the triad of objectives, activities, and assessments in mind. This triad is sometimes called the "Teaching and Learning Triad" or the "Fink Triad," after Dee Fink's (2003) wonderful book *Creating Significant Learning Experiences* (see Figure 7.1).

As this chapter is about facilitating Application Activities, let us for now restrict our thinking to a single class consisting of either one or several Application Activities. Starting with the objectives (or desired outcomes, if you prefer), you need to ask yourself, "What do I want students to be able to do by the end of the class?" Perhaps you would like them to apply a new tool or technique or use new knowledge to solve a problem; perhaps you would like them to critically evaluate a scenario in light of new information or a new perspective; perhaps you would like to expose students to an experience that will help to develop their appreciation for professional practice or another viewpoint. Knowing where we would like students to be by the end of the activity then raises the question "How will we know that students have reached these objectives?" (where "we" ideally includes both the teacher and the students). This is where the assessments come in, as they will provide the data to answer the question about whether objectives were met. And finally, this leads to the class activities themselves: What should students do in class such that they can achieve the objectives you have determined and demonstrate this attainment on the assessments?

We find keeping the Fink Triad in mind is particularly helpful with TBL Application Activities. It is easy to get lost or carried away in designing fun and engaging Application Activities, so the triad gives three simple checkpoints to ensure that your activity is not only fun and engaging but also meaningful and well integrated with the course. The learning objective for the class activity is directly related to the specific course content you would like the students to master, so unfortunately this book cannot provide that piece for you. For now, just take a moment to consider a higher level cognitive learning outcome, perhaps involving critical thinking, synthesis, or evaluation, related to your subject matter. It is not hard to imagine an activity where students working in teams develop these skills or abilities by making a decision about a complex problem with conflicting or incomplete information. Certainly, the opportunity to develop higher level learning outcomes is far superior with this approach compared to conventional lecturing: How can students effectively develop the higher level learning outcomes by copying down notes and listening to someone talk?

Start With the End Point

One of the strengths of this is around the application of knowledge. It's not just acquiring knowledge. It's really giving students an opportunity to apply the knowledge, and that means a different perspective taken by the academic. So you're starting with "What do you want your students to be able to do at the end of the course?" And that, for me, was quite transforming. (Jenny Morris, Nursing and Midwifery, Plymouth University)[2]

The assessment portion of the Fink Triad can refer to formative elements (assessment during the learning process) and summative elements (assessment at the completion of a course or unit). These are sometimes referred to as assessment *for* learning and assessment *of* learning, respectively. For a single Application Activity, I usually interpret assessment in the most general sense as providing feedback to answer the question "Were the learning objectives met?" This could have both formative and summative elements. In a conventional lecture-based course, assessment tends to be heavily summative through examinations and term papers and is normally delayed many weeks after content appears in the lecture. (That is not to suggest lectures cannot be adapted to include forms of formative assessment; tools such as personal response systems, or clickers, can be brought into a lecture to enhance active learning and promote timely feedback. Classroom Assessment Techniques [Angelo & Cross, 2003], or CATs, such as the One-Minute Paper or the Muddiest Point, also help to bring assessment to an otherwise passive classroom.)

Formative feedback permeates good TBL Application Activities. Informal peer-to-peer feedback is ongoing while teams discuss, debate, and work on Application Activities. Likewise, as you circulate and listen in on team discussions, you can provide timely feedback, coaching, or assistance to a team or the class as a whole. Finally, at the conclusion of an exercise, during a classwide debriefing or discussion, appropriate feedback can be shared across the class, whether it originates from you or from the students. During a TBL Application Activity, you (and the students) will likely already know whether the class and course objectives are being met. Of course, there is still room for formal, quantitative, summative assessment in the form of examinations, homework, papers, and so on at other points in the course.

Alignment between the three pieces—objectives, activities, and assessments— is critical, and misalignment is a sure way to create frustration and pushback from students. With this in mind, we will now look at elements of good Application Activities, strategies to develop them, and techniques to manage them in the classroom. Near the end of the chapter, we will turn our attention to what to expect during your first Application Activity and what to do if things do not go as planned.

APPLICATION ACTIVITIES AND THE 4 Ss

So what makes a good TBL Application Activity? I know I have hit the mark on this when the classroom is full of noise and energy, the discussions are focused on the activity at hand, and I have a steady stream of students asking for additional information as they dig deeper into the problem. Most compelling is when students seem oblivious to the clock and the end of the class period; they continue to discuss the activity, and I actually need to tell them to leave the room to make space for the next group coming in. To me, this is a strong indication that the students are engaged with the course material (there is on-task noise and energy), and they enjoy and value the experience (they would rather continue working than leave the room). This is a huge step from the rustle of bags and clicking of binders I used to hear several minutes before the end of a lecture, before I was introduced to TBL.

FIGURE 7.2
The 4 Ss

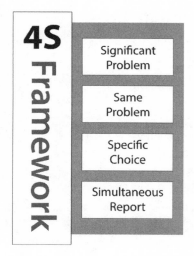

For creating an effective Application Activity, you will use one of the guiding principles in TBL, the 4 Ss: significant problem, same problem, specific choice, and simultaneous report (Figure 7.2).

Significant problem reminds us that the problem must be meaningful to the course and rich enough to engage the whole team. A trivial problem that can be solved by a single person working alone does not make a good team Application Activity. Rather, we should seek a complex problem with incomplete or contradictory information where a diversity of perspectives is an asset. Churchman's (1967) concept of a "wicked problem" captures some of the essence of a significant problem in that it is resistant to resolution or at least does not have an obvious solution. As highlighted in the following quotes, N. Kevin Krane and Michael Nelson have developed good personal tests for what makes a significant Application Activity.

To me, the golden rule is if you can Google an answer, then it isn't a well-written application exercise—which sounds almost too simplistic, but it really does work. Because I've sat with faculty who show me their application exercises and said, "Watch this. I never read your material. I don't know anything about it. But I'm going to answer using Google, and though I've answered the application correctly, I've still learned nothing." And for students, you know, when we emphasize that they can use any resource they want to answer an application exercise, that emphasizes that just "knowing" information is not enough, which means it's really hard to write good application questions. (N. Kevin Krane, Medicine, Tulane University)[3]

A phrase that is mentioned often amongst the faculty when we're reviewing applications and writing new ones is "Is this something that's likely to need the whole team to solve? Will it engage the whole team?" (Michael Nelson, School of Pharmacy, Regis University)[4]

Same problem refers to having the entire class work on the same problem at the same time. The rationale is that by having all teams work on the same problem, they will have a greater engagement and investment when it comes time for a classwide discussion or debriefing. Having a deep knowledge of the problem will allow for a more informed critique of other teams' work, not to mention a more engaged and passionate critique if other teams arrive at a conflicting conclusion for the same problem. This approach is in contrast to the common practice outside TBL of having teams work on different problems so they can share what they have learned; without having everyone work on the same problem, each team becomes the "expert" of its own topic, which does not invite challenges or contradictory conclusions in the same way.

Specific choice requires that teams be able to express their solution to a problem by means of an easy to describe choice. Before we look at some examples of how specific choice can be used, consider the following cases that do *not* require a specific choice: a multipage report, an oral presentation, a demonstration of a functioning device or process, or an ordered list, to name a few. Creating these deliverables may be valuable experiences for students and may even relate to some of the course outcomes, but they do not lend themselves well to TBL Application Activities. Instead, the specific choice of a good Application Activity requires that the team members all come to agreement on a single, clearly defined answer in light of potentially vague or conflicting information. Having teams make a specific choice also makes it possible to quickly see and compare responses between different teams (part of the next "S"). Posing multiple-choice questions is one of the most common ways to require a specific choice, provided the question is not trivial; that is, the problem is *significant*, as described earlier. There are many other approaches too, such as an open prompt requiring a one- or two-word answer; a task involving identifying a specific feature or location on a drawing, chart, or map; or a task involving specifying a value (e.g., minimum profit or maximum safe dosage). As noted by Mark Stevens in the following quote, the choices available to the teams need not necessarily have a clear "right" answer; the purpose is to stimulate discussion and application of the course material and to require teams to support and justify their thinking.

One of the things I struggle with regarding the application exercises is when I give the teams five discrete choices or options to choose from, does there necessarily have to be a right answer? I tend to find that the exercises are both more valuable as well as more realistic, for my field, if there isn't necessarily a right answer. If you can make a case for any of the options, the exercise then becomes about "How do we make this decision when there's no obvious right choice, and how do we justify the decision that we made?" In most cases, my application exercises don't have an obvious right answer. (Mark Stevens, Community and Regional Planning, University of British Columbia)[5]

Simultaneous reporting is the final "S," and it requires that responses from all teams are reported to the class at the same time. Requiring the response in the form of a specific choice (the previous "S") makes simultaneous reporting possible, because a specific choice is easy to report. Simultaneous reporting encourages team accountability, because each team knows its response will be available for all to see, and no team wants to stand out with an unreasonable, hastily chosen answer because it did not put the same thought into the problem as the other teams. Put another way, the public commitment that comes with simultaneous reporting motivates the teams to seriously engage in the activity. There is also a fairness that comes with simultaneous reporting, because no one generally wants to be "picked on" first. More important, there is no opportunity for later teams to unfairly modify their answer based on the responses of earlier teams, because everyone commits to their answer at the same time. Finally, simultaneous reporting creates anticipation, excitement, and engagement in the classroom; teams want to see how their response compares to those of their classmates. Techniques for achieving simultaneous reporting follow naturally from the type of specific choice the teams make, and later in this chapter we will explore a variety of different simultaneous reporting possibilities.

As a final note, it is the *revealing* of the choices to the class that should be simultaneous, not the *recording* of the choices by the teams. For example, teams could report their answer to the teacher or teaching assistant by a certain cutoff time in the class while the teacher records the answers as they come in (perhaps on a laptop or an overhead transparency), and then the teacher could reveal all answers at once using a digital or overhead projector. A common facilitation approach in these circumstances is the "last to report, first to talk" rule.

Before we move on, it may be helpful to examine several example Application Activities to get a sense of what they might look like in practice. Later in the chapter, we will look at many other examples you can consider for inspiration when constructing your own activities.

Example 1: Active and Passive Voice With Voting Cards

Consider the following exercise (adapted from Michaelsen, Knight, & Fink, 2004) to be presented to teams in an English class:

> Imagine you are an English teacher and you are working with your students to develop their understanding of the active and passive voice. You are trying to develop their next assignment. Which wording in the following assignments would best promote higher level thinking and a rich reporting discussion?
>
> A. List the mistakes writers frequently make that detract from their efforts to write in the active voice.
> B. Read the following passage and identify a sentence that is a clear example of (a) active voice and (b) passive voice.
> C. Read the following passage and identify the sentence in which the passive voice is used most appropriately.

In advance, teams are given three large colored cards prominently labeled A, B, and C. After giving teams an appropriate amount of time to discuss and determine their choice, the teacher instructs teams to simultaneously hold up their cards (e.g., "on the count of three, hold up your choice"). A teacher-facilitated discussion of the class responses follows.

The following points highlight the 4 Ss in this example:

1. The problem requires not only an understanding of what differentiates active and passive voice but also an ability to critically evaluate the effectiveness of potential learning experiences in enhancing student understanding (significant problem).
2. All teams work on the same scenario at the same time (same problem).
3. Each team chooses one of three possible answers (specific choice).
4. All teams reveal their choice at the same time by holding up a colored voting card on cue (simultaneous reporting).

Example 2: Location for Dry-Cleaning Business Selected Using a Pushpin

In this second example (adapted from Sweet & Michaelsen, 2012b), imagine an economics course in which teams are tasked with identifying the best location for a business:

> You are consulting for a new business owner who wants to open a dry-cleaning store in Norman, Oklahoma. Where would you recommend locating a new dry-cleaning business (and why)?

A street map of Norman, Oklahoma, is placed at the front of the room, and each team is given a pushpin. At the appointed time, after teams have had time to analyze the scenario and reach a supported conclusion, each team sends a representative to the front to indicate the team's chosen location on the map using the pushpin. The scatter of pins on the map creates a natural motivation to understand other teams' thinking in determining their choices. A teacher-facilitated discussion of the class responses follows.

This example also makes effective use of the 4 Ss:

1. Drawing from their course material, teams must analyze the business and location characteristics, identify and appraise possible locations, and recommend and justify a location based on an evaluation of the potential options they have identified (significant problem).
2. Again, all teams are tasked with the same case to analyze (same problem).
3. Each team has a single pushpin to indicate the location for its business on the map (specific choice).
4. All teams place their pushpins at nearly the same time (simultaneous reporting).

As teams also need to be prepared to support and defend their choice during the class discussion, there is little concern of a team changing its decision at the last second if it happens to see a difference between its choice and those of other teams that have already placed their pins.

Although the 4 Ss are invaluable in guiding us to the elements of an effective Application Activity, it remains to actually construct the exercise, structure a class or classes around it, and facilitate the activity. These are the topics of the next two sections.

STRUCTURING AN APPLICATION ACTIVITY

The organization of an effective TBL Application Activity parallels that of any effective teaching activity; it needs a well-thought-out structure with a beginning, a middle, and an end. There are many frameworks used to describe such structures, but they generally have the same elements grouped in different ways. I will use one of the simpler top-level frameworks to describe structure: Set, Body, Close. Feel free to adapt your personal favorite if you have one.

Set, Body, Close is highly adaptable for almost any size group and any duration (Figure 7.3). It aligns, respectively, with the beginning, middle, and end of an activity or lecture. The Set portion sets the stage and primes the learners for what is to come; most important, it establishes the tone, conveys why the topic is important, and outlines the objectives. The Body is the core of the class; in a conventional lecture, this would be where the teacher delivers content, whereas in a TBL class, this is the Application Activity (including teams working on the exercise, as well as the discussion and debriefing that follow). Finally, the Close wraps everything up. It summarizes the class or activity, emphasizes what has been accomplished, and relates the outcomes to the objectives from the Set.

Setting Things Up

The typical team exercise day will start with an introduction. I usually take anywhere from 5 to 15 minutes to introduce the exercise and talk about the context. One of the things I'm learning to do a better job of, and I think I'll try to do even more, is develop really clear learning objectives for each exercise. I haven't done that as much as I would like to, but I'm kind of learning that as I go. I want to be able to explain, "Here's what we're doing and here's why. This type of situation would come up when you're a practitioner in this type of case," and I can do this both before as well as after the exercise. (Mark Stevens, Community and Regional Planning, University of British Columbia)[6]

FIGURE 7.3
The Set, Body, Close structure

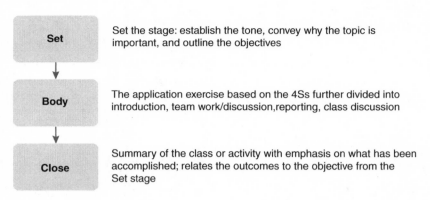

In facilitating a TBL activity, you are important through all phases of Set, Body, Close. The Set and the Close are the primary opportunities for you to engage with the entire class at once. The Set and Close can be particularly useful in a course where learners are new to TBL, as they allow you to highlight why you believe the team Application Activity is superior to some other teaching approach. It is a chance to make a "sales pitch" for TBL and to ease some of the students' trepidation and resistance that might otherwise come forward when trying something new. If an activity falls flat, which does happen from time to time, the Close gives an opportunity to gracefully acknowledge that and still achieve some or all of the learning outcomes that were set forth (more on this later in this chapter).

Put another way, the Application Activity is the Body, and the Set and Close are there to frame and support it and reinforce the learning. With properly designed Application Activities, student focus naturally shifts from identifying the "correct" answer to examining the thinking and supporting evidence behind a decision. Highlighting this to the class and reinforcing this shift in focus is important in the Set and Close. The Body of a TBL Application Activity also deserves special attention; as we will see in the next section, there are many techniques and approaches around which this can be constructed.

FACILITATING AN APPLICATION ACTIVITY

The Body of the Application Activity is based around the 4 Ss introduced previously. As depicted in Figure 7.4, the Body can be further divided into four stages: exercise introduction, team discussion and work time (also called *intra*team discussion), simultaneous reporting, and class discussion (also called *inter*team discussion).

FIGURE 7.4
The stages of the Application Activity Body

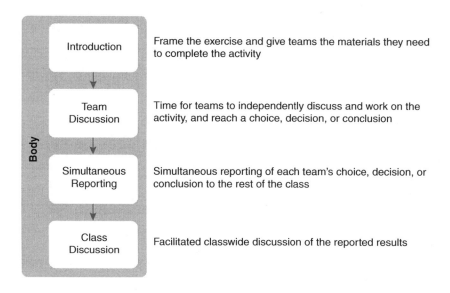

When introducing the exercise, you give teams the required materials they need to complete the task. Having handouts and other materials already prepared in team folders can expedite the distribution process and also conveys the message that thought and effort have gone into the activity and its preparation. The introduction is also used to orient teams to the activity in terms of the time available and the resources, applicable knowledge, and skills they should draw from. Finally, this is an opportunity to remind teams specifically what outcomes are expected, including the specific choice they are to make and any deliverables or supporting information they should have available.

Mary Hadley nicely captured the importance of coming prepared and the smooth simplicity that results when you do so:

> *They come in. I have folders. I put everything for the team in the folder. The application that they're going to be working on is in there. They get it. They start to work on it. I wander around.* (Mary Hadley, Chemistry and Geology, Minnesota State University–Mankato)[7]

The team discussion and work time (intrateam discussion) is the time for teams to complete the activity. Thinking of the 4 Ss, this is where teams apply the course material to study the significant problem and make their specific choice. This is also the time when teams prepare whatever is needed to report their choice, as well as any supporting materials they anticipate may be required during later class discussions.

Although most TBL classes allot this time for the teams to simply reach the specific choice they are prepared to defend, another approach is to require teams to prepare worksheets, summaries, or other deliverables to submit during the activity or at the end of the class. A simple worksheet might have three boxes for teams to complete: their team number, their specific choice in the activity, and a brief written summary of the most compelling reasons supporting their choice. The worksheet could also be extended to include a second part to be completed *after* the class discussion: What is the team's new choice and why, if it has changed based on the class discussion; otherwise, what new information has come forward that strengthens the team's original choice? Two other options for worksheets include using staged questions to formally guide teams step-by-step through an activity (staged questions are discussed at the end of this section) or to have teams summarize their choice and all of the required justification for it in a concise poster or display (as can be used in the hot seat method, described in the next section). If used, worksheets and summaries can help to structure an activity, to clarify and make visible student thinking, to increase accountability if teams are required to submit their work, and to provide artifacts for evaluation and grading, if so desired.

The teacher's role during the team discussion stage is typically an active one and requires the teacher to constantly check in with teams. The teacher's moving from team to team and engaging with students emphasizes that the activity is important and valued. In addition, this gives the teacher an opportunity to track team progress for the sake of activity timing, as well as to anticipate possible issues. Questions from teams can be addressed—or not—as they arise. The role of the teacher, monitoring team conversations and managing the activity time during the team discussion phase, is described well by Mary Hadley and Mark Stevens:

> *They can ask me questions if they like. I don't answer the questions. Specifically, I try to ask a question or several questions so that they can come to the answer themselves. I will often say, "Ah, you might want to go and consult with Team Four. I was looking at what they were doing, and it looked like they were on the right track." So every now and then, they consult with one another. I'm just there wandering around. They pay very little attention to me; they end up in an argument among themselves. They want me to solve the argument. So I never do, but like I say, I try to say, "Well, did you think about that? Did you think about this?" and leave at that point.* (Mary Hadley, Chemistry and Geology, Minnesota State University–Mankato)[8]

> *I spend my time moving around the room, observing, listening, writing, taking notes. I usually write down if I hear a really interesting comment that a student makes, or if common issues are being raised, I take notes on that.* (Mark Stevens, Community and Regional Planning, University of British Columbia)[9]

Knowing how teams are progressing helps you determine if there is a need to pause the activity and provide additional information, clarification, or even a mini-lecture if many teams seem to be excessively struggling. This is not to suggest other views of the teacher's role are not possible; Sandy Cook[10] noted that facilitators at the National University of Singapore found "being in the room meant that the students spent more time trying to weasel the answer out of the faculty," so now the faculty sit in another room while the discussion is taking place.

The simultaneous reporting portion of the exercise is where the different team choices or responses to the problem are revealed to the class. There are many approaches to manage and achieve the simultaneous reporting, and a small sample of some techniques is described in the next section, with additional examples included in Appendix B. Though there are many techniques for this phase, the essential elements are the same: All teams' choices are revealed at the same time (which requires each team to commit to its response prior to seeing any other team's responses), and differences in team choices are immediately and clearly available for all to see.

The class discussion (interteam discussion) follows immediately or shortly after the simultaneous reporting. This is where teams have an opportunity to examine other teams' methodology and challenge their decisions. By the same token, this requires that teams be prepared to defend their own choices and decision-making process. Contrasts in student thinking revealed by the simultaneous reporting naturally lead to the class discussion. In some cases, teams may eagerly seek the opportunity to challenge contrasting opinions or decisions, whereas in other cases, teams may need a little coaxing from the teacher. Either way, the conversation naturally tends to focus on the thought process or support for the decision, rather than which answer is the "correct" one.

The teacher's role during the class discussion stage is to *facilitate* the discussion, while resisting the temptation to *join in* the discussion. It is important to ensure all team voices are heard, and how this is done will depend on the class personality, the norms that have been established, and the confidence teams have in their answers.

One approach to aid in starting the dialog is to begin with the group of teams with the most common response and ask for one of those teams to volunteer, or randomly select one of them to speak first, and have the team defend why it believes its response is well justified. Another approach is to give teams some time, perhaps 2 or 3 minutes, to formulate questions for other teams. Last, it is typical that the teacher calls on an entire team to answer rather than an individual, but it is worth considering whether this is the best approach for your class. As Bill Brescia highlights, there may be merit to asking a specific individual from within a team to speak:

> *We call on a specific student from a team, rather than saying "someone from Team 17." We did that because what we observed after the first year was a team spokesperson was evolving, and whether that person was the smartest*

one in the group or the one who felt the most comfortable speaking in a group or whatever, we wanted to break that down, and we wanted every student to feel comfortable answering the question. (Bill Brescia, Medicine, University of Tennessee)[11]

The discussion and diagram from the start of this section suggest a single-pass, linear progression for the Body from introduction to class discussion, but this is not the only approach. Some subjects and exercises will better lend themselves to staging a large problem in parts, resulting in looping through the process multiple times during a class. As Sandy Cook describes, there may also be situations where such a staged process should be made formal and explicit:

In Application Activities, you don't want a wrong response on one question to send students down the wrong paths for all the following questions, but you also don't want to pre-clue the students to a response by giving the answer in a subsequent question. So a lot of our applications are "staged" questions. What that means is the students get some questions one at a time. They answer one, turn in the responses, and only then receive the next question. That next question may have information that would have helped them answer the previous question. But since they've already turned in their responses, they cannot go back and change their response, but they also can move forward correctly on the next question. (Sandy Cook, Medicine, Duke–NUS Graduate Medical School Singapore)[12]

SIMULTANEOUS REPORTING TECHNIQUES

The character of an Application Activity and the energy and engagement stimulated during the class discussion is largely determined by the simultaneous reporting method used. Two simultaneous reporting methods, voting cards and pushpins, were mentioned earlier in this chapter, but there are many other approaches that can be used. Along with a more detailed description of the voting card and pushpin methods, two more methods, whiteboards and hot seat, are presented next. Additional approaches can be found in Appendix B. The intent through all of these examples is to give a better idea of what simultaneous reporting might look like and to provide inspiration for ideas you might incorporate into your own class.

Voting Cards

The standard TBL approach for simultaneous reporting is for each team to hold up a colored letter card that indicates its decision (see Figure 7.5). (Note how the

FIGURE 7.5
A-B-C-D-E voting cards

ring in the cards in the figure is used to hold everything together.) Voting cards appeared earlier in the chapter, in "Example 1: Active and Passive Voice With Voting Cards" (p. 121). Each team's response is highly visible and clearly linked to it. It is also very easy for teams to compare their response to those from other teams. This kind of reporting can be used as the starting point for a facilitated conversation where student teams defend their positions and challenge the positions of other teams. This technique can be effectively used for both short problems (four or five per hour) and long problems (one per hour or longer), provided the rest of the 4 Ss are met.

Writing good distractors (the "incorrect" or less correct answers) is essential to this technique. The class discussion is largely driven by teams wishing to understand, challenge, and reconcile differences in the thinking processes that led to the different decisions. At the very least, the distractors should all be plausible. To go one step further, an approach to promote lively discussion is to have *no* answer that is obviously correct, as was suggested by Mark Stevens in the "specific choice" portion of the previous discussion on the 4 Ss. Some strategies to deal with the case where all teams immediately agree on the some answer can be found in the "What to Do When an Activity Does Not Go as Planned" section at the end of the chapter.

Getting the Distractors Right

Getting the distractors [right] is key to getting good discussion, because there was [sic] a couple times when all the teams had basically chosen the same distractor, the same correct answer, because in my opinion, my possible answers were not good enough, so there wasn't really a lot of discussion, as much as some of the other ones, where there was a lot of discussion when there were multiple possibly correct answers, and the teams kind of had to defend why they chose what they did. (Ron Carson, Occupational Therapy, Adventist University of Health Sciences)[13]

Having teams report their choices by holding up cards is effective in everything from small classrooms to very large classrooms with 50 teams or more. The greatest challenge in larger classes is to effectively facilitate a whole-class discussion that keeps all students engaged. Some difficulty may also occur in large classes when voting cards go up for only a few seconds, but the reporting conversation takes much longer, because once the cards go down, it is no longer clear which teams had which responses. One solution to this problem is to use flag holders, similar to place card holder stands used on tables at banquets and weddings, that allow teams to indicate when they have completed their work and are ready to report. Voting cards can later be attached to the same stand so they are visible for the duration of the discussion.

Another possible issue is that indecisive teams may hold up more than one choice (A *and* B instead of A *or* B), or they may wait to see what other teams respond with before selecting their card. A quick and effective solution to both of these problems is to inform the class that you will be watching for these occurrences, and those teams will be the first ones called on to explain and defend their choice. After you follow through on this once or twice, very few teams continue to employ these strategies to deal with indecision. (As a side note, I have on occasion had confident teams hold up two cards to make the point that they believe the question is overly ambiguous and two answers are equally well justified.)

Pushpins or Sticky Notes

When students are working with certain kinds of graphical data (maps, charts, drawings, building plans, concept maps, etc.), you can achieve an effective simultaneous report by having teams select a specific location as their answer to the question. Teams can use either pushpins or sticky notes to indicate their location choice. The Oklahoma dry cleaner exercise discussed earlier in this chapter is an example of pushpins on a map. Once each team has decided on a location and made that decision public, you can then facilitate a discussion between teams as they defend their position choice and challenge the decisions of other teams.

The following is an example of this technique from a civil engineering course featuring the use of pushpins:

> An overweight truck has driven onto a bridge. The truck's weight far exceeds the bridge's designed carrying capacity. At which location would the bridge structure likely fail first? Identify the specific point on the drawing, and be prepared to defend your position. Show the specific location with a pushpin on the drawing.

A second example with a "virtual sticky note" requires students to report their choice to the teacher, who then labels each team's selection on a digital image hidden from the class until the teacher is ready to reveal it:

> Carefully disassemble the Lexmark Z615 printer provided and examine the components. Identify the component with the most significant violation of a Design for Assembly guideline (i.e., the component that, if redesigned, would benefit the assembly process most). Report your component to the teacher before 10:30 a.m. A class discussion will follow. Be prepared to justify your choice.

Whiteboards

The whiteboard approach is a variation of the voting cards, but it is more open-ended. Each team writes its decision on a small whiteboard, similar to the one shown in Figure 7.6. The size of the whiteboard limits the possible complexity of the report, so students can easily compare their team's decision to that of other teams. Teams are not alerted to a possible subset of correct answers, as they are with the voting cards.

A whiteboard can be used for student reporting in examples such as the following:

- Given the following investment portfolio, investor profile, and market conditions, which stock would you sell first and when?
- A patient presents at the ER with the following symptoms. What would be your first course of action? What test would you order first?

In each case, after working on the problem, teams write their decision on their whiteboard. In a manner similar to that of the voting cards, the teacher coordinates the simultaneous revealing; for example, "Hold your whiteboards up on the count of three." Classroom size and layout will have a bearing on the use of this technique, as ideally all teams should be able to see all of the other teams' answers.

FIGURE 7.6
Whiteboard report

Keep in mind that unlike a colored voting card, which can be viewed from front and back, whiteboards can be viewed from only one side.

Hot Seat

The hot seat method quickly identifies a single team to begin whole-class reporting—putting the team in the "hot seat." This method has been used in several different settings and can be used in a variety of ways as a means to initiate the discussion or to arrive at the "best" answer. One such approach is the random draw. As depicted in Figure 7.7, you can randomly select teams by (a) drawing from numbered paper slips in an envelope or a jar with numbered balls; (b) rolling dice (hobby stores sell dice in all different numbers of sides; 4, 6, 8, 10, 12, and 20 are common); or even (c) using a smartphone app that allows customizable random team selectors and looks like the wheel on *Wheel of Fortune*. The latter usually creates a great deal of excitement in the class when the spinning wheel is projected onto the screen using a document camera (tip: to really create excitement in the class, include your own name on the wheel with the chance that *you* might have to answer). After the random draw takes place, the selected team then displays its completed worksheet with analysis using a document camera and walks the class through its thinking.

We have discussed four quite different simultaneous reporting methods at length. A selection of additional examples can be found in Appendix B, including two more variations of the hot seat. Of course, there are countless other approaches you can use, limited only by your imagination.

FIGURE 7.7
Sample tools for the hot seat random draw

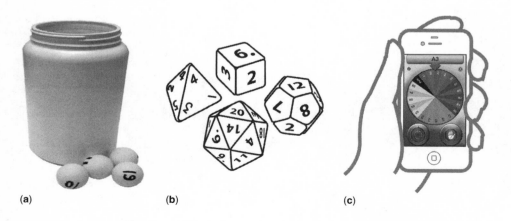

(a)   (b)   (c)

WHAT TO EXPECT: VOICES OF EXPERIENCE

At this point in the chapter, we have the theoretical framework and tools needed to develop outstanding Application Activities. As we all know, theory and practice can feel completely unrelated at times. This section will alert you to a few challenges experienced by others but will also offer their words of wisdom in overcoming those challenges.

First of all, it is important to know what you are getting into. Developing a new course takes a tremendous amount of work, but so does transforming an existing course to a new format, such as converting a lecture-based course to TBL. My personal experience is that the time it takes me to develop a TBL course is similar to what I used to spend developing lecture-based courses. The difference is in *where* that time is spent. In the past, I labored over producing clear, comprehensive, and thoughtfully organized lecture slides that covered all of my content; now most of my time is spent dreaming up potential Application Activities and pondering over how the students might tackle them. This shift is well explained by Jenny Morris:

> *I would argue for a committed teaching team who is prepared to sign up to the importance of the whole process; in particular, writing good test questions and designing good Application Activities and recognizing the centrality of dialectical questioning. It is hard work at the outset, but if you get it right, the process runs really smoothly.* (Jenny Morris, Nursing and Midwifery, Plymouth University)[14]

An important point to keep in mind is that producing good Application Activities is a skill that is developed with practice. This is like any other teaching activity. If you are a good lecturer, you likely developed that ability—preparing great slides, being able to organize content and pace your talk, knowing how to check that students are following, and so on—through practice and refinement. For Application Activities, the challenges are different, but the learning process is the same. You need to figure out what style of activity works best for your students and your course, determine the appropriate difficulty of your activities, develop ways to gauge whether an activity is appropriate before you use it, and so on. Michael Nelson highlights this learning process:

> *Applications. We've learned a lot through the years. Initially, our applications were mostly on paper, and some of us tried too hard to come up with clever application questions. What we ended up doing was writing applications that were too trivial and tricky and really didn't get at the heart of the information. One thing we learned is there are ways to assess students on core concepts, but in a way that brings the team together.* (Michael Nelson, School of Pharmacy, Regis University)[15]

A related aspect is developing strategies for facilitation and facilitation skills. Depending on the size of your class, the level of your students, and the tasks and difficulty of your activities, you may be able to facilitate Application Activities by yourself or you may need a support team. As you initially roll out activities, you may want to consider having additional facilitators present to assist, as Simon Tweddell suggests when speaking of a class of 105 students in a room of 18 tables:

> *We tend to have two or three faculty on our RAPs [Readiness Assurance Processes] and Application Activities, partly because it's new to us and partly because there is a lot going on. As we become more used to it, I think we can probably manage with one academic member of the staff and maybe a teaching assistant, but I think you've got to have at least two people, from my experience.* (Simon Tweddell, Pharmacy, University of Bradford)[16]

Last, it is important to remember that things will not always go as planned, and there will likely be times when you are put on the spot. That does not mean that students will become disengaged or that their learning will stop. It might, as Liz Winter recounts, be quite the opposite:

> *Yes, I was strangely humbled every day. But you know what? That was a good thing. It's sort of a proud moment, at the same time that you're kind of appalled. As I looked at the application exercise as they worked through it, and we started talking about it, I realized that the answer that I had crafted was not so great. I had a very sharp team that essentially took me to task on it, and I said, "Okay. So, you don't like B, and you don't like D, and it's hard to choose between because neither of them feels quite right. How would your ideal answer read?" And there was such clarity from this group; it was a difference of a word, I think. But they nailed it, they absolutely nailed it, and it was a perfect fit. "That's it. I'll take it. You get credit."* (Liz Winter, Social Work, University of Pittsburgh)[17]

Of course, even with our diligent preparation and best efforts in class, things can sometimes go sideways. The next section of this chapter will present a few strategies and ideas for what to do when an activity goes differently than planned.

WHAT TO DO WHEN AN ACTIVITY DOES NOT GO AS PLANNED

Before we give you some suggestions about what to do if an activity does not unfold the way you expected or intended, it helps to consider some of the *ways* an activity might go differently than planned. Over the years I have had my share of these, and in my case, the most common cause is that the Application Activity was either too simple or too challenging for the time available. Other common issues are that teams do not engage in the class discussion or the activity results in all teams making very similar choices (which often also leads to a lack of engaged discussion).

In the case of an activity being too simple, it is possible that the solution is relatively clear to the team from the outset, even if the activity requires considerable time and effort on the teams' part to complete. This can lead to frustration and disengagement in that students may feel they understand and can apply the material, and yet they are still being forced to go through the motions on a long, tedious problem. In terms of the 4 Ss, the issue with an activity like this is likely that the problem posed was not *significant*. A closely related issue arises when one or more teams identify a shortcut to solve an otherwise complex problem. It has happened to me that some students have viewed a problem in a way I had never imagined, and in doing so, they were able to bypass most of the analysis and discussion I had intended. It may not be an issue if only a few teams do this, and in fact, it could turn into a great teaching moment, but if most of the class catches on to the shortcut, a backup plan will be needed (as will be discussed later).

Cases where teams find it difficult to complete the activity in the time permitted can be due to a number of reasons:

- The teacher did not set aside enough time for teams to finish the activity (I am often guilty of underestimating the time required by teams).
- Students do not yet have a sufficient command of the material to apply it to the activity.
- Students are lacking knowledge or skill from a secondary area required for the activity (e.g., an activity in an economics course requires an ability to apply techniques from calculus, which, unbeknownst to the teacher, some students may not be familiar with).
- The instructions provided to teams are missing key pieces of information, overly complicated, or unclear.

These issues too can lead to frustration and a sense of panic or hopelessness during the activity in that, try as they might, the teams cannot accomplish the task that has been set out.

Another possibility is that the activity does not inspire or engage the teams. Over many years of teaching with TBL, I am not sure I have ever found this to be the case except when I made the mistake of giving an overly simple problem that took a lot of work to complete, as described previously. Adhering to the 4 Ss presented in the start of the chapter helps greatly with this potential issue. With teams working on the same problem, with a specific choice and a simultaneous report, there is a natural motivation to come to a reasonable, defendable answer to avoid standing out in the class. I sometimes include a small mark with an exercise, but in the majority of cases, my activities carry no direct grade.[18]

In light of all this, careful planning of activities is essential. Unfortunately, it can be very difficult to predict how teams will react to an activity or anticipate how they will approach it. It helps to have some strategies to deal with activities that run into trouble, as well as some tricks up your sleeve to turn a faltering activity around.

Strategies During Planning

Some strategies to employ during the planning phase are as follows:

- Once you have set your problem, try to approach it from multiple viewpoints to make sure that there are not any approaches that make the answer trivial (i.e., render the problem insignificant) or any that lead down long dead ends where the teams need to put in a great deal of work before they realize their approach will not work. This could lead to designing the activity to be staged, as described earlier by Sandy Cook in the "Facilitating an Application Activity" section of this chapter.
- In planning your class, consider what to do if an activity runs shorter than expected. Can you extend or change the activity by adding additional information or different cases? Do you have other material to fill in with?
- Consider what to do if it runs longer than expected. Do you need to finish on time, or can it spill over to the next class? Is there a natural point at which it can be cut short, or can you provide additional information to simplify the problem?
- Also consider how you are going to check in with the teams to know whether they are on track.

Strategies for Activities That Are Too Simple

When the activity is under way, you need to be active and constantly checking in with teams. Part of your role will be to address, or at least consider, questions from teams as they arise, but you will also need to be tracking team progress to anticipate possible issues. If you find an activity is too simple or students are finishing much more quickly than you allotted for, some options you might consider are as follows:

- Add a complicating factor or alternate scenario. For example, imagine a teacher in medicine saying, "I see many teams are getting close to finishing the exercise on the screen. Once you do, I want you to consider a second case where the patient now presented this additional symptom." This would be followed by a slide or description of a confounding symptom that would change the complexion of the problem or perhaps even directly contradict other information so as to change the team responses. Or in an engineering class, a teacher might say, "In this problem we assumed friction was insignificant; as soon as your team finishes the scenario on the screen, please decide whether your answer would change if it turns out that friction in fact *is* significant."

- Make time at the end of the activity for a team 2-minute paper (which I find usually goes for 5 or more minutes when teams get into discussions). You can have teams decide on what was the most important thing they learned from the activity; have them summarize the best single piece of advice they would give themselves if they were back at the start of the activity; or have them come up with the best argument *against* their choice, decision, or conclusion if they were to play the devil's advocate. A nice aspect of the team 2-minute paper is that it gives you a chance to take a breath and collect your thoughts while the teams are busy in discussion.

- After the activity, ask teams to write a multiple-choice question based on the activity topic, and promise that the best question from all teams will appear on an upcoming test.

- After the activity, acknowledge that the class exceeded your expectations and ask for their input: "Wow! You did great on that activity and finished a lot faster than I was expecting. That's wonderful. Because we have a few extra minutes, I am wondering what about that activity made it easy for you and what would you suggest I do to make the activity more challenging for next year."

- Or it may be appropriate to simply acknowledge the students completed the activity faster than you were expecting and then move on to the next course topic.

Strategies for Activities That Are Too Difficult or Too Long

The situation where the students are not able to complete an activity in the time available poses a different set of challenges. The first step is to determine why they are pressed for time.

If it is due to a lack of command of the course material (or related material, as in the economics and calculus example mentioned previously), early detection and intervention is key. For longer exercises, it may be possible to give a short, impromptu mini-lecture on the necessary material to get teams back on track. In my teaching, I find I do this very frequently. For shorter exercises, particularly ones with multiple-choice responses, it can be effective to keep all teams progressing at a similar pace by pushing the activity to the reporting stage, even if all teams are not confident in their answer. The responses can be discussed as a class without revealing or acknowledging the correct answer, and then teams can be given time to rethink and rereport their answer. A variant of this is to identify a popular but incorrect answer, guide a discussion where teams identify why that is not the best response, and then have teams rework their choices and rereport.

If the issue is due to not making enough time available for the activity, some options include the following:

- Devote more time to the activity (i.e., extend it into the next class if the course schedule permits).
- Simplify the problem (e.g., acknowledge you see teams are pressed for time and then eliminate one or more answer choices or provide them with additional information they can assume to help expedite their work).
- Ask teams to continue working outside of class time and come to the next class with a response selected. This may be an unpopular choice if it is overused or if students are in the middle of a busy week of midterms and papers, so choose this route with care.

An important point to note before moving on is that an activity might run too long not because it is poorly designed but because a sharp eye is not kept on the clock during the team discussion portion, as Mark Stevens describes for his course taught in 3-hour blocks:

> *One of the things I did early on in Team-Based Learning that didn't work so well is I basically just gave teams as much time as they wanted for team exercises, and they basically took as much time as they were given. So at the end of class, there wasn't as much time for synthesis, sharing results, and cross-team discussion. So my time limits now are designed to ensure that we have at least 45 minutes for the cross-team discussion.* (Mark Stevens, Community and Regional Planning, University of British Columbia)[19]

Challenges With the Class Discussion

Even when you select the right activity, design it with appropriate difficulty, and accommodate it with enough class time, challenges can arise during the class discussion. One common issue is that no team wants to volunteer to speak. A silent classroom such as this can be exceedingly awkward and uncomfortable, not just for the students but also for you. Your temptation might be to relieve the discomfort by answering on behalf of the teams or by cutting the discussion short and moving on. Both of these approaches will almost certainly create larger problems down the road, as you have just communicated that even though you *say* you want teams to contribute, all they need to do is remain silent and you will step in and save them. A strategy to address this potential issue that will likely prove more effective in the long term is to simply remain silent and let the awkwardness and discomfort among the teams grow. Remember, although this may seem uncomfortable for you, it will likely be even more so for the teams. This would probably best be accompanied by some firm but supportive and encouraging words, such as "I know you all have thought about this question, and I heard some great points raised during the team discussions, so I am happy to wait for a brave team to come forward to explain its thought process." Another approach is to send teams back into discussion to think about and prepare a response, perhaps adding something like "It appears no teams are quite ready to share their thinking yet, so I want you to take another 2 minutes to prepare your responses." You might add that if no teams volunteer, you will randomly select one (see the random team selection methods in the earlier hot seat discussion). A third approach is to give the teams several minutes to prepare a question to ask of other teams in order to better understand alternative responses to the same problem. This changes teams' contributions from exposing their own thinking to the potentially less threatening task of asking what others did.

A related issue is, when asked to speak, a team gives a brief response that lacks detail, support, or commitment to the specific choice presented. The impulse in a situation like this might be to expand on the students' answer for them or move on to another team, but like the issue described earlier, arguably the best thing you can do is to encourage or press the students to expand on their response themselves. You might do this directly by asking exactly that ("Thanks for your response, but can you elaborate on that?") or by probing for detail in a particular area ("I see you have thought about X, but how did you address Y?"). Another approach is to turn it over to the class: "So this team has said. . . . Are the rest of the teams satisfied with this argument? Do you have any follow-up questions for them?" Bill Brescia has some more tips to help you get the most out of teams, and individual students, during the discussions:

> *Every once in a while we would get a student that can't answer it or feels really uncomfortable, but that's a rare case. . . . When a student is answering, [I tell the faculty] don't walk toward that student, because that's their impulse, to get as close to that person that they're talking to, but that cuts off the rest of the students in the class, essentially, so they kind of pace back and forth in front of the room, or sometimes they circle around and I give them a laminated sheet of all of the students' names, divided up into teams, so that they don't just walk up and say, "Okay, you from Team 16," but they say, "Michelle from Team 16, why don't you tell Ralph over there why his answer's completely wrong?"* (Bill Brescia, Medicine, University of Tennessee)[20]

What to Do When All Teams Have the Same Response

Nothing kills discussion more than when all teams have the same response or make the same choice in an Application Activity. If it turns out the responses are incorrect, you have a great teaching moment on your hands, and you can tell the students that their choice is incorrect and then send them back into discussion, or you can lead them in discussion to think about issues they may have missed so they can uncover the correct response themselves. The point is, your activity is still alive, and the students' engagement with the exercise may actually go up once they realize the problem is trickier than they first thought.

A very different problem is when the entire class converges on the same correct answer. In this case you might have an abbreviated discussion to make sure that the teams actually understood the problem and that their decision making was in fact sound, and then you might move on to the next problem or topic. It might also be appropriate at this point to acknowledge the consensus and ask what it was that led them all to the same answer; this could be a meaningful discussion for the students but might also be instructive for you as to what you might consider changing in your activity for the future. If, for whatever reason, you do not wish to move on, as perhaps you do not have material ready to move on to, you might be able to apply one of the strategies for activities that are too simple that we discussed earlier. If you are using some form of simultaneous reporting involving multiple choice, a great strategy to consider comes from Rick Goedde, as elaborated in the sidebar: Instead of having teams choose the *best* example or *first* choice of something, change the question so they now choose the *worst* example or *last* choice.

Adjusting What You Ask for to Enliven an Activity

[One of my favorite application case studies] deals with deciding which of three candidates to hire to be a vice president at a Toronto bank. Students are given résumés and the answers to interview questions for each candidate. The case is 17 pages long. There's no right answer as to which candidate to hire; each candidate has positives and negatives. The goal is to understand the best process for hiring and to understand which pros and cons for each candidate are most relevant.

A few hours before class, students submit answers to questions about the case, using the quiz feature of Moodle. One of the questions is which candidate is their first choice and which one is their last choice. Most students agreed on the first choice, but there was considerable disagreement on the last choice. I would have normally started the discussion by having the teams vote for their first choice. By looking at their answers on Moodle before class, I decided to start the discussion by asking for their last choice, which led to a much richer discussion. (Rick Goedde, Management Studies, St. Olaf College)[21]

CONCLUSION

To reiterate the opening remarks in this chapter, facilitating Application Activities is very different from lecturing. This can be frightening and unsettling at first, but it has the potential to truly transform for the better how students learn, how they engage with the course material, and what they are able to do. It also has great potential to make the classroom experience fun, energizing, and deeply rewarding for you and the students both, as Mary Gilmartin explains:

> So I think the kind of level of energy and the level of engagement in those classes is probably the best experience I've had in undergraduate classes ever, because students get into the question, and they get into arguing about the question. . . . Very often, students are looking for that right answer, so the idea that there are lots of possible answers and what matters is how they justify their answer can sometimes be a little unsettling. What I love seeing is how they debate, and how they talk, and how they argue about the questions that I've asked. (Mary Gilmartin, Geography, National University of Ireland–Maynooth)[22]

It is my belief that one of the things students value most in a teacher is that the teacher has the students' best interests at heart. My experience has been that students will grant you significant latitude to try new things—and they will be much more forgiving of the occasional class or activity that falls flat—if they believe that you are doing these things for their benefit and to improve their learning experience. The very fact that you are reading this book suggests that your motivation in teaching is not to deliver more content or increase students' test scores but rather to promote students' ability to *use* the course material, to question information they are presented with, to make complex decisions, and to justify their choices. For these reasons, I believe it is critically important that you share with students this desire to give them a better, deeper, richer learning experience and show your commitment to making that happen.

FIGURE 7.8
Application checklist

Application Checklist
Optimized for TBL

☐ **Significant Problem**
Relevant challenging problem

☐ **Same Problem**
All teams work on same problem

☐ **Specific Choice**
Solution expressed by simple choice

☐ **Simultaneous Report**
Teams report at same time

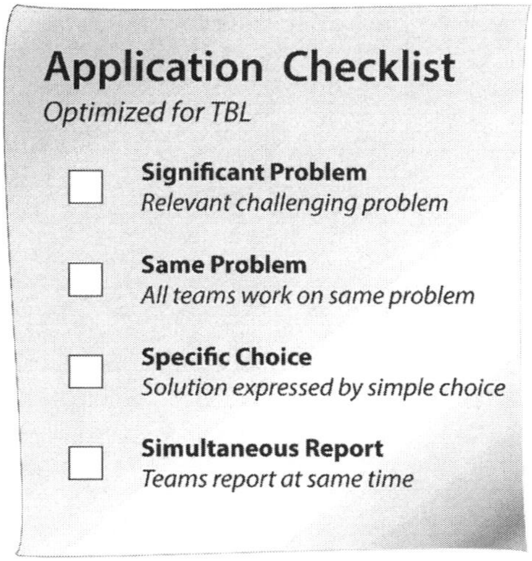

NOTES

1. S. Tweddell, personal communication, January 8, 2013.
2. J. Morris, personal communication, January 9, 2013.
3. N. K. Krane, personal communication, January 18, 2013.
4. M. Nelson, personal communication, January 8, 2013.
5. M. Stevens, personal communication, January 16, 2013.
6. M. Stevens, personal communication, January 16, 2013.
7. M. Hadley, personal communication, January 9, 2013.
8. M. Hadley, personal communication, January 9, 2013.
9. M. Stevens, personal communication, January 16, 2013.
10. S. Cook, personal communication, January 10, 2013.
11. B. Brescia, personal communication, January 11, 2013.
12. S. Cook, personal communication, January 10, 2013.
13. R. Carson, personal communication, January 7, 2013.
14. J. Morris, personal communication, January 9, 2013.
15. M. Nelson, personal communication, January 8, 2013.
16. S. Tweddell, personal communication, January 8, 2013.
17. L. Winter, personal communication, January 4, 2013.
18. A trick I sometimes use to make exercises meaningful to the course grade without actually marking them is to describe them as a "safety net" in case things go wrong. Just prior to the simultaneous reporting, I collect from teams a worksheet or short summary, maybe 100 words, maybe one page, of a team's final choice and its reasoning. I hold on to all of these materials, and if a team has difficulties later in the course, I refer back to the submissions as evidence for or against being lenient when determining its course grade. For example, perhaps a team is unable to fully complete a major project because it either has chosen an inappropriate strategy or has had a string of bad luck; rather than simply assigning a failing grade, I can look back to the team's earlier work to see if the team has otherwise been engaged and committed through the course.
19. M. Stevens, personal communication, January 16, 2013.
20. B. Brescia, personal communication, January 11, 2013.
21. R. Goedde, personal communication, January 23, 2013.
22. M. Gilmartin, personal communication, January 9, 2013.

CHAPTER 8

The Importance of Accountability

This chapter is written to help teachers understand how to develop grading schemes and evaluation processes that fairly reward students for both their individual work and their team work. The goal is to foster improved student behaviors and fairly reward students for their overall contributions.

GRADING AND PEER EVALUATION

There are three things we should do to encourage productive student behaviors in the Team-Based Learning (TBL) classroom:

1. Students must be encouraged to individually prepare.
2. Students must be encouraged to contribute to their team.
3. Students must be made aware that they will be accountable for their contributions to their team.

To accomplish these goals, we must incorporate three important corresponding measures into the overall course design to ensure that we encourage the behaviors we want:

1. Individual performance
2. Team performance
3. Contribution to the team

An important measure of an individual's performance comes from the Individual Readiness Assurance Test (iRAT) scores. These scores give instructors a measure of individual accountability for the quality and completeness of each student's preparation. This component must be a substantial enough portion of the final grade so that a student feels compelled to prepare but not so large that the iRAT turns into high-stakes testing. There are often other measures of individual performance that are not related to TBL, including individual assignments, mid-terms, and final examinations. Students are sometimes shocked at first at the low individual scores on the iRATs. Typical averages are 65%–70%; that's perfectly normal. Students may need to be reassured that the RATs are working as designed, that they constitute only a small portion of their final grade, and that the higher team grade on the Team Readiness Assurance Tests (tRATs), typically 85%–95%, will balance out the lower iRAT score.

The team performance measures come from all team activities that are graded. These include the tRAT scores and, in some courses, the Application Activities.

The measure of students' contribution to their team typically comes from a peer evaluation process. Peer evaluations hold students accountable for their level of participation. Peer evaluations also reassure students that loafers won't benefit from the team grade; this is a happy side effect of the process.

There are a number of different methods you can use to implement peer evaluation. It is important to help your students understand the value of peer evaluation by spending some class time introducing the process, how it will be used, and why it is so important to TBL and the development of their team. Whatever peer evaluation method you use, it needs to have enough teeth so that nonperforming students do not unfairly benefit from the high team scores. Contributing to team success is more than just knowing the right answer. Team members need to be rewarded for supporting each other's learning, mediating conflict, promoting equitable discussion, and supporting the overall functioning of the team.

Students will often express concerns when you announce that you will be using any kind of teamwork. You need to convince them that TBL is designed to address the very issues that they are concerned about. No doubt in the past they have encountered situations where their teammates were not pulling their weight, refusing to contribute, bullying or dominating, or doing low-quality work. During the first-day orientations, many TBL teachers brainstorm with their students to come up with a list of the pros and cons of teamwork (as discussed in chapter 3). The teachers can then explain how the evaluation structures and grading policies in TBL will fairly reward them for their efforts and will not unfairly reward people who have not contributed.

One very major difference worth pointing out is that TBL, unlike many other forms of group work and group projects, does not require teams to meet outside of class time. This may come as a relief to many students.

Because team grades are inevitably higher than individual grades, we need to ensure that if students don't contribute to the team's success, they do not get the benefit of the higher team grade. Conversely, if students consistently show up prepared and contribute well, their grade should reflect this. The structures you put in place around grades and peer evaluation also should address any concerns you might have about grade inflation from higher team marks.

TYPICAL GRADING SCHEMES

There is a wide range of grading schemes found in different TBL courses. Course context, institutional culture, instructor goals, and course goals all need to be considered when you construct the grading scheme that is appropriate for your course. In some institutional environments, policy or local norms may not tolerate having a grade component like peer evaluation where students evaluate other students. For example, in some very competitive environments such as premed, it can be very difficult to sell a grading scheme that incorporates any summative peer evaluation process where one student assesses another student in a way that affects the final course grade. In these environments, the formative styles of peer evaluation are more commonly implemented, because they don't affect students' grades directly. Characteristics of formative and summative feedback are compared in Table 8.1. These can be viewed as end points of a spectrum, as it is possible to have an evaluation with both formative and summative elements.

The TBL grade component in a prototypical TBL course with ungraded Application Activities (i.e., only iRAT and tRAT grades) can be as low as 25%. In these courses, the other 75% of grades might come from traditional components like individual essays, individual reports, midterms, and finals. There is considerable range on how TBL course grades are divided between individual and team work in different courses and contexts. In some courses, the grades are 100% based on TBL components; these courses most often have graded Application Activities.

TABLE 8.1
Comparison of Formative and Summative Feedback

Formative Process Feedback	Summative Outcome Feedback
Process feedback	Outcome feedback
Student-to-student	Student-to-teacher
Open and shared	Confidential
Enhances group process	Guards against grade inflation
Establishes individual and mutual accountability	Reduces social loafing
Ongoing	Final
Provides information to team about how to improve group process and productivity	Provides detail to teacher about how to assign team portion of final grades

Note. From "Peer Feedback Process and Individual Accountability," by Derek Lane, 2012, in *Team-Based Learning in the Social Sciences and Humanities*, p. 54. Adapted with permission.

An effective way to increase student buy-in to TBL is by completing a grade-weighting activity with your students at the start of the course. The activity allows the students to determine the portion of the course grade to assign to each TBL component, usually within instructor-defined limits. Such a first-day grade-weighting activity is described in the sidebar. Whether you or your students determine grade weights, you need to manage two opposing factors: You need to set a high enough weight that the students take each stage of the Readiness Assurance Process (RAP) seriously, but not so high that the RAP is perceived as an intimidating test or exam. I have always used 25% in total for the TBL portion of the overall course grade, dividing it into 10% for five iRATs, 10% for five tRATs, and 5% for peer evaluation. This has worked well for me, but some TBL practitioners have found that 2% for each iRAT is not enough incentive to induce students to prepare. You will need to determine the right numbers for your context, but starting somewhere around 35% might be a safe place to begin. The RAP counts most often for 20%–50% of the total course grade, and peer evaluation usually counts for 5%–10% of the course grade. Just to be clear, RAP refers to the whole Readiness Assurance Process, and the RATs refer specifically to the iRAT and tRAT that are part of the RAP.

Typical Grading Scheme in Second-Year Engineering TBL Course

- Individual Readiness Assurance Tests (5 in total): 10%
- Team Readiness Assurance Tests (5 in total): 10%
- Peer Evaluation: 5%
- Individual Homework Assignments: 20%
- Midterm: 20%
- Final Exam: 35%

To Grade or Not to Grade Team Application Activities

There is no clear consensus in the TBL community on whether Application Activities should or should not be graded.

Some TBL practitioners worry that not grading activities might result in less motivation for grade-driven students. Other TBL practitioners have never evaluated the team Application Activities and have still found no issues with student motivation, engagement, or learning—in fact, they could even make the activities more challenging, as the students did not fear a bad grade. Students will remain motivated if they see that the Application Activities are an integral part of preparation for midterms, finals, or other assessments.

I was worried that the medical students would disengage and not put forth their best effort because the application was ungraded. To my surprise, the quality of work and quality of discussion actually was almost the same. I was happy, because now I could ratchet up the difficulty of the applications as high as I wanted to, and it seemed like the higher I was able to ratchet that up, the better the discussion was, without the pain and suffering and anger that had occurred in the graded situation. (Paul Koles, Medicine, Wright State University)[1]

Even if you don't grade the Application Activities, you still might want to collect the team worksheets. You can use these artifacts for additional evidence if needed later. For example, if a team struggles on a major project and receives a low grade, the unmarked artifacts can be used to determine whether the students do understand the material and some lenience is warranted on the project grade.

If you choose to grade activities, there are some principles to keep in mind:

- Students must fully understand what is expected of them.
- Students need to know what is expected in the classroom and what artifacts will be generated and evaluated.
- Students must understand how the classwork artifact/worksheet will be judged and evaluated.

The classwork artifact created is often in the form of a worksheet, where students capture a very condensed version of their decision and supporting rationales. Often there will be a rubric supplied with the worksheet so students can understand how the worksheet will be evaluated.

Activity Worksheets

Some teachers use worksheets as a deliverable that teams prepare and submit at the end of an Application Activity. The whole team completes the worksheet during the intrateam discussion prior to reporting. These completed worksheets should contain just the "barebones" summaries of decision-making conversation. They might include the following:

- What decision did your team make and why?
- What are the two most important pieces of evidence or arguments that can be made to support your decision?
- What are the two most important pieces of evidence or arguments that can be made to refute your decision?
- If you could ask for one more piece of information, what would it be?
- What is your second-best choice and why?

Not everyone uses worksheets. Some teachers just let students take whatever notes they think are important. Some teachers really like the modeling role that structured worksheets bring to student thinking, whereas others feel that they force too much structure and may rob students of a valuable learning opportunity.

IMPLEMENTING PEER EVALUATION

Peer evaluation is an essential (many would say nonoptional) component of any TBL course. It gives students an important opportunity to give feedback to their teammates on things like preparation, performance, and overall contribution to team success. Team scores are typically much higher than individual scores, so we use a peer evaluation process to adjust the team performance score so it more accurately reflects an individual's performance and contributions to the team.

Whatever peer evaluation method you choose should be fair and defensible: fair in that it rewards and penalizes students appropriately for their teaming behaviors, and defensible in that you can respond effectively to the student question "Why are you doing this to me?" It's important to have your words ready to respond to students' inquiries concerning the necessity of peer evaluation. It's important to help students see that peer evaluation, when done well, can create multiple benefits for them, their team, and their whole course experience.

Potential peer evaluation benefits include the following:

- Preparing students for similar evaluation practices in the workplace
- Fostering individual and mutual accountability
- Motivating team members to use optimal behaviors
- Helping manage conflict
- Developing the team's potential for future activities

The three overarching goals of peer evaluation should be as follows:

1. Helping students learn how to give meaningful and constructive feedback
2. Helping students learn how to receive and act on feedback
3. Helping students reflect on their own preparation, participation, and contribution to their team's success

---

I didn't do the midterm peer evaluation originally, and I've started doing them, and I've been able to see the students respond and change their behavior based on the feedback they get from their teammates. (Mark Stevens, Urban Planning, University of British Columbia)[2]

We recommend having both formative and summative peer evaluation opportunities as part of any peer evaluation plan. In general, formative evaluations are forward-facing, meaning they are focused on changing future performance, and summative evaluations are backward-facing and provide measures of past performance. Often a formative peer evaluation is conducted about a third of the way through the course, and a summative peer evaluation is conducted near the end of the course. Formative opportunities give students feedback from their peers, and this can help students grow, change, and improve. Many TBL teachers report seeing shifts in students' behavior when they are given this important formative feedback. Some TBL teachers now use more frequent peer evaluations, such as one per module, to give additional opportunities for students to get feedback and a richer data set to determine final course grades.

Examples of the types of helpful formative comments that can be expected include the following:

- We wish you would come to class more.
- Speak up more; you have a lot to offer.
- Let someone else contribute.
- You have a negative attitude.
- Don't stop what you're doing—it's helpful.
- You need to be better prepared.

Students appreciate it even though it makes them uncomfortable. I use the analogy about this idea that you can't give two people the same grade: Consider you're the boss of a small business, and these are your employees, and you only have a small pool of money to give raises, and if you give everyone the same raise, everyone's going to be unhappy. So you have to differentiate effort, and they get that. (Janet Stamatel, Sociology, University of Kentucky)[3]

PICKING A PEER EVALUATION METHOD

Four peer evaluation methods are commonly used in TBL. Which method is best for you will depend on your context, goals, and teaching style.

Michaelsen Method

Students are asked to assign a score assessing their teammates' contribution to their team's performance. The evaluation makes up a fixed percentage component of the course grade (typically 5%–10%). The evaluation can be either rubric based or a simple "divide the money" evaluation.

In rubric-based evaluations, students rate their teammates' behaviors using Likert scales on a series of questions about the team experience. Typical rubric criteria include the following:

- *Preparation:* Did your teammates come prepared?
- *Participation:* Did your teammates come to class?
- *Contribution:* Did your teammates contribute to team success?

In simpler "divide the money" evaluations, each person is given a fixed sum to divide among team members. A typical evaluation prompt might be, "Your project team has received a $1,000 bonus. Divide the bonus among your teammates based on their contribution to the project."

Whatever system you choose, students will often attempt to "game the system." Sometimes they will assign perfect scores to all teammates, hoping to ensure that everyone receives the full peer evaluation portion of the course grade. For example, in a course with 5% for peer evaluation, assigning perfect scores to all teammates would result—they hope—in everyone getting the full 5%. Often you can circumvent this by pointing out that assigning full points to all members has in fact made them just average and that an average score will be assigned (maybe 75% of the peer evaluation grade). In addition, if students believe that peer evaluation is a zero-sum game, then assigning a very low score to one teammate will let them assign more points to the remaining teammates. This is normally controlled by setting lower limits on possible evaluation scores, often supported with rules like "If you feel you need to assign an evaluation grade below 6/10, please discuss this with the instructor first." We have also noticed that students are more comfortable giving lower scores to other students if they can justify it. Rubric-based evaluations allow students to "show their work" when they assign a low grade to a teammate. The "divide the money" evaluations might be easy might may rob students of the opportunity to be truly candid with their feedback. Many teachers require both qualitative comments and quantitative scores from students. Others require assigning differentiated scores, where it is not possible to give everyone a 10; someone must get 9 or lower, and someone must get 11 or higher.

I started with the Michaelsen method but have switched to the Fink method.

Fink Method

The Fink method is also known as the course multiplier method. Similar to the Michaelsen method, the Fink method asks students to assign a score based on their teammates' contribution to their team's success; the difference is how that generated score is then used. After the students evaluate their teammates, a multiplier score is computed from their individual peer evaluation score divided by the average evaluation score for the team. The ratio of individual and average evaluation scores is used as a multiplier to adjust the team component of the course grade.

Some examples will likely help.

Example 1

In the *case of a high-performing student*, where the team's average peer evaluation score might be 10 and that particular student has received an 11 overall, the individual score is then divided by the average peer evaluation and yields 1.1. This is then used as a course multiplier. Therefore, the student receives 1.1 times the unadjusted whole team grade (e.g., 80%), adjusting the student's grade upward to 88%.

Example 2

In the *case of an underperforming student*, where the team's peer evaluation average might be 10 and that particular student might have received an 8, the individual score is then divided by the average peer evaluation and yields 0.8, which is then multiplied by the team grade. Therefore, the student receives 0.8 times the unadjusted whole team grade (e.g., 80%), adjusting the student's grade downward to 64%. "Students generally see this as fair because they can give everyone the same score if they contributed to the same degree, or they can give different scores if some teammates contributed more than others" (Michaelsen, Parmelee, McMahon, & Levine, 2007, p. 106).

Koles Method

With this method, students assess their teammates using a large number of quantitative and qualitative measures. But the twist here is that students' scores aren't just what others say about them but also based on the quality of the comments they give others. So students' total evaluation scores are a combination of the quality of the comments they make about their peers and a score that is derived from their teammates' comments about them. A large number of attributes can be assessed using this method. They can include things like cooperation, helping behaviors, attendance, attitude, preparedness, initiative, leadership, communication, and facilitation.

Koles Method: Quantitative Measures

Score each on the following scale: *never, sometimes, often,* or *always.*

Cooperative Learning Skills

- Arrives on time and remains with team during activities
- Demonstrates a good balance of active listening and participation
- Asks useful or probing questions
- Shares information and personal understanding

Self-Directed Learning Skills

- Is well prepared for team activities
- Shows appropriate depth of knowledge
- Identifies limits of personal knowledge
- Is clear when explaining things to others

Interpersonal Skills

- Gives useful feedback to others
- Accepts useful feedback from others
- Is able to listen and understand what others are saying
- Shows respect for the opinions and feelings of others

Note. From "Peer Feedback Form and Peer Feedback Grading," by Paul Koles. Retrieved from www.teambasedlearning.org/misc. Adapted with permission.

In the previous example, the quantitative assessment Likert scale questions are based on three themes: cooperative learning skills, self-directed learning skills, and interpersonal skills. Each thematic element is further subdivided into a series of prompts that are reported on a *never*, *sometimes*, *often*, or *always* scale.

The qualitative component is assessed using two prompts: "What is the single most valuable contribution this person makes to your team?" and "What is the single most important thing this person could do to more effectively help your team?"

The advantage of the Koles method is both the large quantity and the high quality of feedback an individual student receives and the important skills students can develop in learning how to provide effective feedback to others. The disadvantage of the Koles method is the large amount of instructor effort required to review the students' submissions. However, comments like "This effort is worth it" or "It's my favorite part" are very common from teachers who use this method. Like any instructional improvement, we need to weigh the benefits to student learning against recognizing the instructor's time is a limited resource. What is right for a small class may be impossible in a large class.

This method is very similar to Daniel's SKS (DeLong, 2011): Stop, Keep Doing, Start. The SKS prompts are simply as follows:

- What should I stop doing?
- What should I keep doing?
- What should I start doing?

These qualitative components can add significant value to the evaluation for students' personal and professional development, because the quality of feedback is used for grading purposes.

Koles Method: Instructor Guide for Evaluating Student Comments

The following verbatim comments were provided to the same person by five different teammates in response to the question "What is the single most important way this person could alter his or her behavior to more effectively help your team?" Each feedback comment is assigned a value of 0–4 points, using these criteria:

- *4 points:* Very useful to the receiver of feedback
- *3 points:* Fairly useful to the receiver of feedback
- *2 points:* Marginally useful to the receiver of feedback
- *1 point:* Feedback is written but not useful at all to the receiver
- *0 points:* Feedback not written

1. "Continue to find the positive energy in every task that you are required to tackle. You have great knowledge and insight to offer, but this can sometimes be overshadowed by a less-than-positive attitude. You have demonstrated great improvement this semester, and our team thrived off this new, improved energy!" *3 points (useful, but lacks specifics about "less-than-positive attitude")*

2. "On occasion, you have sometimes been hesitant to take a clear stand for a particular answer choice. Since you are often correct in your thinking, our team could certainly benefit from your strong input and support for an answer, even if you are not entirely confident." *4 points (useful, behavior clearly described, expectation clearly defined)*

3. "Sometimes you were wary about giving a definite answer on the group application, which put more pressure on the rest of the group." *4 points (specific, behavior clearly described, defines area to be improved)*

4. "Sometimes your frustrations with the material in team learning are exhibited, which at times affects the group dynamics. So maybe try not to become as frustrated with the material. Also, stop bringing noxious items, like PICKLES, to team learning, as it is disgusting and distracting to other group members, which decreases the effectiveness of the group." *3 points (useful, humorous, but "frustrations" are not clearly defined)*

5. "While you come well-prepared, perhaps you could have come with a little more positive attitude; we would love to see a smile on your face! At times your less-than-cheery attitude brought a cloud to the group and made it hard to get through TL. I know TLs are long and hard, but by being less negative, you could have inspired us to have some hope that we would get out alive that day." *4 points (compared to #1, this is more specific about behavior to be improved)*

Note. From "Peer Feedback Form and Peer Feedback Grading," by Paul Koles. Retrieved from www.teambasedlearning.org/misc. Adapted with permission.

UT Austin Method

In this very simple method, students are asked just two questions:

1. What is one thing you appreciate about this team member?
2. What one thing would you like to request of this team member?

After the teacher compiles the evaluation and comments are put in random order, students get a list of the feedback from their peers about what they are doing well and things that they could improve. This method is sometimes adopted in contexts where teachers have encountered significant student pushback, especially where students might not be happy with the idea of having other students quantitatively assess them.

My own journey with peer evaluation began with the Michaelsen method, where I would assign 5% of the course grade to peer evaluation. I eventually became dissatisfied with the method, because students would game the system, giving everyone the highest marks in an effort to get the full 5%. In a response to that behavior, I started to assign 75% peer evaluation scores to the average evaluation score. This did circumvent the gaming of the evaluation but left me unsatisfied that the evaluation was really doing its job. I had students complain on the first day that because getting 100% was already impossible, the process was unfair. I now recommend the Fink method or course multiplier. If everyone did a good job and contributed equally, then the team grade is the right grade for everyone. I was originally uncomfortable with this method, because I thought it might be possible for a high-contributing student to get a very high team grade, maybe even exceeding 100%. I have never had any such issues and am willing to deal with that "problem" if it ever happens. At our own institution, from a second-year engineering design course, 98% of all evaluations using the Fink method fall between 0.77 and 1.15 (based on over 3,000 evaluations over a 5-year period).[4]

Some teachers continue to tinker with the process to eliminate gaming the system, but other teachers accept the collusion to manipulate the system as a legitimate extension of teamwork.

Helping Students Give and Receive Feedback

Any time we ask students to provide qualitative feedback, we should help them learn how to do this well. Many TBL teachers use the "Making Feedback Helpful" article by Michaelsen and Schultheiss (1989). The article details seven components of helpful feedback:

1. Descriptive feedback, using no judgment or evaluation
2. Specific detail, not general descriptions
3. Honest and sincere

4. Expressed in a helpful format for the receiver
5. Timely and in context
6. Given only when desired by the receiver
7. Usable, only about behaviors that the receiver can control

Sometimes we use the feedback "Sandwich Method" in which a positive comment is followed by a critical comment, which is then followed by a positive comment. This makes any criticisms more palatable to the receiver, and often the feedback is rated as more accurate and credible. We can help make this happen by structuring our reflection prompts first to elicit a positive comment, then a negative comment, and finally another positive comment. Some people find the "sandwich" sends a mixed message that makes the feedback misleading and confusing, so it doesn't work for everyone or in all situations.

Rider and Longmaid (1995) provided a pithy, helpful article that can help students understand how to make the most out of feedback they receive.

Choosing the Right Peer Evaluation Method

The peer evaluation method you choose will depend on the teaching context and goals. Whatever method you choose, you should think through peer evaluation's role in three possible student performance scenarios:

1. *The student who is chronically unprepared and does not contribute.* A well-designed peer evaluation process needs to adjust an underperforming student's overall mark so he or she does not unfairly benefit from the higher team marks.
2. *The student who is well prepared and contributes well.* A well-designed peer evaluation process must reward this student.
3. *The student who overcontributes and dominates or bullies other team members in the process.* A well-designed peer evaluation process must reward only healthy team behaviors and contributions and provide timely feedback to students who disrupt the ability of the team to work as a cohesive unit.

Thinking through these scenarios can help you fine-tune both your grading scheme and the peer evaluation method you choose. The grading scheme needs enough teeth to address these scenarios.

Some Concerns

Some teachers are worried that peer evaluation may hurt trust and team cohesion. A destructive, hurtful comment can do damage to a team, but there are a number of actions you can take to control or at least minimize this. We review the student comments before releasing them back to students as anonymous comments. We are looking for those hurtful or destructive comments that are not helpful. We will suppress these comments. We have suppressed only two comments out of more than a thousand teams in the past 10 years. This doesn't mean that you suppress all negative comments. You suppress hurtful, nonconstructive comments. Negative but constructive comments are fine. We need to coach the students on what constitutes a constructive comment and what constitutes a nonconstructive comment.

Once we've got our teams in place, I explain the grading system and peer evaluations, what role they're going to play. The first time I did peer evaluations, I didn't orient the students well enough, and they didn't have a clue what it was all about. That didn't work. Now I explain it to them in the first class and remind them about the end of the third week. They see the forms. They think about it. They do a practice one early in the course. I share the practice results. There are some students who need to be told they're not pulling their weight. These kids are all freshmen, and peer evaluation scares them, but I find students are very honest and very truthful. We do it again about halfway through the course; I again share the comments with them because it's not too late to pull your socks up. And then we do a summative one at the end of the semester, and that's where it actually counts for grades. (Mary Hadley, Chemistry and Geology, Minnesota State University–Mankato)[5]

A few instructors have reported very significant pushback when they have tried to implement peer evaluation. Some instructors have restated their rationales and stood their ground, and others have been forced to change or abandon peer evaluation altogether. In some institutional settings, especially in very competitive settings, the idea that a student has any control over another student's grade is anathema. Students in these settings often comment that it's the instructor's job to evaluate them, and another student shouldn't be evaluating them. Here you need to sell the rationales for why you're using peer evaluation:

- Feedback is important to help teams function well.
- Team members are in the best position to observe and evaluate other team members' behaviors.
- Peer evaluation brings fairness to the grading.
- Feedback in the workplace is the norm. Other people will be evaluating you, and you will be evaluating others.
- The course experience is probably the safest place to learn these skills.

After we introduce the peer evaluation process on the first day, we will need to revisit the topic multiple times throughout the semester, especially shortly before the formative evaluations during the semester. Although one formative evaluation and one summative evaluation may be the norm, your course may have a different arrangement where a different frequency of evaluations makes more sense. Michaelsen and Fink made me realize the pitfalls of doing just one formative assessment; for example, behaviors that are helpful and valued when a team is in the early stages of cohering can become annoying and overbearing after a team has cohered. We need not only to give students feedback but also to give them reasonable opportunities to change their behavior.

Online Peer Evaluation

As class size increases, the complexity of implementing peer evaluation and the sheer volume of data to be tabulated can become overwhelming. At this point, many people look for a software solution to simplify the work of implementing peer evaluation.

The two most commonly used software tools are SPARK^{PLUS} and iPeer. The SPARK^{PLUS} software was developed at the University of Sydney in Australia and greatly simplifies the peer evaluation process. The SPARK^{PLUS} software can be accessed at http://spark.uts.edu.au. The iPeer software was developed at the University of British Columbia in Canada and lets you create a whole variety of evaluation types and has recently been released in a Blackboard Building Block version. The iPeer software can be accessed at http://ipeer.ctlt.ubc.ca. Both software packages have many happy users, the major difference being SPARK^{PLUS} is a hosted solution and iPeer requires that you download the software and have your IT group install it on a local server.

You need to develop grading schemes and evaluation processes that fairly reward students for both their individual work and their team work. The goal of a well-thought-out evaluation plan is to foster improved student behaviors and properly reward students for their overall contributions.

FIGURE 8.1
Accountability checklist

Accountability Checklist
Optimized for TBL

☐ Uses iRAT - Individual Readiness Assurance
Accountable to Instructor

☐ Uses tRAT - Team Readiness Assurance
Accountable to Peers

☐ Uses Peer Evaluation
Accountable to Peers

☐ Peer Evaluation counts
Impact of Accountability

☐ Feedback is immediate

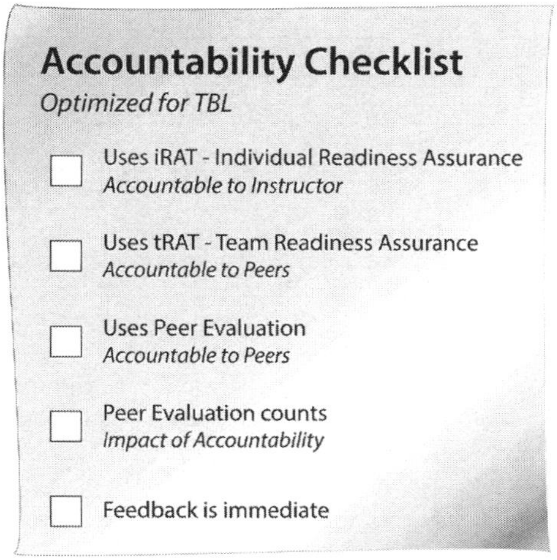

NOTES

1. P. Koles, personal communication, January 24, 2013.
2. M. Stevens, personal communication, January 16, 2013.
3. J. Stamatel, personal communication, January 3, 2013.
4. P. Ostafichuk, personal communication, June 2013.
5. M. Hadley, personal communication, January 9, 2013.

PART THREE

Getting Yourself Ready

CHAPTER 9

The Emotional Journey to Team-Based Learning

Bill Roberson and Billie Franchini

Even with the four essential elements of Team-Based Learning (TBL) in place, new adopters typically do still encounter some issues in their early implementations. This may be due in part to a lack of experience with TBL, or it may be related to the change in attitude and mind-set that is required in moving from lecturing to TBL facilitating. This chapter helps to make the transition to TBL a smooth one by alerting you to some common issues faced by new adopters.

Steve Rogers's adoption of TBL has been an uphill effort. Each change in his teaching has challenged his deeply held beliefs: "If I don't lecture, how can I be sure they'll cover the material?" "If I put them into groups, won't they just waste time?" But he is highly motivated and has been persistent. On this day early in the semester he has managed to carry out his first iRAT [Individual Readiness Assurance Test] and tRAT [Team Readiness Assurance Test]. He is stunned by students' low scores on the iRAT, which he had worried was too easy. The tRAT scores are more heartening. After talking briefly with students about the two questions that several teams missed—and actively resisting his urge to review every idea covered by the test—he nervously puts up a slide and announces the first application task: "In your teams, you have 3 minutes to decide the following: Based on the theory presented in the reading, which of these four outcomes will be the most likely consequence of. . . ." As soon as he finishes the prompt, a loud clamor erupts throughout the room as all the student groups start to talk at once. After class Dr. Rogers comments to a colleague, "I actually had a good time in class today. That hasn't happened to me in many years."

All of the cases used in this chapter, although completely fact based, have been altered so as to protect the identity of the instructors concerned.

Steve's story is representative of one type of instructor experience we have observed at the University at Albany. For many adopters, the process of implementing TBL has become an invaluable opportunity to revitalize their teaching practice and, most important, to transform the way they think about their students and their content. But this change often comes slowly and with a fair bit of resistance on the part of both the faculty member and the students. The tipping point for instructors is usually the kind of experience Steve described, when evidence of changing student behaviors induces a change in instructor attitude. The primary barrier to getting to this tipping point is the difficulty of letting go of old assumptions about teaching and trusting the method long enough to reach the transformative moment.

This chapter attempts to provide a framing perspective for new adopters of TBL who are trying to get to this pivotal moment described in Steve Rogers's narrative. In this chapter, we present an analytic and systematic overview of challenges to be faced and decisions to be made in the run-up to a TBL implementation. Our hope is that you will be able to see yourself within the context of a jagged but well-traveled path to successful TBL implementation.

ISSUES FOR NEW ADOPTERS OF TBL

New would-be adopters of TBL can be observed in various stages of thinking about teaching, and where an individual is in this process will directly affect his or her implementation. These various stages can be loosely represented in a range of dynamic instructor profiles, characterized by factors such as experience in the classroom, feelings about themselves and their roles as teachers, academic discipline, perspectives on students, and attitudes about teaching in general.

Profile 1: The New Instructor With Little or No Teaching Experience and With Both the Liabilities and Advantages That Come With This Profile

This grouping includes many graduate teaching assistants and nonacademic professionals who step into academe for the first time. The group also includes newly hired assistant professors from graduate programs that offered limited opportunities for their graduating students to teach. A primary challenge for those in this group is learning to conceptualize, leverage, and modulate their authority in the classroom. TBL wreaks havoc with the traditional power structure of a college classroom, and this might not be comfortable for a new instructor who is still managing uncertainty and fear. On the flip side, younger instructors in particular sometimes have a desire to remain a peer with other young adults, and this can lead to reluctance to impose a clear structure on classroom activities—with disastrous consequences. The optimal student/teacher dynamic for any given instructor develops over time. In the process, new instructors risk adopting TBL elements either narrowly and formulaically so as not to lose control or randomly, tentatively, and piecemeal so as not to seem excessively authoritative. In addition, many new instructors in tenure-track positions face external pressures: If they are in a department or an institution that does not actively support innovation in teaching, they may be encouraged to avoid experimentation. Convinced that they need to "play it safe" and keep their teaching evaluations just high enough to earn tenure and promotion, these instructors may struggle to engage fully with the TBL method.

On the other hand, we see new instructors who appreciate having a method handed to them and who excel in the implementation because the TBL model is fully coherent.

> *Antonio Cruze has been an engineer for a computing services firm for a decade. Looking to reinvigorate his intellect, he applied to teach a lower division university computer science course and was hired. At that moment he was overtaken by the realization that he had no idea how to teach. He was provided a textbook but had no feel for how to convert the dry text on the page into a lively classroom experience for students. A colleague guided him to one of the TBL trainings that was offered each semester by the teaching center, and the colleague strongly recommended Antonio adopt the method. Having few preconceptions about teaching, he followed the instruction closely and designed his syllabus, RATs, and Application Activities so as to conform as closely as possible to TBL best practices. The training did not eliminate Antonio's anxiety, but it provided immense relief. As a professional, he appreciated the hands-on, action-oriented approach rather than having to create 90-minute lectures that would keep students awake. As he approached the first class meeting, he knew what he was going to do on day one and for the first several classes. He also knew why he was doing these things, which lifted his confidence. Later he commented, "It just made sense. I didn't have to invent all these pieces—they fit together and gave me a structure to work within."*

Adopting wholesale TBL removes from the new instructor's highly crowded perspective some of the unfamiliar decisions that come with planning a course for the first time. When these new instructors fully comprehend the goal and logic of the TBL method and follow the model faithfully, they can be quite successful, even in a first-time-teaching implementation.

Profile 2: The Tinkerer, Who Can Be a Veteran Instructor or a Relatively New One

Tinkerers are TBL adopters who have typically experimented with various techniques but tend to replace one serially with another, sometimes struggling to bring strategic coherence to those efforts. In cases where an instructor has already played with student-centered practices and believes in the value of using class time to allow students to work through problems on their own, the transition to TBL is relatively straightforward. However, one challenge for this individual, as a result of insouciance gained from casual experimentation in the past, can be too little discipline, too little attention to task design, and too much improvisation in the implementation. The result can be a hybrid approach that dilutes the energy of effective TBL. Veteran tinkerers are often confident instructors, and in some cases this is a decided advantage. In others, it may be a liability as they may have strong beliefs about why their past efforts—which don't align with key TBL principles—have (or have not) worked. For example, we commonly hear tinkering instructors express doubt that students will respond well to the exacting structures and processes of TBL, which require them to prepare themselves outside of class. Similar doubts are expressed about whether students should be given the power to hold each other accountable via peer evaluation. Part of the veteran tinkerer's thinking may be related to the perception that the increased structure and the increased burden of student responsibility limit student choice and freedom to decide how they want to participate. Finally, there may be reluctance on the part of the tinkerer to make the attitudinal shift in the instructor role away from ever-present, very involved, hands-on helper to that of less intrusive observer/facilitator.

Profile 3: The Traditional Practitioner, Who Has Rarely Experimented in Using Class Time for Anything Other Than Lecturing

The traditional practitioner who becomes interested in TBL is usually looking to reenergize his or her teaching but is likely to have little experience or feel for designing and managing student-centered activities in the classroom. Although these practitioners will surely face the challenge of learning a completely new skill set, their greater challenges will be those of examining and changing their own deep-seated beliefs. The strongest of these will be about what professors should be seen doing and not doing. Letting students work independently, make determinations about grades, evaluate the quality of each other's participation, or even just talk among themselves can be extremely difficult for some traditional practitioners to accept as valid learning behavior. And there is the inevitable question of integrity. The thought of abandoning the traditional, instructor-centric role to become an observer of students at work can seem ethically suspect for multiple reasons. The potential perception that an instructor "is not doing her job" because she is not talking in the center of the classroom can be a real cause for concern, and when students make the same observation on course evaluations, it can be unnerving. In addition, it is a common fear among traditional practitioners that focusing on students doing work in class (rather than listening attentively) will lead to a substantial loss of content "coverage." Their experience has proven to them over many years that students are unwilling or unable to get the content on their own. What offers hope that a traditional practitioner can succeed in what will be a radical transformation of belief, practice, and identity is the deeply frustrating prospect of continuing to teach in an environment where only a small fraction of students are able to engage.

STAGES OF THE EMOTIONAL JOURNEY

Any new adopter of TBL will most likely have a teaching identity that combines elements of more than one of the profiles we outlined. These profiles are intended not to pigeonhole instructors but rather to provoke reflection on where one's perspectival challenges are likely to lie. Will the transition to TBL be characterized as a mere adjustment, because, as a tinkerer, the instructor has already experimented with student-centered learning processes? Or will the transition be a total rupture of one's persona, as most teaching habits of the traditional practitioner will have to change? Will the anxiety of teaching for the first time be part of this journey? Thinking about one's teaching identity is a useful exercise for developing expectations for what the road to TBL will look like.

Although the specifics of the process may vary across individuals, on the basis of personality and level of experience, we have found that many adopters (with the exception of totally new instructors) of TBL follow a pattern of emotional changes akin in some ways to the grieving process, with variation (Kübler-Ross, 1969).

Stage 1: Waving the White Flag (I Give Up—Nothing Is Working)

Many of the successful adopters we work with have considerable teaching experience and are highly motivated. They have already reached awareness that their classrooms are not currently what they envisioned when they decided to become university instructors. The factors that drive them to this awareness are occasionally extrinsic, as in recurring low student ratings that threaten to affect their career advancement. More often, though, the factors are intrinsic, expressed as personal dismay that students are not learning to their potential; as disappointment in the lack of student engagement; as feelings of futility in connecting with students because of the abstruse nature of the content; or, finally, as just the lack of enjoyment in what should be exciting and satisfying professional work. Whatever the specific driver, the strong motivation for change is what makes it possible for potential adopters to manage the stressors that sometimes come with learning to teach with TBL, such as student resistance or colleagues' expressions of doubt and even disparagement.

A key dimension of this White Flag stage is the individual's awareness that he or she is missing some critical piece of information or a particular perspective that is making it impossible to solve the problem alone. In many cases, the instructor has already tried labor-intensive changes that haven't yielded substantial results. This state of "I just don't have the answer" creates an opening for an authentic conversation about teaching and learning. The White Flag stage is an indicator of readiness to learn and openness to new ideas—even those that, in the past, might have seemed too radical and too high risk to entertain.

Stage 1 Primary Need: Conversations with someone sympathetic who will commiserate without passing judgment.

Stage 2: Doubting Thomas
(TBL Pushes Me Too Far—I Can't Change That Much!)

Even after instructors wave the white flag, their first encounter with the TBL model will often provoke resistance and even derision: "What? You want them to read and take a test *before* the lecture? That's crazy talk—they won't do it! You want me to turn the classroom over to the students? You want students to work together—without my direct input—the whole class meeting? I'm supposed to let them evaluate each other? What does that leave *me* to do?" These are very legitimate concerns, based on instructors' extensive experience watching poorly prepared, uninspired students sitting passively in class and years of observing good-faith efforts gone bad. However, the belief system has to change if the Doubting Thomas is to be successful, which means that his or her assumptions need to be challenged strategically and convincingly.

It is at this stage that the presence of empathetic colleagues who have adopted TBL successfully is particularly helpful. Their stories, inevitably laced with humor and humility, recount the doubt and uncertainty leading to surprise and excitement when the model works, in spite of a flawed implementation and low expectations. No one wants to be the pioneer in a high-risk, high-stakes endeavor, and would-be adopters at the Doubting Thomas stage need assurances that others have gone before and been successful. This is also where having a formal faculty development process (see Appendix C), where new adopters can express and discuss their anxieties freely in a supportive environment, can make an enormous difference.

Stage 2 Primary Need: Contact with other successful TBL instructors; conveniently packaged, easy-to-access research on improving outcomes through active learning.

Stage 3: Reluctant Concession (I'm Desperate, So I'll Give
Some Parts of It a Try—But I'll Do It My Way!)

Instructors at this stage may still be deeply attached to their earlier teaching persona, which means that they are often willing to make changes that are only piecemeal and tentative. Usually this manifests as a desire to adopt certain elements of TBL (most often the RATs—"If I can just get them to read, everything else will work out!") but also as a problematic belief that the tools can simply be transposed onto their previous course design. What these instructors have not yet fully confronted is the reality that low levels of learning and tepid student engagement are usually the result of more than the lack of a single magical technique. A more complete rethinking of the learning enterprise might be needed, and to this end, TBL is a full-blown method of teaching, composed of elements that are designed to work in concert with each other. The catalyst for the change, furthermore, is the shift in the role and working assumptions of the instructors.

Getting instructors to let go of their former classroom identity is, predictably, one of the most difficult transitions for many TBL adopters, and it rarely begins to happen before starting (usually by a leap of faith) an actual first-attempt implementation. The true change of instructor persona begins once the course is under way and positive feedback begins to be generated, especially from students. As we reported in our opening case of Steve Rogers, once an instructor sees firsthand the effect of TBL on students, the journey to a new teaching identity begins.

Stage 3 Primary Need: Reassurances; models of TBL components; encouragement to experiment with all TBL components before dismissing them.

Stage 4: Resignation and Commitment (Okay, I'll Jump in All the Way but Only Because I Don't Have a Better Idea— And I'm Still Scared to Death)

A sizable fraction of instructors who might attempt TBL will proceed no further than Stage 3 and end up with what has been labeled "TBL Lite": traditional teaching overlaid with small-group activities or an interactive assessment component using tRATs. In many cases this is not a failure; what they are doing in class will provide a better experience for students than most full frontal lecturing but will not have the transformative effect on learning and intellectual maturation seen in the most successful TBL implementations.

Instructors with the persistence needed to do a full TBL implementation often do so as an act of stoic commitment within complete resignation. They have considered the prospects of further tinkering and rejected it as an inadequate solution, given their strong motivation for change. They have weighed the risks and potential downsides (students might resist, course evaluations might go down, colleagues might smirk) but have decided that these are an acceptable price for the potential payoff of a more engaged classroom and higher performing students.

This new phase represents an important psychological shift and a change in energy level. We have reached a turning point in thinking about students: Resistance and pushback are now a foreseeable, predictable consequence of changing, not a vague threat. In fact, the much-feared student resistance has now been co-opted by the new perspective: It has become highly anticipated evidence that the classroom culture is changing. When it comes, it will be a positive sign that students have been meaningfully implicated by the new and surprising approach. The primary worry is no longer about *whether* the method will work but rather about *how* to respond to surprises such as activities that do not work as planned.

Stage 4 Primary Need: Opportunities to debrief and reflect on tasks and class meetings with a "coach" or informed, experienced, sympathetic colleague.

Stage 5: Relief and Pleasure (Hey, It Kind of Worked, and It's FUN!)

Once the implementation is under way, the adopter of TBL finally has real data to respond to rather than pictures and scenarios conjured in his or her imagination. The quality of student thinking rises visibly and measurably, as students process information in teams, report their thinking, and defend publicly their reasoning. And because students visibly engage with the content and with other students, they magically evolve from nameless entities into real people having real conversations and discovering new friends in the process. For some instructors, this may be the beginning of a new grieving process as they mourn the loss of their earlier teacher persona, but this will be overshadowed by the evidence of improved student engagement and learning.

Stage 5 Primary Need: Continued evidence and assurances of improved student learning; feedback to refine practice.

ATTITUDE ADJUSTMENT

Although TBL imposes a clear design structure and set of protocols that ensure its success, mastering the mechanics of TBL course design and course management is not the most difficult part of the journey. As our faculty support strategy has evolved, we have learned to focus much more deliberately on addressing old beliefs and fostering the new attitudes and mind-set needed in order to be successful. We have learned that changes in belief and attitude do not occur just through preparation and planning. These happen slowly, through learning moments that resemble those experienced by students. Throughout the process instructors need frequent reassurances and examples from colleagues, early positive experiences of their own, meaningful feedback from students, continual encouragement from their peers, and opportunities to celebrate victories. These considerations have all entered into our TBL support strategy.

Furthermore, over time we have distilled this process of changing beliefs and awareness into a set of target attitudes necessary for successful TBL implementation. When new adopters of TBL already possess these attitudes, they are ready to focus on the reconceptualization of their course, along with the mechanics and related skills needed to plan and manage the learning process. In cases where these attitudes are not already apparent, the preparation of the instructor focuses on support that will foster, encourage, or induce the targeted attitudinal shift. The following is a list of the top four attitudes we target for adjustment.

Be Playful, and Expect to Have Fun

Janet Hale had been teaching a general education humanities course for 3 years. It was a course that attracted many first-year students outside of the major and with no experience in the subject area. She was growing increasingly frustrated with her students, who were not reading, not attending class, and rarely participating when they were present. Over time she found herself becoming increasingly skeptical of the value of the course and feeling increasingly negative about the ability of her students. She tried using clickers to increase interactions with students and to ensure their preparation but was disappointed that students still seemed to exploit every possible loophole to avoid full engagement. When she discovered TBL and learned to set students to work independently in their teams, she immediately noticed changes in her students' behavior and their learning. What really sold her on the method, though, was the change in herself. She no longer dreaded going to class!

For some of us, teaching has become a chore fraught with fear of failure and of losing control. To make matters worse, even when things are obviously not going well, we are inhibited from making changes as a consequence of both a system that does not reward risk taking and our own entrenched personal beliefs—reinforced by our peers—that teaching and learning have to look a certain way. Making a change in teaching can be a high-stakes endeavor: A decline in student evaluation scores, for example, can have real and immediate implications for some faculty. Doing something unusual in the very public world of students is a high-wire act: "What if students won't do what I ask them to do?" "What if they ding me on the evaluations?" What is really at stake for most instructors, though, is even more personal, existential, and intangible: their own sense of their identity in the classroom. Seasoned instructors have worked to develop their teacher persona, and for many of them the prospect of deep changes in their relationship with the course content and with their students causes great anxiety. This kind of fear can inhibit a teacher's ability and willingness to adopt an absolutely essential mind-set for a TBL instructor: playful experimentation expressed as "Let's see if this will work." Therefore, a key part of faculty preparation for using TBL is to develop an expectation that the classroom can and should be a place we go to in order to take some risks and have some fun—even when making mistakes and seeing a clever idea become a dud.

This notion will also be especially alien to instructors who feel a deep sense of responsibility for delivering a specific quantity of content to their students (see "Profile 3: The Traditional Practitioner," discussed previously). In many cases, they fear that there simply isn't time to be playful. These instructors, when dabbling in TBL, often buy in to the idea of holding students accountable for reading, via the Readiness Assurance Process (RAP), but they struggle with giving over the remainder of a unit to student-centered Application Activities. At root is the casting of doubt on one's identity and on the value of commitments to and investments in teaching practices of the past. For some traditional instructors, even the positive results of an initial implementation can be overshadowed by the cognitive dissonance between their former identity and the new one. For these instructors (stuck at Stage 2 of the journey), having a peer support system to hold them focused on their students' successes is essential to keep them from abandoning the method too early.

Have Faith in Your Students (Both in Their Intelligence and in Their Willingness to Learn)

On the afternoon that I visited Jane Meyer's class, she was administering the first iRAT and tRAT of the semester. Students were deeply engaged in the tRAT, arguing about key concepts, debating the differences between answer choices, groaning when they didn't find the correct answer, and yelling excitedly when they did. After time was up for completing the test and the Appeals Process, the instructor called an end to the chaos by putting a slide on the overhead: "Question #1. The correct answer was . . . ." I watched the enthusiasm drain from the room as Dr. Meyer spent the next 30 minutes reviewing every question on the RAT, one by one.

This is one of the more common scenarios that we witness in our visits to first-time TBL instructors' classrooms, and it is one of the most potentially destructive. In Dr. Meyer's class, the RAP has clearly worked—the students have begun engaging with the content and are prepared for challenges. Now the instructor has violated the contract that TBL makes with students, in which they prepare themselves outside of class so that in-class time can be spent discovering how to use the content in specific situations. Dr. Meyer has also short-circuited the process by reminding them that *she* is the only real expert in the room. Not only are the immediate consequences palpable in the loss of energy in the room, but the long-term consequences for the whole course are dire. Dr. Meyer's students will inevitably come to resent the fact that the RAT process has now become simply an exercise of coercion to get them to read rather than a real learning experience, and this ultimately threatens to derail the course. Not only does reviewing material that the students have already covered at least *four* times (reading, iRAT, tRAT, appeals) risk insulting their intelligence and their work ethic, it leads students to distrust both the instructor and the process.

For any instructor, especially those who, as former students, have been successful in the traditional "chalk and talk" model, it can be hard to imagine that undergraduates are capable of reading and comprehending information on their own *without hearing it from the instructor*. Taking this leap of faith is often the single difference between success and failure in a first-time implementation of TBL. Of course, students will sometimes make this journey more difficult, as they will push back, both directly ("You aren't teaching us!") and indirectly ("Your lectures are so great! Please do more of that"). Some of them won't immediately recognize that your use of TBL is demonstrating respect for their intelligence. For many of our students, this is a new and uncomfortable experience, as it places a greater burden of responsibility on them. They need to be continually reminded of their abilities, and we need to be reminded that they are capable of learning many things outside of our presence, without our direct assistance.

Get Your Expertise, Authority, and Especially Your Ego out of Students' Way—And Let the Method Do Its Job

Jim Barnes came to us because of low teaching evaluations and realized that he needed to do something to revolutionize his teaching. In his first adoption of TBL, he was optimistic but guarded, not having fully bought into all elements of the method. When he invited us to observe his class for the first time, he resisted our suggestion that he include appeals as part of the RAP because he believed that inviting students to argue with him would undermine his authority and create a class full of "grade grubbers."

Professor Barnes is representative of many of the new adopters we work with each semester. They can intuitively see how certain elements of the method could have immediate and tangible benefits (e.g., the iRATs and tRATs), but they resist those elements that they believe would most radically restructure power relations in the classroom (appeals, peer evaluation, student input on grade weighting). First-time adopters often don't recognize the extent to which the different elements of the TBL method are designed to work in ways that are integrated and reinforcing, so they take the "smorgasbord" approach, selecting only those items that fit into their preexisting notions of their students, their content, and their role as instructor. In essence these instructors embrace parts of the new strategy, but they haven't yet re-envisioned their role beyond that of authoritative expert. Successfully converting a course to TBL not only induces but also requires a higher level of reflection and self-awareness.

This reflection is particularly challenging because for many of our would-be TBL adopters, teaching is the ad hoc accumulation of practices and techniques adopted from personal experience; borrowed from colleagues; or, occasionally, gleaned from reading articles on teaching. They know that students need practice applying information and thinking critically, and they have tried isolated ways of making that happen. Many of them, however, have never taken ownership of a full-blown method or considered adopting a comprehensive approach based in a theory and supported with evidence from educational and cognitive research. Consequently, one of the attitudinal changes we seek to foster in new TBL adopters could be summarized as "suspend disbelief" and have confidence in the thoroughly tested set of TBL protocols. Trust the method enough to let it work.

Dr. Barnes's story has a happy ending: Although he didn't immediately overcome his doubts, he did eventually integrate appeals into the RAP. What he learned was that giving this level of ownership to his students did indeed change the dynamic of the course and his role within it. His students adopted a more assertive critical thinking perspective with respect to both content and test questions. What he had not expected, though, was that allowing students to appeal answers reinforced—counterintuitively—his role as expert rather than undermined it. He found himself engaged in questions and discussions at a level never imagined through earlier teaching practices. Ultimately, he also found his students taking responsibility for their own efforts in ways that he had never seen and never expected. Although he feared that students would use the Appeals Process to complain about "unfair" questions, he reports instead that students struggling with a difficult RAT question say, "Wow! I just didn't read that part of the article carefully enough!"

Tolerate the Errors, Uncertainty, and Messiness of Authentic Student Inquiry

Dr. Foster was looking forward to her Introduction to Political Theory course on Monday because she had designed a series of very engaging questions that would require students to apply concepts they had read about for homework. Students took the iRAT and tRAT to test their comprehension of the reading, and the process had gone well. She was convinced that they were ready for the challenging application exercises she had prepared. She began by giving students a mini-case, which she had drawn from the research on election reform. Students were asked to read a short case about a complex voter redistricting problem, analyze a list of possible solutions, and predict which solution had been successfully implemented. After students read the case, they delved into very animated discussions within their teams. After about 5 minutes, Dr. Foster forced them to stop and agree on an answer. This is how the ensuing discussion went: "Okay, let's see what your answers were. When I count to 3, everyone hold up your cards. 1, 2, 3! Wow, that's interesting! It looks like most of you chose option B, which draws heavily on X theory. Actually, in this case the solution that was chosen was option C. Why do you think that was?" The same students who had been eagerly discussing the case in their teams fell silent. "Come on, guys! I know you have answers—you were all talking about this before!"

This is another fairly common scenario we see when working with new TBL practitioners. When instructors have not quite relinquished their role as authoritative expert and don't yet fully trust their students' ability to reason at a high level, they can become so focused on making sure that students know the "right" answer that they fail to assess how students are thinking. This was a moment where expert knowledge needed to be withheld from the discussion. Knowing *why* most of the teams arrived at incorrect option B would be useful data for Dr. Foster to use going forward: Did they not understand a key concept? Were they falling into a common misconception? Were they actually applying a more complex set of principles in their attempt to answer the question? The design of this task was excellent and meets the Michaelsen 4 S design principles, but Dr. Foster's debrief ultimately short-circuited the purpose of the task (Michaelsen & Sweet, 2008). Instead of allowing students to develop their own agenda for investigating the problem— and risking an unanticipated direction in the conversation—Dr. Foster intercepted their thought process and inserted her own agenda. The students ceased being owners of their thinking and fell back into a posture that reflected their lack of agency in the classroom.

EMBRACE THE EMOTIONAL JOURNEY

As academics we are the product of an institutional environment that discounts the role of emotions in learning, both the learning of our students and our own. The last several years of research in cognition and brain functioning, however, have provided conclusive evidence that there can be no separation of our emotional reality and the workings of our intellect. This helps to explain one dimension of positive student response to a well-implemented TBL experience: The social element provides an essential emotional framework for learning.

A parallel emotional framework for university professors is more difficult to conceptualize and construct, even when we have been cast back into the role of "learner" by attempting to adopt a new teaching method. It is nevertheless important for us to become more conscious of how our emotions play out in the choices we make as teachers and in the efforts we make in learning how to teach more effectively. Inevitably, our own emotions are projected into our classrooms by way of our teaching practices. In some cases our practices express a fear of chaos and the resultant need for extreme order and control. In happier cases, our practices express a deep-seated optimism that students will respond energetically to authentic, respectful challenges designed to provoke their intellectual development.

The path to effective use of TBL can be summarized as the distance between these two emotional states. One of the primary goals of TBL practitioners is to learn to minimize in themselves the prevalence of those emotions that respond to fear and the need for control and to foster those that express confidence in students' ability to take responsibility for their own learning.

CHAPTER 10

The Last Word

Now you have the tools and knowledge you need to succeed at Team-Based Learning (TBL). In this final chapter, we want to highlight 10 things you can do to ensure that you get to enjoy the fun, learning, and excitement that can be part of TBL when it is implemented well.

TBL can transform the student-and-teacher experience. It naturally creates wonderful opportunities for deep student learning by harnessing the power of social learning as part of well-designed teamwork. It lets teams do what teams are naturally good at: making decisions. TBL effectively scales to large classroom settings so that having more people in the room actually leads to even more powerful learning opportunities. This point was driven home for me when a faculty member complained her class of 18 was too small to do anything really powerful, and she had hoped for 70 students to get deeper and richer conversations. The TBL method gives you a powerful framework to develop and implement your course. You can rely on this framework with its well-thought-out self-correcting and synergistic structures that work in classes of all sizes.

I hope that I have successfully convinced you that TBL is right for you. But you need not believe only me; many teachers sing the praises of TBL. Let's listen to a few faculty members describe their joy:

What do I see when TBL is implemented well? Students excited about learning, and faculty falling in love with teaching. Lots of energy in the room. Lots of engagement. The way learning should be. (Holly Bender, Veterinary Pathology, Iowa State University)[1]

It means fun! I don't have to lecture, which I hated. I get to know my students. TBL is a heck of a lot more work than lecturing, but it's also a lot more fun. (Mary Hadley, Chemistry and Geology, Minnesota State University–Mankato)[2]

I love the enthusiasm and energy of students. It's just so much more fun. (Larry Michaelsen, Business, University of Central Missouri)[3]

The rewards are incredible. The energy in the classroom is phenomenal, and the feedback we've gotten from faculty is sky-high in terms of preference for TBL and not wanting to go back to lectures. (Chris Burns, Microbiology, University of Illinois)[4]

I would say if you're motivated to have fun in the classroom and want to enjoy every class, and you want the students to leave energized about your subject, this is for you. Now I will not teach a course without Team-Based Learning. (Brenda Collings, Accounting, University of New Brunswick, Saint John)[5]

TEN TIPS FOR TBL SUCCESS

Here are my final 10 ideas to help you get yourself started right on the journey to all the learning, engagement, and excitement that can be part of the TBL classroom:

1. Ask the right question the right way.
2. Reconsider the function of content.
3. Embrace backward design.
4. Be very organized.
5. Remember, RAPs are about readiness.
6. Expect student resistance and marshal your evidence.
7. Help students see the value.
8. Build a local support network.
9. Get connected to the greater TBL community.
10. Have fun.

1. Ask the Right Question the Right Way

When I recently asked a very experienced TBL colleague what the most important thing in TBL is, he stated very emphatically, "Asking the right question!" The holy grail of TBL is asking the right question the right way. When you do this, the other pieces of TBL seem to fall easily into place. Those deep, rich, interesting questions, the ones that are seminal to the discipline, the ones that help inform how we practice our profession well and how we succeed in our daily lives, are the questions we are looking for.

Use good questions and the 4 S framework as your compass to guide you to consistently successful and powerful activities. The 4 S framework lets you build questions so they consistently lead to all that wonderful learning, engagement, and excitement. Some teachers do stray away from the 4 S framework, but this should be done only with large amounts of caution. When you are new to TBL, there is often an impulse to ignore one of the 4 Ss, because you may have been using group activities in your classroom for years and you may not want to conform to what you see as unnecessary constraints. This can sometimes still work, but more often it leads to activities that fall flat.

TBL novices may shy away especially from the "specific choice" component of the 4 S framework, fearing that forcing students to make a specific choice may inhibit their creative energies. On the contrary, using specific choice quickly changes the reporting discussion from simply listing facts or right answers to discriminating between reasonable choices and examining the process for arriving at a particular decision. How are you using the facts to support your decision? Which facts are most important to this problem, and why? Specific choice also forces the teams to commit to a position. It is absolutely critical to generate a simple, comparable decision that drives the rich reporting discussions and leads to deep student learning.

2. Reconsider the Function of Content

Caution: Adopting TBL may require a change in beliefs about what constitutes good teaching. A new approach often necessitates a shift in our views about the function of content. Course content becomes the vehicle that allows students to solve significant relevant problems, not just regurgitate the same material back to you. The content is the means to the desired end: helping students learn how to use the course concepts to solve real, significant problems. But don't worry; students will indeed learn all the content they need to solve those problems. You might feel like the students won't learn the material if it's not coming out of your mouth during a lecture, but the TBL literature is very clear: Students actually learn *more* content in a TBL course (Levine et al., 2004; Vasan, DeFouw, & Compton, 2011). That's in addition to other important skills they acquire, like problem solving, peer teaching, public speaking, negotiation, argumentation, and peer mentoring.

3. Embrace Backward Design

Backward design is crucial to designing powerful educational experiences, whether it is a whole course experience or a single activity. When I first encountered backward design, I would dutifully rearrange my existing course components into backward order, but I had not truly embraced the idea. I still had a content-first mind-set and fundamentally hadn't shifted my thinking to the primary question "What do I want the students to be able to do?"

What exactly do you want your students to be able to do? If you overheard a student conversation, what could the students say that would make you really think they achieved deep understanding? Knowing what you want your students to be able to do or say lets you effectively design situations, problems, or performances that give opportunities for students to show us they really know.

> *You must be prepared to design your course backward to forward, and that's not easy. Most of us sit down, we read the textbook, and we design our course from the textbook. I'm guilty of that. To do Team-Based Learning, it must be a reverse design process, and it's not easy. It was not easy for me to think about "What do I want students to be able to do?"* (Ron Carson, Occupational Therapy, Adventist University of Health Sciences)[6]

4. Be Very Organized

Prepare, prepare, prepare. It is one of the keys to success with TBL. Be highly organized. Students are very intolerant of disorganized teaching, even more so when they might be anxious about their new roles and responsibilities in the learner-centered classroom. Being organized can help your students with this transition or at least not add to their anxiety. Preparation gives you mental space to respond to and embrace teachable moments when they appear. When we are not organized enough and just barely hanging on as a teacher, we often can't capitalize on these teachable moments when they arrive. The students might not thank you for being organized, but they *will* complain loudly if you are not. Don't give them the argumentative fuel. You will be glad you took the time to prepare well.

> *I think the difference between TBL and other methods of teaching is that with other methods of teaching, you can be a lot more "just in time" in your preparation, and so people don't notice the work so much since it's spread out. With TBL, to be successful, you have to do it all up front. Doing TBL doesn't seem like any more work to me than any other teaching I do. I know some of my colleagues will dash out a lecture the morning before class in the afternoon. Unfortunately, it's taken them down that path that even if a student asks a really interesting question, any teachable moment will likely pass them by.* (Peter Smith, Business and Economics, University of Auckland)[7]

5. Remember, RAPs Are About Readiness

Remember that the Readiness Assurance Process is *only* about getting students ready for the activities that follow. It's not about testing. If students come to believe it is about testing rather than preparing them for the activities that will follow, they will complain.

The RAP should begin the process to build a mental schema for the students and give them the conceptual understanding and vocabulary to begin problem solving effectively. The RAP is about giving students a clear entry point to the activities. Ask yourself, "What is the minimum that students will need to know to begin problem solving?" The RAP shouldn't try to cover everything that students need to learn. They will naturally extend and deepen their understanding as they complete their Application Activities. Trust the method.

6. Expect Student Resistance and Marshal Your Evidence

When you orient your students to TBL on the first day, most students will buy in and be willing to try out TBL with you. But a few students will resist. This is normal and should be expected. What is important here is to acknowledge and respond constructively to the resistance but not be derailed from moving forward. Practice what you will say. Be ready to respond to questions and complaints: "Why are you using TBL?" "Testing before teaching makes no sense!" "This isn't working for me! I learn better from lectures." You should plan well-thought-out responses to these common student assertions. Having your evidence and rationales prepared is key to responding effectively. You need to do your homework and build your case by investigating the TBL literature (see chapter 4) and establishing in your own mind the value of TBL. You need to persuade yourself to be ready to convince others. Do not underestimate the importance of this step. Most students have had a series of poor team experiences, and you may need to manage any anxiety and fears they may have about teamwork. You need to make it clear that TBL is different. TBL has been carefully thought out and has accountability structures that effectively control dysfunctional team behaviors. Point out that TBL will help students achieve learning outcomes that are important for the course, their lives, and their future work. Be positive. Be ready.

During the interviews for this book, I uncovered a personal misconception. Even though my own TBL experience has had positive responses from the students, I was convinced that some student resistance was an unavoidable problem in any TBL class. But in interview after interview, people spoke of overwhelmingly positive responses from their students. I have revised my own belief and now see that when we thoughtfully implement TBL, when we thoughtfully orient our students to the TBL process, and when we thoughtfully and openly respond to student concerns, TBL will be a success.

> *The challenge is figuring out how to pitch the course and then managing the pushback, the resistance, and knowing in advance that the resistance is coming and there's nothing wrong with it—it takes you two or three rounds to get to the point where you say, yeah, that's okay.* (Bill Roberson, Faculty Member and Faculty Developer, University at Albany)[8]

Just stick with the game plan. If you start feeling uncomfortable, don't revert. Trust that it's going to work out. It may take a little bit of time and unease. Worry about what you're going to say to the students if they do start push-ing back, but it's so worth it. (Trudi Jacobson, Librarian, University at Albany)[9]

7. Help Students See the Value

Without huge piles of lecture notes, students sometimes have difficulty perceiving just how much they have truly learned. Remind them. As part of the closure for any activity, module, or course, you can remind and reinforce all that has been cov-ered. At the end of the course, you can brainstorm a list on the document camera, overhead, or whiteboard of the things you have learned together during the module or course. This simple activity quickly becomes a multipage document and helps reassure students that they have in fact learned a lot.

> *After the first couple of activities, at the end of the class, I try to save a few minutes to help students realize how much they have learned and to sort of translate what they just did into what a lecture could have looked like, so that they can see that all of the information that could have been in that lecture is what came up in their conversations.* (Laura Madson, Psychology, New Mexico State University)[10]

8. Build a Local Support Network

You should try to find and build a support network. We all need someone to listen to us. Maybe you can find a like-minded colleague to lend an ear or someone from your local teaching center to work with or reach out on the TBL LISTSERV and find someone in your discipline to work with. TBL teachers are passionate about TBL and are happy to talk to others who are just starting out.

It is extremely important to have someone look at your materials before you take them to the classroom. What appears obvious to one person may not to another. This has been made very clear to me when I have shared my materials with a colleague, and the colleague always seemed to pick the "wrong" answer. Get feedback. Test your materials.

> *If at all possible, do field-testing with a group of students. It doesn't have to be the whole class. But get yourself a group of volunteer students, just for an hour, to test out your questions, test out the process before you go live.* (Dean Parmelee, Medicine, Wright State University)[11]

> *In terms of adopting TBL, what I found the most helpful was having another colleague who was also using TBL. Having somebody else I could run*

questions by, and I could talk through application exercises with, and then talk with after I'd finished the class, I found this to be really, really helpful. (David Raeker-Jordan, Law, Widener University)[12]

9. Get Connected to the Greater TBL Community

There is a whole community of TBL teachers out there. Get connected. Start by getting yourself to www.teambasedlearning.org. There you can join the Team-Based Learning Collaborative and get access to sample TBL modules, instructional material samples, and other resources. You can also join the free TBL LISTSERV, where over 900 TBL teachers from all over the world share their struggles and advice with each other. You will find that the TBL LISTSERV is one of the most helpful educational LISTSERVs you have ever seen. People will often post queries to it about what happened in class that day and receive multiple thoughtful responses in the same day.

> *The LISTSERV for TBL is great. People jump in, and it's a real community. It's really unusual to find a LISTSERV where people give of themselves so freely. I think on the TBL LISTSERV, people really put a lot of time and love into their postings. And they really authentically want people to do well in TBL and to be successful. On the TBL LISTSERV, I know that if a question goes up, it's not going to take very long for somebody to come back and throw in an answer. I think it's a wonderful way for people to keep in touch, especially if you're teaching at a school and you don't have somebody else using TBL, and you kind of feel like you're on your own. This really keeps you plugged in to the community and keeps you motivated to keep learning and thinking and trying out things, taking chances.* (David Raeker-Jordan, Law, Widener University)[13]

You can also attend the annual TBL conference, which is a great opportunity to meet TBL teachers with all levels of experience and teachers from many different disciplines. The annual conference includes workshops and sessions specifically designed for teachers who are new to TBL.

Come join us!

10. HAVE FUN

TBL is fun for both teachers and students. When everyone is learning more, the classroom can become a highly charged environment where students (and faculty) are deeply engaging with the course material. Give yourself permission to experiment and have fun, and remember that not all of your experiments will work out, but try to learn the lessons they contain. Having that playful, experimental attitude can make all the difference as you transition to the TBL classroom.

> *I try to help faculty get into a playful, experimental mood. Most university professors are horrified by surprises. You have to get them to the point where that's no longer an issue, that surprises are good. So when students don't want to do something and push back because they say, "You're not teaching us," that's a compliment. You've got them where you want them. You've started to provoke what I call "productive frustration." We want our students to be pushed to a point of productive frustration. That's when learning begins. Sometimes it's an uncomfortable moment for you, the teacher, as well as for the students. But we have to accept the responsibility of having provoked it and enjoy that because that's our job as a teacher.* (Bill Roberson, Faculty Member and Faculty Developer, University at Albany)[14]

You can do this! The TBL method isn't about confining structures and restrictive prescriptions; it's about proven structures and methods that you can rely on. You will be transformed, your students will be transformed, and the classroom experience will be transformed. TBL gives you the key to unlock the instructional possibilities in your classroom.

Have fun.

Learn lots.

Let us know how it turns out.

NOTES

1. H. Bender, personal communication, January 9, 2013.
2. M. Hadley, personal communication, January 9, 2013.
3. L. Michaelsen, personal communication, January 2, 2013.
4. C. Burns, personal communication, January 7, 2013.
5. B. Collings, personal communication, January 15, 2013.
6. R. Carson, personal communication, January 7, 2013.
7. P. Smith, personal communication, January 17, 2013.
8. B. Roberson, personal communication, January 2012.
9. T. Jacobson, personal communication, January 4, 2013.
10. L. Madson, personal communication, January 2012.
11. D. Parmelee, personal communication, January 15, 2013.
12. D. Raeker-Jordan, personal communication, January 4, 2013.
13. D. Raeker-Jordan, personal communication, January 4, 2013.
14. B. Roberson, personal communication, January 2012.

Appendices

Additional Resources

TBL Website: www.teambasedlearning.org

The TBL website has a wealth of information and resources, links to many videos on TBL, and information on joining the Team-Based Learning Collaborative (TBLC). Joining the TBLC entitles you to members-only access to its resource bank and discounts for attending its annual Team-Based Learning conference. You can also find a list of TBL consultants who are willing to visit your campus.

TBL LISTSERV: www.teambasedlearning.org/listserv

Workshops: There are a number of workshop opportunities to learn more about TBL.

The day before the TBLC Team-Based Learning conference each year, there are preconference workshops (sign up at the conference website). Also each year the TBLC hosts a 1-day regional workshop. These workshops are typically held at a major airport hotel. For more information, visit the TBL website.

The University at Albany (State University of New York) runs the TBL Academy a few times a year and accepts outside guests when space is available. Look for announcements and other information on its TBL support program at www.itlal.org or contact the Institute for Teaching, Learning, and Academic Leadership at 518-442-5521.

The Duke Medical School at the National University of Singapore offers a fellowship in TBL. More information is available at www.duke-nus.edu.sg/education/faculty-development/fellowship-team-based-learning-tbl.

Consultants: www.teambasedlearning.org/consult

There are two times when a visit from a TBL consultant can be very helpful. First, early in your learning about TBL, a visit from a consultant can show faculty what TBL is all about, why it is so powerful, and how to get started. A second important time for a visit, especially in large implementations of TBL, is just before you "go live." A consultant can review your materials and plans, helping optimize your first TBL delivery.

Not long after reading the original *Team-Based Learning* (Michaelsen, Knight, & Fink, 2004) book, one of the authors of this volume contacted Larry Michaelsen to visit campus and give a day of workshops. It really helped the campus get excited about TBL and get started well.

Other Books: www.teambasedlearning.org/NewBooks

There are a number of other books on TBL. You can find links to these books on the TBL website.

More Simultaneous Reporting Options

In chapter 7, four different approaches to simultaneous reporting were introduced (voting cards, pushpins, whiteboards, and the hot seat). There are many other approaches to simultaneous reporting beyond these four, and this appendix gives a collection of additional methods to help inspire you when you are designing your own activities. In many ways, the simultaneous reporting method you use is limited only by your imagination; however, the fundamental principle that makes a simultaneous reporting method work well is that teams need a simple way to report complex thinking and decision making. It is this simple report that allows comparability of one team's decision to another's, which is what drives the reporting conversation. If the decision product is too complex, students will have difficulty comparing their decision to those of other teams.

The additional methods described in this appendix are:

- Stacked transparencies
- Hot seat variation 1: performance metric
- Hot seat variation 2: answer key
- Gallery walk
- Best solution tournament
- Google Drive
- Classroom response systems (clickers)
- Scissors and glue sticks (nonsimultaneous)

STACKED TRANSPARENCIES

Stacked transparencies is a useful method for activities where teams need to identify features in graphical data (maps, charts, X-rays, ECGs, stock market trends, images, etc.) or generate a line on a graph or an image. Each team is provided with a colored marker and a transparency. The graphic of interest can be printed directly on the transparency. Each team's response consists of students using the marker to identify a requested feature directly on the transparency.

In large classes, it may be preferable to print the graphic separately on a sheet of paper and give the teams blank transparencies. When too many copies of the same graphic are stacked on the projector, the graphic overlaps so many times that it becomes black and obscures student responses and all other information. If teams are provided blank transparencies and a separate image printed on paper, they need simply to align the transparency over the paper when doing their markup. In this case, make sure to have teams indicate the alignment of a transparency, such as by writing their team name in the top right corner—you don't want to inadvertently stack one team's work upside down or backward!

Here are some examples:

- Circle the feature(s) in this ECG that would most likely lead to a misdiagnosis of left ventricular hypertrophy.
- On the basis of the ground-penetrating radargram shown, identify the excavation site boundary you would recommend to most quickly determine whether the region likely contains an ancient human settlement.
- Draw on your map the location and size of the breakwater you would recommend to mitigate the beach erosion at this site. Your recommended breakwater should achieve the protection at minimum construction cost.
- Given the introduction of this invasive predatory fish species to this lake, draw on the graph the approximate curve representing kokanee salmon population versus time you would expect. Indicate steady-state levels and time to reach them.

The example shown in Figure AB.1 is from a course in earth and ocean sciences (Jones, 2009). The image on the left is the original data graphic provided to teams, and the image on the right is an overlay of the responses from two teams, each using its own color. Teams were required to interpret the data by identifying two linear features with lines and the location of one additional feature with a circle. The specific details of what teams were identifying are beyond the scope of this book, but there are clearly both similarities and differences in the decisions made by these two teams.

To report their results, teams bring their completed transparencies to the front of the class. You will stack them all together (for a small number of teams) or stack a representatively diverse subset (for a large number of teams) and use the document camera or overhead projector to display the simultaneous report to the class. A facilitated discussion follows, revealing for all students how different teams interpreted and applied basic concepts to the exercise.

FIGURE AB.1
(a) Stacked overhead source graphic; (b) student responses

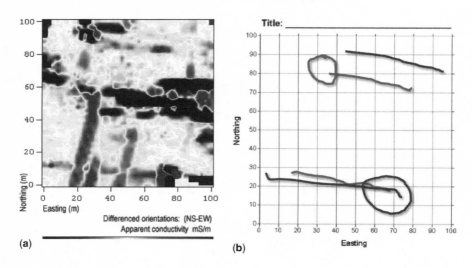

(a)

(b)

HOT SEAT VARIATION 1: PERFORMANCE METRIC

The hot seat method was introduced in chapter 7; here, two variations will be presented. As described, the method quickly identifies a single team to begin whole-class discussion, putting them on the "hot seat."

For the performance metric hot seat variation, imagine an Application Activity in which the answer involves optimizing some measure or performance, such as maximizing profit, minimizing chances of user error, or minimizing recovery time. The teams report their optimized performance measure for the problem. After ranking, the team with the most favorable performance measure is put on the hot seat and must defend its approach and conclusions. Other teams attempt to show that the hot seat team did not properly consider all aspects of the problem, in which case the team is eliminated and the team with the next most favorable performance measure takes over the hot seat. The "winning" team is the one that can withstand the challenges from the class and successfully defend its approach and decisions. If desired, you can assign a nominal grade based on ranking at the end of the activity after all challenges have been heard.

Figure AB.2 shows an example of a hot seat simultaneous report drawn from an engineering design course. In this case, teams were challenged to design the least expensive device that could achieve a particular set of functional requirements. Teams reported their choices directly to the teacher, who in turn recorded and graphed them in an Excel spreadsheet. In this particular case, the teacher augmented reporting by also collecting and displaying the primary technology used in the teams' solutions—roller chain (RC), timing belt (TB), or V-belt (VB)—as shown beside the team names in the figure. This extra data enriched the discussion

FIGURE AB.2
Sample Excel plot report from a hot seat activity

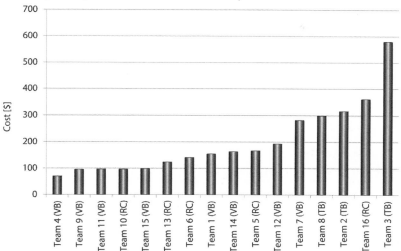

and brought patterns forward; for example, the least expensive designs in this exercise tended to employ V-belts, whereas the most expensive ones tended to use timing belts. Another approach to manage this reporting is to use Google Forms in conjunction with a Google Drive spreadsheet (discussed further later); students report using a prepared form, and the results are automatically ported into a spreadsheet linked to the forms. This must be set up and tested well in advance, and clear instructions must be provided to the teams about how and when they are to report.

A low-tech alternative to achieve these same results is to have teams write their team number and performance metric on a sticky note and place that into a class-wide ordered list on the blackboard, whiteboard, or wall. For this example, instead of using a projected spreadsheet, you could mark several anchor points on the board (e.g., $0, $50, $100, $200, $400, and $800), and teams would report by arranging their sticky notes in order based on those anchor points (see Figure AB.3). The team farthest to the left would be on the hot seat, and if its solution is eliminated, its sticky note could be removed.

FIGURE AB.3
Sample blackboard report from a hot seat activity

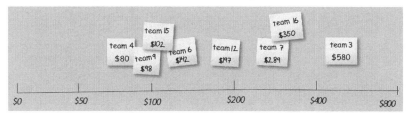

HOT SEAT VARIATION 2: ANSWER KEY

Another variation with the hot seat technique is to use one of the random draw methods from chapter 7 (balls in a jar, dice, or the smartphone app) in order to establish the grading key for assignments or even exams with multiple questions. After the teams have handed in their official answers, you simply use a random draw technique to select the first team for the hot seat. The team gives its answer, and if it is unchallenged by the rest of the class, it becomes the "official" answer for grading all team submissions. This creates a strong incentive for any team with a different answer to challenge the proposed answer. (Of course, if it turns out an answer accepted by the class is incorrect, you must address that at some point.) Additional random draws can be used to determine the next team in the hot seat for each subsequent question.

GALLERY WALK

Gallery walks are useful for problems where the solutions cannot be conveyed by a simple A, B, or C choice (well suited to voting cards) or a short phrase (well suited to whiteboards). Commonly, solution deliverables such as long equations, sketches, and concept maps lend themselves well to the gallery walk technique. This can also be used to distill a long, complex solution into its most pertinent elements as teams prepare a concise solution to a complicated problem.

You generally need to make sure that the team responses have some structure to ensure comparability between team outputs. In some activities, this might be to require that teams first state on their poster their choice or decision, and then use the rest of the poster to list further detail such as three strengths, three weaknesses, and two concerns with their choice.

Another approach is to ask teams to distill a complex work into key elements. For example, a 20-page technical report could be condensed onto an $11" \times 17"$ poster with a minimum font size limit equivalent to 18 points. Ideally, the poster is structured such that a specific choice is prominently highlighted; perhaps this is a recommended course of action or perhaps a performance metric, as described in the first hot seat activity variation. The rest of the poster then contains the most essential information to defend the choice or support the metric. It can be a requirement to include a chart or sketch or, for a fun challenge, to use only pictures—no text.

As an example, Figure AB.4 shows an information-dense sample poster from an engineering course on machine design. This is the output of a project that the students work on for 2 weeks and represents the distillation of a technical report that is 15–25 pages long. The "specific choice" in this case is the performance metric (cost), shown at the bottom right, which is really the overall measure of

FIGURE AB.4
Sample gallery walk poster for an engineering design activity

the cumulative effect of a long series of smaller choices. This use of a performance metric provides a single number by which all teams' designs can be compared. The remaining information is there to explain and support the process used to arrive at that metric. (The team is likely not nearby to answer questions, so the poster must do the talking for the team.)

Whatever method teams adopt, the posters are evenly spaced around classroom walls using masking tape. Some teachers require team names on the posters, which encourages everyone to take the task seriously, whereas others prefer that the posters remain anonymous and randomly placed on the wall. Some teachers go so far as to anonymously add their own poster to the gallery as a way to further stimulate the teams and arouse curiosity.

With the posters on the wall, the actual gallery walk involves having teams review and critique the work of others. In smaller classes, teams can wander around and view the other posters, but in larger classes it helps to coordinate the movement from poster to poster. You will also need to decide how many posters each team should view. I normally budget for 5 minutes per poster and rarely have each team review every other poster in the class.

FIGURE AB.5
Sample team worksheet for a gallery walk

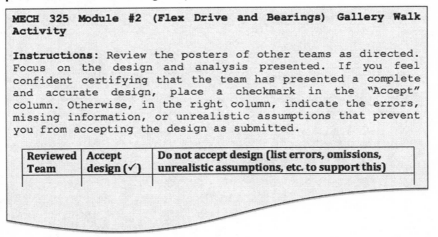

```
MECH 325 Module #2 (Flex Drive and Bearings) Gallery Walk
Activity

Instructions: Review the posters of other teams as directed.
Focus on the design and analysis presented. If you feel
confident certifying that the team has presented a complete
and accurate design, place a checkmark in the "Accept"
column. Otherwise, in the right column, indicate the errors,
missing information, or unrealistic assumptions that prevent
you from accepting the design as submitted.
```

Reviewed Team	Accept design (✓)	Do not accept design (list errors, omissions, unrealistic assumptions, etc. to support this)

Two options for the review-and-critique portion of the activity are either to have teams carry around a worksheet that they use to assess each of the other posters or to have teams annotate and comment directly on the other poster. In the case of the worksheet, in my classes I usually have teams assume the role of a senior manager and imagine they are signing off on the work from a team they supervise. I usually preprint a three-column worksheet similar to the one shown in Figure AB.5, and I give one copy to each team.

You could also have students identify the best idea in each poster that they overlooked in their own poster, or you could have them identify the weakest point of each poster. The advantage of doing all of these things on worksheets is that each team's work remains private, and each team must do its own thinking. Yet another approach is to have teams use sticky notes to add their comments directly to the posters they review. This is a very public approach to critique, and it has the advantage that each team can learn from each other team that has commented before it. Also, when teams return to their own poster, they have a wealth of very rich and targeted feedback from a variety of perspectives.

Whatever approach you use in the gallery walk, it facilitates a whole-class discussion of the posters and critiques, as well as any questions at the end. For this reason, it is very important that you circulate around the class during the activity to view the posters and to listen in on the discussions that are taking place.

BEST SOLUTION TOURNAMENT

Teams prepare a poster or worksheet similar to what they would do for the gallery walk, but they have many copies; the exact number depends on the tournament

FIGURE AB.6
Sample best solution tournament flowchart

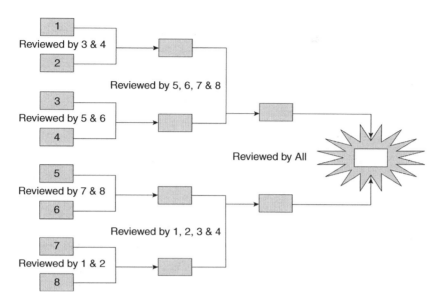

format. Out of class, you will work through the evaluation order and prepare a slide showing the process in table or flowchart form, as shown in Figure AB.6.

Teams are usually also given instructions in terms of the criteria and their importance for ranking the posters. For example, with an engineering design activity similar to the one highlighted in the gallery walk, these criteria might be, from most to least important, as follows:

- The design as presented will work (e.g., it does not violate the laws of physics).
- The solution is free of major errors in analysis, the assumptions are plausible, and all key information is presented.
- The solution is free from minor errors in analysis, and the assumptions are realistic.
- The design has a high performance metric.

The goal of the class activity is to have teams review and rank the solutions of other teams such that by the end they identify the best solution in the class. The activity proceeds in rounds; in each round, the top-ranked designs advance to the next round and go to other teams for review, as per the table or flowchart. The flowchart must be visible to all so students know which teams' work they are to review, and then either the posters can circulate between teams at their desks or teams can move between posters on the wall, as in the gallery walk. With the flowchart projected overhead, you can fill in the advancing team information after each round.

As the number of teams' posters being considered diminishes each round, duplicate copies of the posters still in the tournament are needed in order to avoid a very large number of students crammed around one poster. This technique lends itself best to activities either where posters are very quick and easy for teams to produce or where teams have an opportunity to print their posters before class and can easily produce many duplicate copies.

A word of warning: Although this activity can be a lot of fun for teams as they watch their solutions progress to become the best in the class, it does require a lot of effort to coordinate. For a class with 10–15 teams, this usually means bringing in at least one teaching assistant, ideally two, to help with coordination and distribution.

GOOGLE DRIVE

Google Drive allows multiple users to simultaneously contribute to the same document. In large classes, this can be very helpful in facilitating simultaneous reporting. In this activity, one approach is to create a form (i.e., a survey) in Google Drive and use that to collect data from teams. Google Form allows a variety of question types, including multiple choice, numerical, text, and rating scales, to name a few. Be sure to include a question in the survey that requires teams to enter their team number so you can identify responses later. You only need share the URL for the survey, and then teams can enter their responses from a laptop or smartphone. The survey data are sent to a spreadsheet in Google Drive, which you can design in advance to create charts or tables of responses. When you are ready, you reveal the formatted data to the class (i.e., you initiate the simultaneous report). Another more direct approach is to format a table in a Google Drive document with a pre-filled team number column, a blank team-reporting column, and a blank column for a short rationale or supporting evidence. You then provide document access to each team; you do this within Google Drive by e-mailing an invite to at least one member from each team. (At the start of the course, I ask teams to create their own shared team Gmail address I can use to communicate with them.) At the appointed time, the teams use laptops or smartphones to update their information simultaneously. Display the resulting table (see Figure AB.7) on the classroom screen, and facilitate a discussion that examines the various positions, solutions, and evidence presented in the table. An advantage of this second approach is that teams can communicate and contribute in real time. In particular, a "questions for this team" column is invaluable in a large class in order to consolidate and manage questions in an orderly manner; teams with questions simply type them in Google Drive, and they appear in real time on the screen.

FIGURE AB.7
Sample Google Drive table

	Team	Cost	Actuator Type	Transmission Type	Questions for this team		Rank	Top Teams Cost	Team
A1	$751.93	DC Motor	Power Screw						
A2	$406.42	AC motor	Rack and pinion				1st	$43.93	B3
A3	$641.32	AC motor	Gear drive				2nd	$130.57	C5
A4	$442.99	AC motor	Pulley System				3rd	$169.71	C2
A5	$407.46	DC motor	Power screw				4th	$302.68	C4
B1	$360.69	AC Motor	Timing Belt Pulley						
B2	$1,047.95	DC Motor	Rack and Pinion				Average	$499.31	
B3	$43.93	DC Motor	Direct Drive	Motor stall torque? Do you have a controller?					
B4	$412.17	Air Pump	Air piston						
B5	$543.74	AC Motor	Cable and Pulley						
C1	$470.36	AC Motor	Power Screw						
C2	$169.71	AC Motor	Power Screw	How are you reversing the AC motor?					
C3	$644.23	DC Motor	Pulley						
C4	$302.68	DC Motor	Power Screw						
C5	$130.57	Air Compressor	Air cyclinder	How did you quiet the compressor below 75dB?					
D1	$1,177.10	DC Motor	Rack and Pinion						
D2	$456.60	AC Motor	Cable						
D3	$867.00	DC Motor	Power Screw						
D4	$403.80	DC Motor	Pulley						
D5	$305.58	Electric Motor	Power Screw	AC or DC motor?					

CLASSROOM RESPONSE SYSTEMS (CLICKERS)

Classroom response systems or clickers are commonplace in higher education, and some teachers have adopted them for use in the TBL classroom. The benefits of clickers include an ability to quickly collect information from a large number of teams and to maintain a permanent record of each team's response. Clickers generally provide only aggregate data in class in the form of a histogram of anonymous responses, which can be very useful in trying to foster participation through low-stakes, anonymous activities. In TBL classrooms, this anonymity can be an obstacle, as teams are not forced to stand behind their choice when using clickers; unlike voting cards, no team knows any other team's response. Some TBL practitioners overcome this by requiring teams to vote both with clickers (for the permanent record and the ability to show the histogram) and with voting cards (for the public presentation of choices).

SCISSORS AND GLUE STICKS (NONSIMULTANEOUS)

The scissors and glue sticks approach is useful when teams are working on activities involving writing, something that is notoriously difficult to turn into a collaborative team task. Although this technique is not exactly a simultaneous reporting activity on its own, it is so powerful that it is worth considering as a lead-up to one of the other activities such as the gallery walk or hot seat.

Prior to the class meeting, each team member prepares his or her own response to a writing assignment on a well-defined topic. In an English class this might be an expository essay, in a journalism class it might be an editorial, or in a law class it might be a legal brief. It is critical that everyone writes on the same topic. The students bring their written assignments to the class meeting and review each other's work, most often in light of a supplied grading rubric. The teams then use the scissors to cut the best passages from each member's work and the glue sticks to paste these passages into a unified whole document. Not only does this activity get the team to critically review each member's work using the supplied rubric, but it also requires the students to identify the most valuable parts of each individual document for the team compilation and arrange them in a logical and cohesive manner.

Lessons Learned in Faculty Preparation

A Retrospective

Bill Roberson and Billie Franchini

Implementation of Team-Based Learning (TBL) often takes place on an individual course level and is accomplished by a single teacher working alone. There are also examples where implementation is supported on a much larger scale, as in the TBL Academy at the University at Albany featured in this appendix. The TBL Academy is a training program that has helped hundreds of teachers to implement TBL, and the materials presented here offer insights for new adopters. This appendix is likely of even greater interest to faculty developers or those interested in training other TBL teachers.

In chapter 9 we attempted to distill for would-be adopters of TBL some of the critical issues that they will encounter on their journey. We have by no means addressed all of them, but these observations represent the experiences of two veteran faculty development specialists. Our writings here distill much of what we have learned from working with approximately 300 university instructors who have experienced varying levels of success in converting to TBL. In this appendix, we will describe in detail the evolution of the formal training strategy we have developed to support faculty in redesigning their courses and doing a first-time TBL implementation. We will also present some of the lessons we learned during the process. We think this description will be useful for both instructors and faculty development specialists, who may want to see the evolution of ideas intended to increase the probability that new adopters will fully succeed.

It is important to state, however, that you can individually embark on a successful journey to redevelop your course for TBL without having access to a program like University at Albany's TBL Academy.

Since 2007 the Institute for Teaching, Learning and Academic Leadership at the University at Albany has worked closely with a wide range of instructors to use TBL, from those with decades of teaching experience to first-time instructors. In our initial attempts we saw a fairly low rate of successful implementation: Fewer than 30% of adopters who completed TBL training managed to implement a complete instance of TBL without major dilution of the method or complete reversion to traditional practices midway through. Observing the experiences of faculty members such as those featured in our short cases in chapter 9 has taught us a great deal, and we have developed a variety of strategies to support individual efforts in TBL adoption.

In early iterations of our TBL Academy, we focused so extensively on the mechanics of implementation that we overlooked the enormous attitudinal shifts TBL requires for many instructors—just as it does for students. A high percentage of our early clients adopted TBL by the book, but they were not psychologically and emotionally prepared for the shock and pushback that is sometimes produced when students are placed in an authentic adult learning situation—often for the first time in their college career. These instructors tended to see student surprise, discomfort, and resistance as indicators of failure rather than as a normal, positive, and often inevitable step in student learning. Our faculty development programs for TBL now focus directly on helping instructors understand *why* students resist even when TBL is working very well, *when* to expect resistance, and *what* to do when it happens.

A TALE OF TWO ADOPTERS

Our story begins with what turned out to be a natural experiment. In an early iteration of our training process, we worked closely with two professors during their TBL implementations. Their respective experiences became a comparative case study. We assisted both instructors in planning their courses, writing their syllabi, developing Readiness Assurance Tests (RATs) and team tasks, and managing the first few classroom meetings. And because these were large classes of over 100 students each, we met with their teaching assistants (TAs) to make sure the classroom assistance was as consistent as could be hoped with the implementation plans. We also helped out by attending in person and assisting in the first few classes; then we gradually reduced our Academy staff presence as the courses got under way.

Our learning moment came as we discovered (too late) that the same amount of coaching and assistance did not work for both instructors. One of these TBL adopters, whose profile was consistent with what we called a "tinkerer" in Part One, found comfort and early confidence with TBL and had a transformative experience. There were the usual moments of doubt and stress, but this person initiated regular contact with the support staff and sought feedback, and as each crisis emerged, we were able to provide a sounding board, perspective, and guidance. In spite of a few knocks, by the end of the semester it had become evident that the implementation was a huge success. Students who had begun as vocal skeptics now praised the effort. The exams and papers that had typically been assigned in the course in the past turned out to be too easy to challenge students in the new design. The instructor had to set about revamping them in subsequent semesters in order to make them more appropriate for students who were no longer passive recipients of knowledge but were active critical thinkers. The instructor emerged from the implementation feeling relief that the investment in TBL had paid off and feeling satisfaction that this course provided a decidedly improved, more dynamic, and intellectually rigorous experience for students.

The other faculty member, whose profile resembled that of the "traditional practitioner," lost confidence in the method about a quarter of the way through the course. One issue was task design. To create good tasks in TBL, instructors need to rethink their and their students' relationship with disciplinary content so as to convert conceptual thinking into concrete actions that engage students. This instructor worked in a discipline in which student problem solving required thinking disruptively about the discipline and disciplinary teaching conventions in order to invent concrete inquiries of substance and of high interest. He had no easy-to-adopt models. Another issue was the traditional practitioner's resistance to giving up the instructor-centric role of expert and scholar in order to make time for students to do their own analysis and investigation in class. Faced with the challenge of creating effective tasks, along with his underlying doubt about the value of the new facilitator role, he took the first signs of student resistance as a critical blow. To make matters worse, this instructor had also been less successful in converting the TA to the new system, which accelerated the overall confidence crisis. In hindsight, it is clear that a much more present, proactive support structure was needed to help generate examples, provide encouragement, and mitigate the bumps—but this realization on the part of the support staff occurred beyond the point at which the disappointing outcome of the implementation could be avoided.

For many of our clients who are initially intrigued by the idea of TBL, the magnitude of change required in order to transition to the new model is difficult to imagine until the implementation is well under way. Over time we have become more attentive to this gap. We have found ways to help instructors conceptualize the challenge earlier and more realistically in terms of a project to be accomplished in manageable increments and with particular attention to specific TBL protocols. We focus a great deal of time on task design. We also help instructors anticipate student resistance and help them develop ways to manage it. The result has been a faculty development process consisting of honest self-examination, thorough orientation, experiential learning, coaching, peer consulting, candid feedback, and friendly assessment. All of these elements find their place in the program we call the "Instructional Leadership Academy."

THE SHAPE OF THE INSTRUCTIONAL LEADERSHIP ACADEMY

The name of the Academy is significant. Among our goals is to elevate the value of innovation for faculty members and honor those who are willing to take a risk. Through the name we intend to communicate that adopters of TBL are leaders and pioneers, responsible for establishing a new culture of teaching at the university.

The Academy itself is an extended, semester-long program that takes would-be adopters of TBL through the complete process of transforming a traditionally taught course into a full-blown instance of TBL. In early iterations, when the success rate for full TBL implementation hovered at a disappointing less than 30%, we at first concluded this was normal and to be expected. Over time, however, we have come to understand better how to recruit new adopters and how to support the processes of course reconceptualization, role adjustment, and course implementation. As a result our track record has improved recently to a rate of close to 90% as we have gained greater understanding of the various journeys required by instructors with different needs, different assumptions, different attitudes, and different skill levels. What follows is a description of the entire process, from scheduling to management to conclusion.

TIMING AND SCHEDULING OF THE ACADEMY

Timing is crucial because the commitment is substantial. The Instructional Leadership Academy requires an initial 3-day commitment (2 daylong workshops plus a day in between of design and planning). This is followed by a 2-hour consultation the following week, for which participants bring their new syllabus and completed first TBL learning sequence (readings, RATs, tasks, assessment). In this interview we do a walkthrough of the learning sequence and discuss activity design, communication strategies, and classroom management for each step. We also work through the syllabus to ensure that all parts are consistent with the new goals and classroom culture.

The months of the year when faculty are most available and professionally undistracted (May, December) turn out not to be most productive for learning a new teaching method. Furthermore, the stated preferences of instructors contradict behavior. Through trial and error, we have discovered that too much time between the Academy and the actual implementation is problematic for the development of the necessary attitudes, perspectives, and skills. A sense of immediacy during the Academy has proven to be highly motivating for many instructors, and the logistics of TBL are still fresh in their minds when the semester begins. Also, any delay in transitioning from the planning phase to the implementation phase allows doubt and second thoughts to enter into an instructor's thinking, exposes the would-be adopter to the skepticism of colleagues (which is not trivial, especially if you are pretenure at a research-intensive institution), and diminishes the benefit of the peer-cohort learning experience. *Once the process of reflection and planning begins, the implementation needs to follow immediately.* For this reason we schedule our primary Academies for early August and early January, allowing 2 weeks before the start of classes. We also schedule a May Academy for those who want to adopt TBL for a summer course, an opportunity exercised by many University at Albany graduate students, who are frequently given teaching assignments during the summer session.

Pre-Academy Processes

In early iterations of the Academy, the criteria for recruitment of potential TBL adopters were simple: "Do you want to do this?" and "Can you come to the meetings on Monday and Wednesday?" Because we offered a modest stipend to faculty members who were willing, it was relatively easy to find the targeted 10 candidates for each cohort. This minimalist approach, however, was based on the flawed assumption that applicants who signed up were already cognizant of the size of the commitment necessary for wholesale adoption of a new method of teaching. When we experienced a high attrition rate, even before the implementations were attempted, we realized not only that the support process was flawed but also that the recruitment process needed to be more intentional. It needed to induce reflection and be more informative to candidates. In later iterations of the Academy, we required applicants to fill out an electronic survey, asking them to respond to the following set of questions:

1. What is your experience with asking students to work collaboratively? (Choose from five examples.)
2. Describe what happens when things are going well in your classroom. What does it look like?
3. What changes do you want, expect, or hope to see in your students as a result of their participating in your course? [This allows us to understand their goals and values as teachers.]
4. What are some innovations that you have tried in the past (e.g., something you did to increase student engagement with the course and the material)? What was your experience with those?
5. Please describe in 200 words or less your goals and expectations for participating in this project.

In answering these questions, applicants begin characterizing their individual journey and reflecting briefly on past practices, both successful and less than successful. We have found that a significant number of applicants, confronted with these reflections, stop midway through the survey and decide not to apply for the Academy. The questions make it clear that this is not a workshop that simply assembles random teaching techniques. This self-screening ensures that those who decide to join the cohort have already articulated a clear goal, are conscious of the choice they are making, and are more likely to be prepared for what will be asked of them.

The answers to the survey questions also tell us a lot about the applicants and help us judge whether the Academy is a good match for their goals and whether their beliefs and past experience will be a positive or negative factor in their ability to adopt a new method. When we sense that there is an oversized misalignment of instructor assumptions and Academy goals, we contact the applicant individually and guide him or her as needed, sometimes away from the Academy toward the appropriate resources or services.

To drive home expectations for the work that participants will need to do, we provide a short, descriptive list of principles of TBL and communicate that these will need to be observable in any implementation that qualifies for funding:

1. Students work in permanent groups so they can improve as a team over time.
2. All team work is done during class to eliminate scheduling problems.
3. Students are held accountable for preparing, thanks to the Readiness Assurance Process.
4. During class meetings students use content to make decisions, then analyze their decisions through comparison with other teams.
5. Immediate feedback techniques motivate students to work productively.
6. Students are held accountable to each other by means of graded peer evaluation.

These principles are communicated at multiple points and inform the evaluation criteria we use in bringing each project to closure.

We also ask applicants to commit to concrete benchmarks in order to create specific expectations for each step of the implementation and to help them visualize the entire process:

This Instructional Leadership Academy will take you through the process of transforming a traditional course into a TBL course. A modest stipend will be made available to University at Albany faculty members who implement TBL in the coming semester and meet the following benchmarks:

- Attend an orientation meeting (date provided) the week before the Academy begins.
- Attend the 2-day Academy (dates provided), 9:30 a.m. to 3:30 p.m.
- Complete substantial homework and reading assignments before the Academy begins and between meetings.
- Undergo a presemester review of the syllabus and early lesson plans by Academy staff (week before classes begin).
- Schedule and complete observation of the class by Academy staff before the midterm of the semester.
- Conduct a midterm survey of students before the midterm of the semester.
- Meet with Academy staff members to reflect on both classroom observation and midterm survey data and to redirect efforts for the remainder of the semester.

- Meet with other Academy participants for a mid-semester update (lunch provided).
- Write a brief, one-page reflection essay on the experience of implementing TBL (format to be provided).

Pre-Academy Orientation

In spite of the reflection required in the application form, in early instances of the Academy some would-be adopters would apply, attend the first workshop, then decide to drop, expressing that they did not realize what was expected of them. This departure typically proved disruptive for two reasons: (a) It undermined the cohesion of the individual's team during the Academy, and (b) it announced to those whose commitment was still tenuous that failure was possible. We therefore added one more step in the run-up to the first day of the Academy: an orientation meeting designed to convey through an informal interview those things that the application process failed to communicate. This step usually filters out one or two additional candidates. From initial application through orientation, it is typical for the number of applicants to shrink by as much as 50%. If we start with 25 applicants, we will normally have 12–15 in the Academy.

The goal of the orientation is to demonstrate the scope of the change that a TBL implementation will require in a traditional class. We begin the session by asking all of the instructors to reflect on and verbalize a description of their current teaching personae. Next, we spend time showing (through video footage) and explaining what a TBL classroom looks like, focusing specifically on the limited instructor role in the classroom setting and the change in instructor role from content delivery expert to learning sequence designer. After we share these insights, we ask the instructors to begin reflecting on the journey they will be undertaking to move from their current persona to this new instructor role. We also share a case study about student pushback and discuss the changing power dynamic of the classroom and the various ways in which students might respond to the new challenges that a TBL classroom will present. At the end of the session, participants are provided a list of six readings, some from the original *Team-Based Learning* by Michaelsen, Knight, and Fink (2004) and some from other sources on active learning and student engagement. These become the basis for the Readiness Assurance Process on Day One of the Academy.

Day One

After our experimentation with a variety of approaches, Day One has evolved into a daylong simulation of the experience of being a student in a TBL course. We use the content from the readings on TBL to provide the material for team-driven activities. Our approach is to allow participants to discover inductively how a TBL course functions and to experience the full effect of being on a team that has to make decisions for which students are collectively accountable. Course design, policies, grading schemes, and other teaching concerns are therefore pushed into Day Two. In earlier versions we began with course design but discovered that dealing with course design before the concrete experience of being a student was too abstract. Courses that looked fine at the macro level would be undermined by a misunderstanding of the TBL classroom dynamic and by failure to address the student perspective. In the current version of the Academy, course design makes more sense because participants now know—from having been TBL students themselves—the types of student behavior and attitudes that the course redesign needs to foster.

With no prelude or discussion, Day One begins immediately with a 10-question Individual Readiness Assurance Test (iRAT) on the six assigned readings. This is followed by a demonstration of TBL team formation. We form the teams by distributing levels of experience in using collaborative learning approaches to teaching, having participants self-assign a score based on their experience. They then form a line around the room to be counted off into teams of approximately five each. We then debrief the activity and discuss with participants the added value of public team formation. We also walk through examples of ways to distribute human assets. This activity always engenders a lively discussion about the assumed merits of using student GPAs in group determination and assigning students to teams in order to ensure academic heterogeneity. We take the opportunity served up at this point to emphasize the importance of trust in the TBL classroom. The visible distribution of assets assures students that they have not been manipulated and that they have not been secretly chosen for their team based on a perception of their intelligence or characteristics that can become highly politicized, such as ethnicity and gender. For many participants this discussion marks the beginning of the transformation: They are not simply designing a course—they are developing a complete, fully functioning community.

The newly gathered teams are given just 30 seconds to come up with a team name, then are asked to take the Team Readiness Assurance Test (tRAT) using Immediate Feedback Assessment Technique (IF-AT) forms. After the tRAT and the comparative posting of team scores, we allow participants to identify potential places for appeals and have a brief discussion on managing the Appeals Process. We then pause to remind everyone where we are in the TBL learning sequence. After questions and clarifications, we remind participants that what we have just completed (reading, iRAT, tRAT, appeals, Q&A) fully replaces traditional lecture. We emphasize that if we were now to ask them to sit through a lecture on TBL (as content), there would be frustration and eventually resentment. To demonstrate the way TBL turns students into owners of their learning, we move immediately into application of course content—which consists of the six articles assigned before the workshop.

The application exercises vary over time, but one of the more effective tasks we assign is the analysis and evaluation of a somewhat vague TBL implementation as recorded on videotape. The teams are asked to watch a 5-minute clip, then make a judgment by scoring the implementation on a scale of 1 (*no evidence of TBL*) to 10 (*a complete textbook implementation of TBL*). There is always great divergence of judgment among the teams, and this sets up a very lively interteam debate, fueled by questions such as, "What is the evidence that makes you conclude that this was not TBL?" and "Where did you see something resembling a TBL best practice?" We then step back and debrief the task itself, to show how we modeled 4 S design in the way we structured and managed the activity. We explain that we asked them to use their newly gained knowledge about TBL to analyze an unfamiliar teaching scenario and to reach a conclusion that was represented in a focused, select-style decision. We discuss with participants how, counterintuitively, the focused, selection-style format *did not* lead to a simplistic discussion but rather created the conditions for us to explore their understanding of a complex theory.

For those participants who are suspicious of anything that looks like multiple choice, we are able to explain that multiple choice used as a single instrument to measure student learning at the end of a process is, indeed, suspect. But in TBL, multiple choice and other limited option formats are used to launch the learning process. The forced choice is the doorway into the content, as students must engage deeply with the content to justify their choice. We further explain the psychological dynamic of a selection-style question rather than an open-ended question: that a selection not only allows the instructor to set the terms of the discussion but also turns the answer into a clear decision. Collective decision making is what fosters intrateam debate, critical thinking, and team development.

The experience of this first 4 S task leads directly to an exercise in which all the participants are given a list of typical group work tasks from various disciplines and asked to work individually to rewrite them as 4 S tasks. As teams they then work to identify the best example of each, and these are reported to the whole class.

During lunch we remind our Academy participants that there are many colleagues across campus, in many different disciplines, who have been successful at adopting TBL. We do this by inviting two or three users of TBL to join the cohort for lunch. We ask the guests to describe their experience, warts and all, and to describe how their perspective on teaching has evolved. These stories are sometimes quite dramatic and always intriguing:

- "I am notorious in my department for getting the all-time lowest student evaluations—*ever*. Now, using TBL, I get the highest."
- "I was becoming weepy in my distress about how badly my large lecture class was going. Now I love going to class. It has given me new energy as a teacher."
- "My students are much more active than they were before. But I'm a little jealous. They now come to class to be with each other, not with me."

- "Before I converted to TBL, I kept dumbing down the course so that my grade distribution would not be so embarrassing. Now, every semester, I have to keep toughening up the exams so that they'll be challenging enough for students."

After the lunch break, we return to the topic of RATs. We provide two pages of a textbook from a discipline that no one in the room is familiar with and ask participants to work alone, using the text as a source, to write questions that demonstrate (a) basic comprehension and (b) simple application. Then we ask them to conceive a higher-level, multiple choice question by creating a scenario or short case where the content of the text is required to make an informed judgment. At the end of 15 minutes, we ask the teams to select the best examples and write them on the whiteboard. In the debrief we exchange observations as a whole class on which strategies were used to generate questions and which ones work the best.

As the Day One workshop draws to a close, we model principles and an activity designed to help instructors help their students learn to read more accurately. The task asks participants to read two paragraphs from a text, then to make a judgment (choosing from five possibilities) about what the author intended to imply in the selection. The exercise demonstrates how the 4 S format can be used to encourage students to conduct close, analytical readings of texts.

Day One closes with a written reflection that sets up the homework assignment. Participants are asked to write the profile of a student who has successfully completed their course. The template for this profile includes skills and protocols that students will have mastered, key concepts students will now own, and new attitudes and habits of thought that students will have developed as a result of their experience in the course.

Between Day One and Day Two

The homework to be done between Day One and Day Two is critical to the success of the Academy. The assignment requires participants to focus on one element of the student profile they created for their course and then to develop a complete learning sequence (over 2–4 days) around changing students in the targeted way. This assignment normally takes participants 3–5 hours to complete.

1. Identify the readings that will be used.
2. Write a set of RAT questions on the readings.
3. Develop a sequence of team tasks in 4 S design format that will allow students to practice thinking in the targeted way.
4. Create an assignment that will measure student progress in the targeted way of thinking at the end of the learning sequence.
5. Prepare a single-page summary presentation of your learning sequence.

Day Two

Day Two begins with a team task designed to continue fostering new faculty attitudes about themselves and their students. Using data from a recent study that examines student perceptions of instructor credibility, we ask workshop participants to make predictions (in the format of a 4 S task) about what the students in the study reported. The data from the study are, on the one hand, intuitive: Many of the behaviors that we would expect to result in loss of credibility—such as inconsistency, rudeness, and so on—do in fact appear in the results. On the other hand, the data can be counter-intuitive to many faculty, as they show that students do not expect professors to know everything and to have every answer. What matters to students is the faculty member's effort to engage them, meet them where they are, provide a clear path to success in the course, and structure a sound learning experience. Revealing how participants' predictions compare to the actual results of the study allows us to make the case—once again, in case there are doubts—that TBL practices and the consequent instructor's role align nearly perfectly with what students value in their teachers. At the same time, we remind TBL adopters that students will not always at first recognize or appreciate these practices because they are unfamiliar within their range of educational experience.

The remainder of the morning of Day Two consists of a highly structured round-robin conversation in which participants describe their learning sequences to their teammates and receive direct feedback, with a time limit of 7 minutes for each presenter. This process is highly energizing for everyone, as participants' abstract understanding of TBL now has to be expressed in concrete action and made visible to scrutiny by colleagues.

Starting Course Design

Now that participants have had the opportunity to build their own learning sequence, get an outside perspective on their work, and give feedback to others on their sequences, they are primed to begin thinking about their course as a whole. By the time we get to this pivotal moment, participants have already become fully attuned to the dominant feature of TBL course design: A TBL course is designed to be an experiential, integrated learning sequence for students. Framing and structuring this sequence of experiences requires a great deal of thought and planning from the perspective of "What will the students do?" at any given moment. Effective design of each learning sub-sequence organizes student work in ways that ask students to make relevant, significant decisions using course content, leading to useful—and even desired—feedback from peers and the instructor. Effective application questions and activity design are essential to the process. The right task will aim students in a targeted direction but also provide them with the autonomy they need so as to accept responsibility for what they do and decide.

Figure AC.1 uses the image of a tunnel to communicate the dynamic of an effective task design and team discussion. At the outset of the process is the frame that establishes

FIGURE AC.1
The core shape of learning in a TBL course

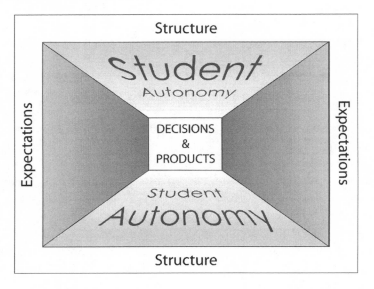

the field of action. The format of the question structures the task discussion and sets expectations for how it will be reported. At the other end of the process is the moment of public accountability, in the form of the proposed solution (product or decision) that emerges from the team discussion. Between these two moments the teams experience a sense of autonomy. Within the confines of the established frame, they are free to exploit any means at their disposal to find and evaluate all relevant possibilities, in the process of narrowing down the options to the one most preferred by all team members.

The design of effective tasks therefore demands realization and acceptance of a fundamental change in planning and behavior for many traditional instructors: Once the activities are designed and planned, there comes a point when the instructor has to launch it and let it go and accept that students may go in surprising directions. The instructor's control is limited to identifying the target and structuring the work so that it points students toward the target.

The instructor then meets students on the other end of that process and makes public all of the thinking in the room. This serves as a form of accountability, as students compare their responses with those of the other teams. It also provides data to the instructor, who can now guide and redirect student thinking through the debriefing process.

The Role of Peer-to-Peer Accountability

It is at this point that the Academy addresses a key attitudinal factor that has proved to be a stumbling block for many new adopters: giving students the authority needed to hold their peers accountable for productive behavior. For many of our participants, peer evaluation is the most suspect element of TBL: It represents an abnegation of their responsibility for evaluation of students. It risks pitting student against student. Another fear is the amount of time and management that the process will require; we have adopted iPeer and encourage faculty with classes over 25 or 30 students to use this electronic solution. We offer one-on-one training to learn the system.

We know that our arguments about peer evaluation are not 100% effective for a new adopter. We are adamant about the importance of peer-to-peer accountability, but we also know that this is a leap that is too big for many instructors. For those who resist, and who are not convinced even by the veteran TBL guests who talk frankly about their troubles resulting from failure to use peer evaluation, we are fully aware that the system is self-correcting. We know that those who fail to use peer evaluation in the first semester will have to confront the issue when students who are teamed with irresponsible peers have no way to influence their behavior. It is rare that TBL adopters fail to introduce peer evaluation by the second semester of using the method.

Backward Design

The core segments of Day Two are devoted to the backward-design process and reconceptualization of course content, followed by tasks and conversations focused on the development of a syllabus and course policies that are well aligned with a TBL approach. The homework assignment that participants complete between the 2 days of the Academy is a rehearsal, at the unit level, of course design. During Day Two, we devote more time to development of authentic learning goals for their courses, focusing on the skills and perspectives that students need to acquire in order to approximate expert thinking in the targeted discipline.

We ask participants to think about their course goals on three levels and to express this thinking by responding to three prompts:

- What are the "big ideas" that you want students to take from the course? This is not a list of content. These are the life-altering, seminal ideas of your discipline that will forever forward be a part of student thinking.
- What are the skills, procedures, and actions that students will henceforth be able to carry out in whatever they do—when working both within your discipline and outside it?
- What are the attitudinal and perspectival shifts that are being targeted? In other words, how will students see the world differently as a result of your course? What values that were not present in their worldview before will now factor into their thinking?

Proceeding from these initial thoughts, participants are asked to select one of the most important changes they want to see in their students as a result of their experience in the course. Next to this goal they now write down a specific concrete action that their students will carry out at the end of the course to demonstrate how they have changed in this particular way. This action is then written in the form of an assignment or exam question.

To complete the thought process, we ask participants to pair off with a partner. One person presents his or her goal and the final action-assignment that will show student progress toward it. The partner listens and makes a list of all the kinds of practice a student would need in order to be effective in carrying out the action-assignment. This list then passes back to the author of the goal and becomes the basis for reflection on the kinds of daily practice activities that students will need to experience in order to be effective in the final action-assignment. Finally, we ask participants to design an activity that they will ask students to do in the first week of class, to begin practicing the kind of thinking identified in their selected goal.

We spend time at this point on coaching participants to write their course goals in active language so that they communicate to students more forcefully and graphically the kinds of behaviors that will be required of them in the course. For example, we ask participants to take the language of invisible learning—such as "understand," "become familiar with," "appreciate," and "know"—and convert it into language that represents these same notions through action: "summarize," "narrate," "predict," "analyze," "evaluate," "advocate," "persuade," and so on.

Only after participants have articulated these essential ways of student thinking and acting do we ask them to turn their attention to the content of their course. Using examples from previous Academy participants, we offer them a set of strategies for organizing their course content into TBL units or "learning sequences" by principles that guide disciplinary thinking. These examples can be seen in chapter 2.

Reenvisioning content in this way is a challenge for instructors, especially if they have entered the Academy with the belief that they can just "add" TBL to their previous course content. For many instructors, finding the best content organization requires experimentation in the first semester, but they come to realize that it is essential to communicating TBL to their students.

Adjusting Tone and Atmosphere

We now begin addressing the importance of using the syllabus to communicate the TBL course to students effectively and consistently. The language of a course syllabus reveals much more about an instructor than many realize, particularly in its tone. For example, we ask participants to examine their syllabi and determine whether the document is ultimately about the students or about the instructor. One sign we ask them to look for is the number of times the word *I* in its various declensions (*me, my*) appears in the syllabus. We ask them to delete every instance of *I* and rewrite the language so that students—and only the students—are the agents of action in the course.

It is this moment when we provoke a lively discussion by asking participants to articulate the difference between these two policies:

- Late papers will be penalized a letter grade for each day they are late.
- For this paper, students may choose their submission date. Papers that are turned in on April 3 are eligible for 100 points. Papers turned in on April 5 are eligible for 80 points. Papers that arrive after April 5 are accepted and will receive feedback but are eligible for 0 points.

This discussion launches a segment of the workshop called "Don't Let Your Policies Undermine Your TBL Implementation." In many cases, this is the moment when faculty members' potential to change their beliefs about their students will be tested. Many of our participants will initially follow the impulse to carry over the language and policies of a more traditional syllabus, including strict policies about attendance and disruptive classroom behavior. As committed as some instructors are to key principles of TBL, they will struggle to believe that they can trust their students to behave consistently like adults and to self-monitor. We remind participants that the TBL method is going to place students into the role of autonomous decision makers and agents of their own destiny. Students will be *busy* in the classroom and will not need as much control as in the past. The student teams, furthermore, will take care of many behavioral issues that might have emerged in the past. But most important, policies that communicate an instructor's overt need for control of student behavior will undo all the good work that TBL is designed to accomplish.

We present a distilled summary of the old and new course dynamics to drive home how the TBL version of a course will be different in every aspect:

- *Old way:* Try to control, contain, or modify student behavior (You must come to class! You must not talk! You must talk! Turn off your cell phone! Do your homework!) in order to improve their learning.
- *New way:* Let the learning process generate the need for behavior modification. Hold students ultimately accountable for their learning, not specific behaviors. Put students to work on meaningful tasks using the content: Keep them active. Ask students to make meaningful choices for themselves and deal with the consequences of those. Provide immediate feedback so students see themselves learning.

We close Day Two by presenting a set of best practices for writing policies that promote autonomous, responsible agency on the part of students:

- Strip down your course policies to the bare minimum (safety policy, policy for accommodating disabilities, policy for academic dishonesty) and build back from there, as needed.
- Try to write all policies in the form of "student choices with consequences."
- Let students help set the rules (cell phones, disruptions, etc.) so they will be implicated in maintaining a respectful atmosphere.

When Day Two of the Academy comes to a close, participants are generally enthusiastic but often drained from the work they have done. To capitalize on the energy (and downplay the exhaustion), we offer as the final act of "initiation" into our local TBL community the addition of the Academy participants to our local LISTSERV and a message publicly welcoming them. This list serves as a resource for creating conversations among implementers across the university. Although the teaching center is always available as a resource (and our support will continue intensively, as described next), we have found—true to TBL principles—that creating a sense of camaraderie among instructors provides an even greater sense of support, as well as opportunities for mentorship among peers.

POST-ACADEMY BENCHMARKS

Post-Academy Pre-First-Class Interview

Within a week after the Day Two workshop, an Academy staff member meets with each new TBL adopter to review the new syllabus and do a careful preview of the first one or two learning sequences. This allows us to provide concrete, individualized feedback on new course conceptualization and organization, policies, RATs, and team tasks. We typically are able to point to and head off one or two common problems, such as too many RATs and too many learning sequences, RATs that are too hard or too easy, team tasks that are too vague or open-ended, policies that still have an authoritative tone, and goals that do not inspire student interest.

Classroom Observation

In early iterations of the Academy, we allowed instructors a lot of latitude to make the determination of when to request their classroom observation. As a result, the requests usually came too late in the semester to be of any use. When we did visit, in some cases we were able to see problems that could have easily been mitigated early on. In a few cases we discovered that too much damage had been done to salvage the implementation.

More recently we have tightened the requirement and now insist that the observation occur within the first three learning sequences and no later than midterm. This allows us to identify issues before they mature into real problems that become cemented into the culture of the classroom.

In spite of extensive modeling in the Academy, by far the most difficult challenge for new instructors is team task design and debriefing. Problems emerge when newly forming teams are given too few clear-cut decisions to make. Because instructors want team work to be complex and multifaceted, and because they also carry a deep-seated belief that complexity cannot be embedded in a focused decision format, there is a common tendency to have students work on multiple-step tasks, such as a worksheet with multiple subtasks. These kinds of tasks not only dilute team energy but also allow dominant students to do the work while other students sit back and play with their iPhones. Our recommendations are for these instructors to break complex tasks down into their parts and have teams focus on each part, one decision at a time, before moving—as a whole class—to the next decision.

Another practice that instructors commonly struggle with is the strategic delay of certitude. In cases where the instructor has designed an excellent team decision task, where the students have debated energetically in their teams to reach consensus, and where the reporting has been done simultaneously to produce a full array of different team answers across the classroom, it is not uncommon to see the instructor reveal the correct or preferred answer too early in the debrief. Once students sniff the correct answer—whether iterated overtly or hinted at through body language or gestures—all motivation to defend and argue for their response vanishes. The opportunity to promote critical thinking disappears.

Midterm Survey

The paper-based midterm survey is essentially a snapshot of students' mood, taken before the actual midterm of the semester and often as early as a third of the way through a course. The Likert-style instrument, plus three open-ended questions, has been developed specifically for instructors using TBL, with several of the items asking students to reflect and comment on the course, with a focus on their experience working in teams. Because the survey captures data at a point where students are still learning to accommodate the new approach, it is common to see a bimodal distribution.

If problems are brewing in the course, the survey will usually show it. More often, however, the survey data confirm the value of the effort the instructors have made. Whether generally positive or generally negative, the data provide a context for a discussion with the Academy staff member who has conducted the observation. The two activities provide a basis for rich feedback and fact-driven encouragement.

Regardless of what the data show, we encourage instructors to share the feedback with their students, using this as an opportunity to remind them of the principles by which their course was designed, what their goals are, and why they are using this approach. Many instructors report that this conversation is invaluable, especially in cases where the surveys reflected substantial student pushback against the method. Soliciting students' feedback and taking their responses seriously are closely aligned with TBL principles and reinforce students' role as responsible agents in the classroom.

Celebration and Follow-Up

Just after the midpoint of the semester, all participants in the Academy are asked to attend a luncheon with their peers to exchange stories and generally celebrate. There will be moments of commiseration as well, but the goal of this event is to provide a public measure of success for the work of the participants. The celebration is also another opportunity for community building among our TBL instructors, some of whom come from departments that do not actively support teaching innovation. In many cases, we will invite some of our veteran instructors to the celebration luncheon to share additional perspectives and to reinforce the sense that these instructors have entered a broader community of leaderly practitioners. Although we, as consultants, are often their first line of support through the Academy and initial implementation process, other instructors ultimately make excellent mentors and resources for their peers.

Reflection Statement

Closure to the formal relationship between TBL adopters and the Academy staff comes in the form of brief reflection statements by participants. Near the end of the semester of their initial implementation, we ask participants to consider the following questions:

1. Which elements of TBL seem to be working as you expected or hoped?
2. What needs to be reworked, further developed, or refined?
3. How will your next iteration of the course (or any TBL course, for that matter) be different?
4. In general, what has been the impact of this project on you as a teacher? What are the takeaways, lessons learned, insights, and so on?

These statements serve three purposes. First, they help us to assess the success of instructors' implementations and to get a sense of where they are in their thinking about TBL. Second, we can look for patterns of struggles in their statements and use these to make adjustments to future Academies. Finally, the reflection encourages instructors to self-assess and begin using that assessment to think forward, reminding them that their TBL journey is still in a nascent stage and that they should continue to grow as instructors.

Long-Term Impacts

The outcomes for individual faculty have been varied, largely depending on instructors' motivation and the place where their journey to TBL began. Many of our successful adopters have reported improved student evaluations and increases in student learning. Those who have gone on to use TBL in multiple iterations find that the time they invested in initial course redesign has paid off in subsequent semesters, as they have been able to reduce class prep time dramatically. Perhaps most exciting, many faculty who were experiencing burnout either with teaching in general or with teaching a particularly troubling class have found themselves reenergized around their teaching and newly optimistic about their students. As a result, the TBL community is starting to inspire and change the conversations about teaching and learning on our campus. This is particularly true in the handful of departments where a cluster of faculty have successfully implemented TBL.

After 6 years and having worked with approximately 300 instructors, we have seen promising pockets of attitudinal and cultural change across the university. We have also benefited from the more consistent image of TBL across campus, as a result of our persistent acculturation efforts. In earlier days we found that many faculty on campus who claimed to be using TBL but in fact were not were contributing to campus misperceptions about the method and were damaging its reputation. Over the years this has been changing, as more instructors have adopted TBL and have helped educate the broader community on what it is. It is common now to hear reports that on the first day of class there is at least one student in the class who says to apprehensive team members, "Oh, yeah, I've had a TBL class before. Don't worry. This is going to be great!"

FOR TBL ADOPTERS IN GENERAL

For TBL adopters who do not have access to institutional support on the same scale as that at the University at Albany, we hope our experience will nevertheless inform other efforts to establish new, local communities of TBL practice. Our experience has taught us that the work of supporting new adopters, whether through formal training or one-on-one consulting, is that of fostering changes in beliefs and encouraging the replacement of old, comfortable habits with new, uncomfortable ones—often in the face of strong resistance. For this reason the road to TBL can be more of a psychological and socialization journey than one of simply mastering a new instructional method. A community of practice therefore needs to be built around a broader conversation of how best to align what we do in the classroom with our deepest institutional values and our commitment to students.

List of Interviewees

A total of 46 phone interviews were conducted for this book. The interviewees are TBL teachers from all around the world (Australia, New Zealand, Singapore, the United Arab Emirates, the United Kingdom, Ireland, Canada, and the United States). They are mostly university teachers, and a large number of disciplines are represented, including nursing, math, psychology, occupational therapy, business, accounting, sociology, library science, law, criminology, medicine, pharmacy, social work, kinesiology, geography, literature, chemistry, human development, veterinary medicine, auto mechanics, religious studies, and global studies. We also used a series of interview transcripts from 2012. Loretta Whitehorne and Jim Sibley conducted the 2012 interviews in preparation for the poster *Team-Based Learning Activities Reporting and Facilitation* presented at the 2012 Team-Based Learning Collaborative annual meeting.

2013 INTERVIEWS

Gail Feigenbaum
Nursing
Central New Mexico Community College
December 27, 2012

Allyson Brown
High School Math
St. Mark's School
January 1, 2013

Marie Thomas
Psychology
CSU San Marcos
January 2, 2013

Cynthia Evetts
Occupational Therapy
Texas Women's University
January 2, 2013

Larry K. Michaelsen
Business
University of Central Missouri
January 2, 2013

Mary Gourley
Psychology
Gaston College
January 2, 2013

Ruth Levine
Medicine
University of Texas Medical Branch
January 3, 2013

Frank Gersich
Accounting
Monmouth College
January 3, 2013

Janet Stamatel
Sociology
University of Kentucky
January 3, 2013

Liz Winter
Social Work
University of Pittsburgh
January 4, 2013

Trudi Jacobson
Information Literacy
University at Albany
January 4, 2013

David Raeker-Jordan
Law
Widener University
January 4, 2013

Judy Kissack
Pharmacy
Harding University
January 4, 2013

Meghan Gillette
Human Development
Iowa State University
January 7, 2013

Lindsay Davidson
Surgery
Queens University
January 7, 2013

Peter Balan
Business
University of South Australia
January 7, 2013

Ron Carson
Occupational Therapy
Adventist University of Health
Sciences
January 7, 2013

Chris Burns
Microbiology
University of Illinois
January 7, 2013

Simon Tweddell
Pharmacy
University of Bradford
January 8, 2013

Michael Nelson
Pharmacy
Regis University
January 8, 2013

Karla A. Kubitz
Kinesiology
Towson University
January 8, 2013

Brent MacLaine
Literature
University of Prince Edward
Island
January 8, 2013

Jenny Morris
Health Education
University of Plymouth
January 9, 2013

Mary Gilmartin
Geography
National University of Ireland,
Maynooth
January 9, 2013

Holly Bender
Veterinary Medicine
Iowa State University
January 9, 2013

Mary Hadley
Chemistry and Geology
Minnesota State University, Mankato
January 9, 2013

Sandy Cook
Medicine
Duke-NUS Graduate Medical School
Singapore
January 10, 2013

Bill Brescia
Medicine
University of Tennessee
January 11, 2013

Tim Dwyer
Auto Mechanics
Oklahoma State University
January 11, 2013

Lynne Esson
Nursing
University of British Columbia
January 14, 2013

Dean Parmelee
Medicine
Boonshoft Medical School
January 15, 2013

Brenda Collings
Accounting
University of New Brunswick, St. John
January 15, 2013

Mark Freeman
Business
University of Sydney
January 15, 2013

Joel Dubois
Religious Studies
CSU Sacramento
January 16, 2013

Melanie Carlson
Administrator
Drake University
January 16, 2013

Mark Stevens
Community and Regional Planning
University of British Columbia
January 16, 2013

Peter Smith
Business & Economics
University of Auckland
January 17, 2013

Esam Agamy
Medicine
University of Sharjah
January 17, 2013

N. Kevin Krane
Medicine
Tulane University
January 18, 2013

Brian Dzwonek
Medicine
Marshall University
January 18, 2013

Shawn Bushway
Criminology
University at Albany
January 18, 2013

Rick Goedde
Management Studies
St. Olaf College
January 23, 2013

Sarah Mahler
Global & Sociocultural Studies
Florida International University
January 22, 2013

Paul Koles
Medicine
Boonshoft Medical School
January 24, 2013

Judy Currey
Nursing
Deakin University
January 22, 2013

2012 INTERVIEWS

Holly Bender
Veterinary Pathology
Iowa State University

Peter Ostafichuk
Mechanical Engineering
University of British Columbia

Gail Feigenbaum
Nursing
Central New Mexico Community
College

Laura Madson
Psychology
New Mexico State University

Mary Gourley
Psychology
Gaston College

Bill Roberson
Faculty Member and Faculty
Developer
University at Albany, The State
University of New York

William Ofstad
Pharmacy
California Northstate University

References

Andersen, E. A., Strumpel, C., Fensom, I., & Andrews, W. (2011). Implementing team based learning in large classes: Nurse educators' experiences. *International Journal of Nursing Education Scholarship, 8*(1). doi:10.2202/1548-923X.2197

Angelo, T. A., & Cross, P. (1993). *Classroom assessment techniques: A handbook for college teachers* (2nd ed.). San Francisco, CA: Jossey-Bass.

Angelo, T., & Cross, P. (2003). *Classroom assessment techniques: A handbook for college teachers.* San Francisco, CA: Jossey-Bass.

Barton, L. (2007). *Quick flip questions for the revised Bloom's taxonomy.* Madison, WI: Edupress.

Bigge, M. L., & Shermis, S. S. (1999). *Learning theories for teachers* (6th ed.). New York, NY: Longman.

Bloom, B. S., Engelhart, M. D., Furst, E. J., Hill, W. H., & Krathwohl, D. R. (1956). *Taxonomy of educational objectives: The classification of educational goals; Handbook I: Cognitive domain.* New York, NY: Longmans, Green & Co.

Bransford, J. D., & Schwartz, D. L. (1998). A time for telling. *Cognition and Instruction, 16*(4), 475–522.

Brickell, J. L., Porter, D. B., Reynolds, M. F., & Cosgrove, R. D. (1994). Assigning students to groups for engineering design projects: A comparison of five methods. *Journal of Engineering Education, 7,* 259–262.

Bruner, J. S. (1966). *Toward a theory of instruction.* Cambridge, MA: Belknap Press of Harvard University.

Chickering, A. W., & Gamson, Z. F. (1987, Fall). Seven principles for good practice in undergraduate education. *AAHE Bulletin,* 3–7.

Chung, E. K., Rhee, J. A., Baik, Y. H., & Oh-Sun, A. (2009). The effect of team-based learning in medical ethics education. *Medical Teacher, 31*(11), 1013–1017.

Churchman, C. (1967). Guest editorial: Wicked problems. *Management Science*, *14*(4), B141–B142.

Clark, M. C., Nguyen, H. T., Bray, C., & Levine, R. E. (2008). Team-based learning in an undergraduate nursing course. *Journal of Nursing Education*, *47*(3), 111–117.

Collins, J. (2006). Writing multiple-choice questions for continuing medical education activities and self-assessment modules. *RadioGraphics*, *26*, 543–551.

Dana, S. W. (2007). Implementing Team-Based Learning in an introduction to law course. *Journal of Legal Studies Education*, *24*(1), 59–108.

DeLong, T. J. (2011, August 4). Three questions for effective feedback [blog post]. Retrieved from http://blogs.hbr.org/hbsfaculty/2011/08/three-questions-for-effective-feedback.html

Drummond, C. K. (2012). Team-based learning to enhance critical thinking skills in entrepreneurship education. *Journal of Entrepreneurship Education*, *15*, 57–64.

Feichtner, S. B., & Davis, E. A. (1984). Why some groups fail: A survey of students' experiences with learning groups. *Journal of Management Education*, *9*, 58–73.

Fink, L. D. (2003). *Creating significant learning experiences: An integrated approach to designing college courses*. San Francisco, CA: Jossey-Bass.

Freeman, M. (2012). To adopt or not to adopt innovation: A case study of team-based learning. *International Journal of Management Education*, *10*(3), 155–168.

Fujikura, T., Takeshita, T., Homma, H., Adachi, K., Miyake, K., Kudo, M., & Hirakawa, K. (2013). Team-Based Learning using an audience response system: A possible new strategy for interactive medical education. *Journal of Nippon Medical School*, *80*(1), 63–69.

Grady, S. E. (2011). Team-Based Learning in pharmacotherapeutics. *American Journal of Pharmaceutical Education*, *75*(7), 136. doi:10.5688/ajpe757136

Grant-Vallone, E. (2010). Successful group work: Using cooperative learning and Team-Based Learning in the classroom. *Journal on Excellence in College Teaching*, *21*(4), 99–121.

Haidet, P. M., Kubitz, K. A., & McCormack, W. T. (in press). Analysis of the Team-Based Learning literature: TBL comes of age. *Journal on Excellence in College Teaching*.

Howell, D. (2013). *Statistical methods for psychology* (8th ed.). Belmont, CA: Thomson.

Jacobson, T. E. (2011). Team-Based Learning in an information literacy course. *Communications in Information Literacy*, *5*(2), 82–101.

Jones, F. (2009). *TBL course talk* [webinar]. Retrieved from http://vimeo.com/26639358

Kelly, P. A., Haidet, P., Schneider, V., Searle, N., Seidel, C. L., & Richards, B. F. (2005). A comparison of in-class learner engagement across lecture, problem-based learning, and team learning using the STROBE classroom observation tool. *Teaching and Learning in Medicine, 17*(2), 112–118. doi:10.1207/s15328015tlm1702_4

Kloss, R. J. (1994). A nudge is best: Helping students through the Perry scheme of intellectual development. *College Teaching, 42*(4), 151–158.

Koles, P., Nelson, S., Stolfi, A., Parmelee, D., & DeStephen, D. (2005). Active learning in a Year 2 pathology curriculum. *Medical Education, 39*(10), 1045–1055. doi:10.1111/j.1365-2929.2005.02248.x

Koles, P., Stolfi, A., Borges, N. J., Nelson, S., & Parmelee, D. X. (2010). The impact of Team-Based Learning on medical students' academic performance. *Academic Medicine: Journal of the Association of American Medical Colleges, 85*(11), 1739–1745. doi:10.1097/ACM.0b013e3181f52bed

Kübler-Ross, E. (1969). *On death and dying.* New York, NY: Macmillan.

Lane, D. (2012). Peer feedback processes and individual accountability in Team-Based Learning. In M. Sweet & L. Michaelsen (Eds.), *Team-Based Learning in the social sciences and humanities* (pp. 51–62). Sterling, VA: Stylus.

Letassy, N. A., Fugate, S. E., Medina, M. S., Stroup, J. S., & Britton, M. L. (2008). Using Team-Based Learning in an endocrine module taught across two campuses. *American Journal of Pharmaceutical Education, 72*(5), 1–6.

Leupen, S. (2011). *Chapter 14: Reading guide and goals.* Retrieved from http://www.teambasedlearning.org/misc

Levine, R. E., O'Boyle, M., Haidet, P., Lynn, D. J., Stone, M. M., Wolf, D. V., & Paniagua, F. A. (2004). Transforming a clinical clerkship with team learning. *Teaching and Learning in Medicine, 16*(3), 270–275.

Masters, K. (2012). Student response to Team-Based Learning and mixed gender teams in an undergraduate medical informatics course. *Sultan Qaboos University Medical Journal, 12*(3), 344–351.

Mennenga, H. A. (2012). Development and psychometric testing of the Team-Based Learning student assessment instrument. *Nurse Education, 37*(4), 168–172. doi:10.1097/NNE.0b013e31825a87cc

Michaelsen, L. K., Knight, A. B., & Fink, L. D. (Eds.). (2002). *Team-Based Learning: A transformative use of small groups.* Westport, CT: Praeger.

Michaelsen, L. K., Knight, A. B., & Fink, L. D. (Eds.). (2004). *Team-Based Learning: A transformative use of small groups in college teaching.* Sterling, VA: Stylus.

Michaelsen, L. K., Parmelee, D. X., McMahon, K., & Levine, R. E. (2007). *Team-Based Learning for health professions education: A guide to using small groups for improving learning.* Sterling, VA: Stylus.

Michaelsen, L. K., & Schultheiss, E. E. (1989). Making feedback helpful. *Journal of Management Education, 13,* 109–113.

Michaelsen, L. K., & Sweet, M. (2008, Winter). The essential elements of Team-Based Learning. *New Directions for Teaching and Learning, 116,* 7–27.

Michaelsen, L. K., Watson, W. E., & Black, R. H. (1989). A realistic test of individual versus group consensus decision making. *Journal of Applied Psychology, 74*(5), 834–839.

Nelson, C. E. (1996). Skewered on the unicorn's horn. *Inquiry: Critical Thinking Across the Disciplines, 15*(3), 49–64.

Nicoll-Senft, J. (2009). Assessing the impact of Team-Based Learning. *Journal on Excellence in College Teaching, 20*(2), 27–42.

Nieder, G. L., Parmelee, D. X., Stolfi, A., & Hudes, P. D. (2005). Team-Based Learning in a medical gross anatomy and embryology course. *Clinical Anatomy (New York, NY), 18*(1), 56–63.

Parmelee, D., Michaelsen, L. K., Cook, S., & Hudes, P. D. (2012). Team-Based Learning: A practical guide: AMEE Guide No. 65. *Medical Teacher, 34*(5), 275–287. doi:10.3109/0142159X.2012.651179

Perry, W. G. (1999). *Forms of intellectual and ethical development in the college years: A scheme.* San Francisco, CA: Jossey-Bass.

Persky, A. M. (2012). The impact of Team-Based Learning on a foundational pharmacokinetics course. *American Journal of Pharmaceutical Education, 76*(2), 1–10.

Rider, E. A., & Longmaid, H. E., III. (1995). Feedback in clinical medical education: Guidelines for learners on receiving feedback. *Journal of the American Medical Association, 274*(12), 938.

Shabani, K., Khatib, M., & Ebadi, S. (2010). Vygotsky's Zone of Proximal Development: Instructional implications and teachers' professional development. *English Language Teaching, 3*(4), 237–248.

Sibley, J., & Parmelee, D. X. (2008). Knowledge is no longer enough: Enhancing professional education with Team-Based Learning. *New Directions for Teaching and Learning, 2008*(116), 41–53. doi:10.1002/tl.332

Sisk, R. J. (2011). Team-Based Learning: Systematic research review. *Journal of Nursing Education, 50*(12), 665–669.

Smith, G. A. (2008). First-day questions for the learner-centered classroom. *National Teaching and Learning Forum, 17*(5), 1–12. doi:10.1002/ntlf.10101

Smith, G. (2013, November). *Selling active learning to faculty requires a student purchase, too.* Session presented at 38th Annual POD Meeting, Pittsburgh, PA.

Smith, M. K. (2002). Jerome S. Bruner and the process of education. *The encyclopedia of informal education.* Retrieved from http://infed.org/mobi/jerome-bruner-and-the-process-of-education/

Sweet, M. (2010, March 30). *Discussion posting subject: Definition.* Retrieved from http://list.olt.ubc.ca/cgi-bin/wa?A0=TEAMLEARNING-L

Sweet, M., & Michaelsen, L. K. (Eds.). (2012a). *Team-Based Learning in the social sciences and humanities: Group work that works to generate critical thinking and engagement.* Sterling, VA: Stylus.

Sweet, M., & Michaelsen, L. K. (2012b). *Team-Based Learning: Small group learning's next big step.* San Francisco, CA: Jossey-Bass.

Thoma, G. A. (1993). The Perry framework and tactics for teaching critical thinking in economics. *Journal of Economic Education, 24*(2), 128–136.

Thomas, M. D., & McPherson, B. J. (2011). Teaching positive psychology using Team-Based Learning. *Journal of Positive Psychology, 6*(6), 487–491. doi:10.10 80/17439760.2011.634826

Thomas, P. A., & Bowen, C. W. (2011). A controlled trial of Team-Based Learning in an ambulatory medicine clerkship for medical students. *Teaching and Learning in Medicine, 23*(1), 31–36. doi:10.1080/10401334.2011.536888

Tuckman, B. (1965). Developmental sequence in small groups. *Psychological Bulletin, 63*(6), 384–399.

van de Pol, J., Volman, M., & Beishuizen, J. (2010). Scaffolding in teacher-student interaction: A decade of research. *Educational Psychology Review, 22*(3), 271–296. doi:10.1007/s10648-010-9127-6

Vasan, N. S., DeFouw, D. O., & Compton, S. (2011). Team-Based Learning in anatomy: An efficient, effective, and economical strategy. *Anatomical Sciences Education, 4*(6), 333–339.

Walters, D. (2012). Team-Based Learning applied to a medicinal chemistry course. *Medical Principles and Practice, 22*(1), 2–3. doi:0.1159/000342819

Wheelan, S. A. (1994). *Group processes: A developmental perspective.* Boston, MA: Allyn & Bacon.

Wood, D., & Middleton, D. (1975). A study of assisted problem-solving. *British Journal of Psychology, 66*(2), 181–191.

Zingone, M. M., Franks, A. S., Guirguis, A. B., George, C. M., Howard-Thompson, A., & Heidel, R. E. (2010). Comparing team-based and mixed active-learning methods in an ambulatory care elective course. *American Journal of Pharmaceutical Education, 74*(9), 160.

Zull, J. E. (2004). The art of changing the brain. *Educational Leadership, 62*(1), 68–72.

About the Authors and Contributors

AUTHORS

Jim Sibley is the director of the Centre for Instructional Support at the Faculty of Applied Science at University of British Columbia in Vancouver, Canada. He has 30 years of experience in faculty development, facilitation, and educational software development. He is an active member of the Team-Based Learning Collaborative (TBLC). He has served on the TBLC's board, Train the Trainer committee, Membership committee, and Web Strategy Committee (as a member of the Web Strategy Committee, he served as the original webmaster for www.teambasedlearning.org). He continues his work as a mentor in the TBLC's Train the Trainer program. He is an international TBL consultant, having worked in schools in Australia, Korea, Pakistan, Lebanon, the United States, and Canada to help others develop TBL programs. You can learn more about his work at learntbl.ca.

Peter Ostafichuk is a professor of teaching in the Department of Mechanical Engineering at the University of British Columbia (UBC). His primary teaching area is engineering design, but he has taught a variety of other topics, including aircraft aerodynamics, naval architecture, engineering principles, and even some physics, math, and statistics. He is the cocreator and former coordinator of the multi-award-winning Mech 2 program that integrated 15 previously disparate courses into a fully integrated, hands-on, team-taught curriculum. From his first course as a new faculty member at UBC in 2004, Pete has been teaching with TBL. He has taught almost 2,000 students, from sophomore to doctoral level, in 20 TBL courses in the years since. He has delivered numerous faculty workshops, conference papers, and webinars on the use of TBL. He also helps mentor faculty members making the switch to TBL.

227

CONTRIBUTORS

Billie Franchini is the assistant director of the Institute for Teaching, Learning, and Academic Leadership at the University at Albany (SUNY). She entered faculty development after more than a decade of teaching at the high school and university levels. She teaches both undergraduate and graduate courses using TBL and has worked with scores of faculty to support them in implementing TBL in their own courses.

Karla A. Kubitz is an associate professor in the Department of Kinesiology at Towson University in Towson, Maryland. She teaches classes in sport psychology, exercise psychology, motor learning, and the psychology of sport injury and rehabilitation and has been teaching with TBL since 2005. Karla is an active member of the Team-Based Learning Collaborative and is currently serving the TBLC in several roles. She is a member of the Steering Committee (i.e., the Member-at-Large for Higher Education), and she is cochair of the 2015 conference organizing committee. In addition, she is editor of the *TBLC Resource Bank* and a mentor in the Train the Trainer consultant program. Karla has published two book chapters on TBL, one in *Team-Based Learning for Health Professions Education* (Stylus, 2008) and another in *Team-Based Learning in the Social Sciences and Humanities* (Stylus, 2012). She also published several teaching modules in the *TBLC Resource Bank*.

Larry K. Michaelsen is David Ross Boyd Professor Emeritus at the University of Oklahoma, a professor of management at the University of Central Missouri, a Carnegie Scholar, a three-time Fulbright Senior Scholar, and former editor of the Journal of Management Education. He earned his PhD in Organizational Psychology from The University of Michigan and has received numerous college, university, and national awards for his outstanding teaching and for his pioneering work in two areas. One is the development of Team-Based Learning. The other is an Integrative Business Experience program that links student learning in three core business courses to their experience in creating and a start-up business financed by real-money bank loan and then executing a hands-on community service project that is funded by the profits of the start-up business.

Bill Roberson directs the teaching and learning center that serves the Albany campus of the State University of New York. He is a former faculty member and now faculty developer and has focused his career on the integration of critical thinking into the university classroom. To that end, he has been a practitioner of TBL since 2000 and has consulted with faculty at approximately 75 institutions in North America, South America, and Europe on course design for critical thinking, active learning, assessment of teaching, and the use of TBL to promote critical thinking. He has held positions in faculty development at UNC–Chapel Hill, Indiana University, and the University of Texas at El Paso, where he was founding executive director of that university's division for instructional technology, classroom design, digital media production, and distance learning. He came to New York in 2006 to create the Institute for Teaching, Learning and Academic Leadership at the University at Albany, State University of New York (www.itlal.org).

Index

Team-Based Learning in the Social Sciences and Humanities
Group Work that Works to Generate Critical Thinking and Engagement
Edited by Michael Sweet and Larry K. Michaelsen

This book introduces the elements of TBL and how to apply them in the social sciences and humanities. It describes the four essential elements of TBL—readiness assurance, design of application exercises, permanent teams, and peer evaluation—and pays particular attention to the specification of learning outcomes, which can be a unique challenge in these fields. The core of the book consists of examples of how TBL has been incorporated into the cultures of disciplines as varied as economics, education, literature, politics, psychology, and theater.

22883 Quicksilver Drive
Sterling, VA 20166-2102

Subscribe to our e-mail alerts: www.Styluspub.com

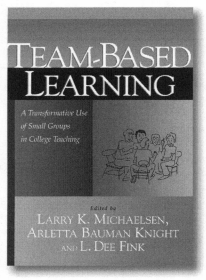

Team-Based Learning
A Transformative Use of Small Groups in College Teaching
Edited by Larry K. Michaelsen, Arletta Bauman Knight, and L. Dee Fink

"Includes all the wisdom, inspiration and practical advice needed to implement TBL in the classroom."—Jane Connor, *Professor of Psychology, Binghamton University, SUNY*

This book is a comprehensive guide to implementing Team-Based Learning (TBL). Part One covers the basics, beginning with an analysis of the relative merits and limitations of small groups and teams. It then sets out the processes, with much practical advice, for transforming small groups into cohesive teams, for creating effective assignments and thinking through the implications of TBL. In Part Two, teachers from disciplines as varied as accounting, biology, business, ecology, chemistry, health education, and law describe their use of TBL. Part Three offers a synopsis of the major lessons to be learned from the experiences of the teachers who have used TBL.

Team-Based Learning for Health Professions Education
A Guide to Using Small Groups for Improving Learning
Edited by Larry K. Michaelsen, Dean X. Parmelee, Kathryn K. McMahon, and Ruth E. Levine
Foreword by Diane M. Billings, RN, EdD, FAAN

"Educators who use this book will transform their classrooms and find renewed satisfaction in their teaching. Students who participate in Team-Based Learning will develop the requisite knowledge, skills, and abilities of 'thinking like a professional' and face a smoother transition from student to health care provider. The patient is the ultimate beneficiary when the health practitioner has been well prepared to provide safe and effective health care."—Diane M. Billings, *Indiana University School of Nursing*

This book is an introduction to TBL for health profession educators and includes chapters in which instructors describe how they apply TBL in their courses.